This book, which combines a deep understa~~~~~~~~~~~~~~~~~~al world and the latest findings of psychology, is essential reading for music educators, therapists, and parents—indeed, for all who are concerned with the relationship of temperament to musical development, and of music to other areas of human experience. Original in concept and lucid in expression, it investigates a subject of great importance to the lives of all musicians, and provides a firm basis for the further research demanded by the penetrating questions it raises.

Jack Dobbs, music educator

The Musical Temperament

The Musical Temperament

Psychology and Personality of Musicians

ANTHONY E. KEMP

Department of Arts and Humanities in Education
University of Reading

OXFORD NEW YORK TOKYO
OXFORD UNIVERSITY PRESS
1996

Oxford University Press, Walton Street, Oxford OX2 6DP
Oxford   New York
Athens   Auckland   Bangkok   Bombay
Calcutta   Cape Town   Dar es Salaam   Delhi
Florence   Hong Kong   Istanbul   Karachi
Kuala Lumpur   Madras   Madrid   Melbourne
Mexico City   Nairobi   Paris   Singapore
Taipei   Tokyo   Toronto
and associated companies in
Berlin   Ibadan

Oxford is a trade mark of Oxford University Press

Published in the United States
by Oxford University Press Inc., New York

A catalogue record for this book is available from the British Library

Library of Congress Cataloging in Publication Data
Kemp, Anthony.
The musical temperament / Anthony E. Kemp.
1. Musicians–Psychology.   2. Choice (Psychology)   3. Personality
and occupation   4. Music–Instruction and study.   I. Title
ML3838.K46 1996   781'.11–dc20   95-39981
ISBN 0 19 852363 7 (Hbk)
ISBN 0 19 852362 9 (Pbk)

Typeset by AMA Graphics Ltd., Preston, Lancs

Printed in Great Britain by
Biddles Ltd,
Guildford & King's Lynn

Foreword

by Raymond Cattell

This is a great book. It is the uniquely happy combination of the mind of a master musician and the mind of a man who has mastered the most recent findings of scientific psychology. The author had the advantage of studying psychology with the remarkable John Butcher of Sussex University, the co-author of the landmark publication, *The prediction of achievement and creativity*.

The field of personality measurement is at present in a mess. It suffers from hundreds of psychologists setting up, by subjective choice, scales for all kinds of supposed unitary traits. There is, fortunately, a way out of this jungle: the use of the statistical 'state of the art' factor analysis. But this is a very complex procedure from which the unhappy majority seek to escape. I understand that Dr Kemp chose not to pursue a technical discussion of methods of factor analysis to avoid the lengthy diversion that this would require. He is probably correct as far as the general reader is concerned. And in any case Dr Kemp makes his choice of evidence, deftly choosing what is firm in the jungle. He follows, in fact, a superb course avoiding what he knows to be false measurement, though he mentions all research, with whatever instrument, has been done. He notes, for example, that Eysenck's three 'basic' factors are only rough approximation to the true 'second-order' factors, from which, however, conclusions can be cautiously drawn.

Kemp's method is, naturally, to take a large sample of musicians of all types—practitioners, composers, teachers, and so on. He comes out with a clear finding that they are more introverted than the average person. They are also more anxious and higher on the second-order Independence and Pathemia factors. It is obviously a complex personality.

Next he examines separately males and females, students, composers, practitioners, teachers, and others. The teachers show, as might be expected, a reverse deviation, in the direction of being more extravert than the majority of people. Composers show the same deviations as were found by Butcher for outstanding scientific investigation and activity. There is a general pattern of deviation among all truly original people: low super ego strength, high radicalism, high self-sufficiency, marked dominance, and so on. Such a personality is not everybody's 'cup of tea'—particularly for a marriage partner. Dr Kemp also studies the evidence from a large number of biographies. In the course of this he demolishes the myth that great musicians all showed a startling early brilliance. They grew up gradually, like the rest, but they went further.

This book has an excellent supply of tables and diagrams, valuable for those who wish to work further in the area. It represents a great deal of labour and searching among over 1100 references.

One would hope to see a volume like this dealing with mathematicians in the modern world. And the same for artists and business giants. Terman's work on 'genius' badly needs to be followed up with the personality measures that have since become available. Where are the Kemps to undertake such work? The mainstream of psychological work seems at the same time to have stagnated in a morass of relatively trivial 'cognitive psychology'. As Kemp powerfully shows, attention to broad traits of personality alone brings insight into the real phenomena of psychology.

Preface

The study of musicians' personalities promises to open up for us a new vista of understanding concerning the nature of musicianship. Although the study of music psychology has loosened itself from the straight-jacket of music ability measurement, the inheritance may well have engulfed us in a predominantly cognitive view of our art. Outside this endeavour there exist a number of very different questions that invite a rather more humane and less mechanistic view of humanity and of the musician. Some of these questions relate to fairly fundamental issues concerning the personality characteristics that predispose an individual to pursue music in the first place, the internal drives that motivate people to practise music for extended periods and with such zeal, and the consuming need that some individuals appear to possess that leads them to engage in a musical life as an inherent part of their self-concept formation.

Occupational psychology demonstrates that the personalities of exceptionally skilled members of society, say airline pilots and brain surgeons, deviate in highly significant ways from those of the general population. From this one might reasonably expect that those types of musician who devote much of their lives to the development of particularly specialized skills would also possess a characteristically deviant profile. Such a profile might be viewed as a window into the musician's deeper psychology and as an indicator of the demands that the development of these musical skills constantly makes upon the individual. By addressing these kinds of questions we are able to develop a broader understanding about the nature of musicianship and the ways in which musical skill interrelates with temperament, thus providing a more comprehensive view of what musicians do and why. In other words, it is not only what people are able to do that determines their life's work but also what kind of people they are.

The study of the musician's personality can, moreover, offer additional insights: by clarifying the musical temperament in all its features we might be able to gain a deeper awareness of the very nature of music itself. After all, music has been performed from the beginning of time; wherever humans exist, music in some form or other manifests itself. Because music is generated by humans, it is reasonable to assume that its purpose is to meet a specific human need and, therefore, by studying the personalities of musicians, who presumably are particularly driven by this need, we may be able to develop a deeper understanding of the nature of music as a direct reflection of the mind and temperament that create it.

It is with these kinds of consideration in mind that this book is principally written, not that it will necessarily be in a position to answer all these questions, but certainly it is meant to provide the basis from which future research may edge ahead. There will be those who will wish to adopt the research findings presented here for the purpose of predicting talent, but it is my view that, at the present state of the art, this is still something of a dubious intention. I take this stance if for no other reason than because we have still not been successful in separating out the direction of causal effects. For example, do people become musicians because they have the appropriate temperament, or does the process of developing the requisite skills also stimulate personality development? Cause and effect are often difficult to disentangle empirically and, for the time being, we may prefer to take the view that both are operative in the musician's development. What perhaps emerges from research in this field is, first, a description of the types of person initially drawn into music—those who tend to be successful and continue to pursue it—and, secondly, the establishing of those aspects of personality that appear to be altered or developed as a result of engaging in musical activity over extended periods. In other words, temperament can be viewed as conducive to musical development or, alternatively, consequential to it. Certainly one suspects that by adding personality data to data on ability we will considerably enhance the power of the latter to predict the future development of musical talent.

To talk, however, about the musician's personality as a homogeneous configuration of traits would be naïve, and certainly those researchers who have undertaken investigations on this basis have been surprised by the variability of their results. Seashore (1936) very early on suggested otherwise when he wrote

We may classify professional musicians as composer, conductor, performer, and teacher. Each of these types has its very distinctive battery of requirements of the musical organism. To make reasonable individual prediction of success in one of these fields far more extensive data (than those furnished by talent tests) must be available. The talent required for each of these four groups is radically different; the necessary education is different; *the resultant personality is different.* [My italics] (p.25)

Besides making the case here for extending the range of predictive tests, Seashore was clearly raising the important notion that, not only would each of these four groups of musicians reflect specific talents, but that each would also reveal characteristically different personalities. This book pursues this kind of model: whilst it is possible to develop a general description of the personality pattern of the musical individual, out of this emerges a composite structure of specific patterns for the composer, conductor, performer, and teacher. Each group has its own particular life-style, body of knowledge, and set of skills, and therefore it will not come as a surprise to find each specialism revealing its own particular modification of the musician's general personality profile. Whether this is resultant, as Seashore suggests, remains to be clarified.

But there are additional areas that need investigating. A kind of folklore exists within musical circles, particularly orchestras, involving beliefs, often quite seriously held, that fundamental personality differences exist between the players of different instruments. Davies (1978) went some way towards investigating the patterns of differences among orchestral players by interviewing members of a professional orchestra and encouraging them to talk about players from other sections. Subsequently, research using personality inventories with larger samples has demonstrated that there exists a firm empirical basis for believing that such differences exist; these are described later in this book.

A rather more contentious area of research is that relating to personality and musical preferences. Although musical preferences may interact with instrumental choice, for example, a person deciding to play a brass instrument because he or she is attracted to the brass band repertoire, nevertheless it is reasonable to hypothesize that the musical preferences of discriminating non-performing listeners might also reveal stable patterns of personality correlates. Certainly, the few pieces of research that have pursued this notion suggest that there are indeed some interesting links. For example, it appears that those attracted to the music of the romantic period might display higher levels of anxiety than those who tend to prefer classical or baroque music.

This book consciously sets out to operate outside the area of ability development and its concomitant concerns with learning theory and teaching method. What it *does* attempt to achieve is a description of the patterns of individual differences that occur as outcomes of the teaching practices and methods that are currently prevalent in school music as well as in colleges and universities. The book therefore has important things to say about the education and training of musicians in studios, schools, and colleges, but from a more unusual perspective.

The book is principally focused upon musicians of the Western classical tradition; this is not entirely through choice but reflects research availability. Certainly, where research has been published concerning, for example, the personalities of pop, rock, and jazz musicians, this has been reviewed as important additional information in the attempt to develop as composite a picture of the musician as possible. Pursuing musicians of different cultural origins raises all manner of additional problems. Quite apart from research accessibility, cultural differences in terms of personality norms are a notorious intervening variable. That these have been shown to be manifest between British and American samples, for example, should serve as a warning to the researcher tempted to embrace more disparate cultural groups, unless, of course, cultural personality differences are incorporated as an additional variable.

The book stems from research that I began in the early 1970s; some of this has remained unpublished, and other material has appeared in research journals. The research belongs to the Cattellian tradition, growing naturally out of Raymond Cattell's monumental work along with his collaborators at the Institute of Personality and Ability Testing at the University of Illinois. Their research, spreading over more than four decades, not only generated several types of personality inventories, but also more importantly developed a comprehensive model of the total personality, as well as accumulating extensive data on large numbers of occupational and clinical groups. At the time of embarking upon this research it appeared important to supplement Cattell's data on musicians with something more valid than the very restricted information that was currently available to him. Encountering the late John H. Butcher at the University of Sussex at about this time was, for the writer, one of life's good fortunes. John Butcher had recently completed a period of collaboration with Cattell at Illinois during which they had jointly authored *The prediction of achievement and creativity* (1968). As a musician with gathering interests in developmental psychology, my research intentions were to 'clarify the nature of musical creativity' as I recall describing them to him. This appeared to excite his curiosity, linked as it clearly was with the recent work of Cattell and Drevhahl concerning the personality patterns of artists and writers. Thus began a relationship during which he agreed to supervise my pilot research at masters level and encouraged me to embark on more extensive doctoral work.

Generally speaking, books on the psychology of music have, for one reason or another, tended to steer clear of the field of personality. This is rather surprising given the trickle of published papers on the topic appearing since the mid-1960s. Recently, however, we have witnessed a resurgence of interest in the field resulting in a steady flow of research articles pursuing various samples of musicians and adopting a diversity of inventories and research strategies. The appearance of this book is therefore timely, and, because it is possibly the first in the field, it attempts to review all the important research available and to present an up-to-date picture of what has been achieved up to the point of going to press.

This book is written with musicians, music educators, and psychologists in mind, and with such a broad intended readership it may not succeed wholly in satisfying everyone at all points. For those who may not be conversant with the essential aspects of personality on which the book depends, an introduction is offered to ease the reader into the field. It specifically deals with those theories that tend to feature most frequently in the research pertinent to our particular interests. Because most of the available research in the field is psychometrically orientated, the introduction inevitably focuses on this, but makes every attempt to avoid any unnecessary technicalities. Clearly some readers may well wish to bypass this introduction, particularly if they are already conversant with its contents.

The early chapters attempt to take the reader a little more deeply into the field by pursuing individual aspects of personality that the research shows to be particularly relevant to musicianship and that appear to exercise an important role in its development. I hope that these chapters will help the reader to develop key insights into the more important facets of musicians' personalities and their aetiology. The chapters that follow continue the search for further enlightenment concerning music–personality links but from the point of view of particular musical skills and specialisms. In doing this, further clarification of the nature of these musical roles and the ways that they relate to the earlier issues is attempted. The closing chapter briefly takes a look at some of the educational implications of personality research for the education and training of the musically gifted.

In pursuing these topics, I have not been reticent about engaging in speculation, sometimes in what may be perceived as quite an unscientific manner, particularly in those instances where research results may be somewhat flimsy, inconclusive, or in conflict. In doing this I am aware of leaving many questions unanswered, but very much hope that through reading this book future researchers will wish to pursue a number of these. Neither do I apologize for allowing my gathering interest in psychoanalytic theories to show itself occasionally. In a curious way, or so the reader may think, I have Cattell himself to thank for this, together with just a little help from some of the writings of Paul Kline.

Finally, I wish to thank several colleagues at the University of Reading who by their generous covering of some of my teaching and administrative duties allowed me to finish this book within the deadline I had set myself. I am indebted also to Pat Parry for her secretarial expertise and kind support. I would like to thank those who reviewed the manuscripts of this book on behalf of Oxford University Press, and particularly my friends Arnold Bentley and Rosamund Shuter-Dyson (Mrs Bourke), who, by their invaluable comments on the draft chapters, have considerably assisted in the process of improving the final copy. At the same time by their encouragement and criticisms they have helped make the process of writing the book a much less lonely and introspective experience than it would have been otherwise. To my wife, Valerie, and our family to whom this book is dedicated with gratitude, I offer my grateful thanks for their love and support, and give my promises to be less heavily preoccupied and more human than I have appeared within recent months.

University of Reading A. E. K.
June 1995

Acknowledgements

Table 1 (p. 6) and Fig. 1.2 (p. 29) are reproduced from *The scientific analysis of personality and motivation* by Raymond B. Cattell and Paul Kline, Academic Press, Inc., 1977, with permission of the publishers.

Figure 2 (p. 9) is reproduced from *Fact and fiction in psychology* by Hans J. Eysenck, published by Penguin, 1965, with permission of the author.

Figure 3 (p.11) is reproduced from *Knowing me—knowing you* by Malcolm Goldsmith and Martin Wharton, published by SPCK, 1993, with permission of the publishers.

Table 3 (p.12) has been modified and reproduced by special permission of the publisher, Consulting Psychologists Press, Inc., Palo Alto, CA 49303 from *Gifts differing: understanding personality type* by Isabel Briggs Myers. Copyright 1980 by Consulting Psychologists Press, Inc. All right reserved. Further reproduction is prohibited without the publisher's written consent.

Similarly, the Myers–Briggs Type Indicator questionnaire items that appear on pages 13 and 14 are modified and reproduced by special permission of the publisher, Consulting Psychologists Press, Inc., Palo Alto, CA 49303 from *Myers–Briggs Type Indicator—form F* by Katherine C. Briggs Myers. Copyright 1977 by Peter B. Briggs and Katherine D. Myers. All right reserved. Further reproduction is prohibited without the publisher's written consent.

The Maudsley Personality Inventory items that appear on page 13 are reproduced by the kind permission of Hans J. Eysenck.

Table 4 (p. 16) is reprinted from *Personality and Individual Differences*, Volume 13, Costa and McCrae, Four ways five factors are basic, pp. 653–65, Copyright 1992, with kind permission from Elsevier Science Ltd, The Boulevard, Langford Lane, Kidlington OX5 1GB, UK.

Contents

Introduction: personality assessment

The study of personality has a long and in some ways a rather chequered history. From the beginning of time an important feature of human interaction has been our inclination to make judgements about one other and to interpret behaviour patterns as consistent temperamental predispositions or traits. Aristotle and Plato were amongst the early speculators, as well as Hippocrates, whose celebrated typology of temperaments was based upon the four body substances, blood, phlegm, and yellow and black bile. It was this typology that Galen adopted several centuries later leading him to develop the sanguine, phlegmatic, choleric, and melancholic classification of temperament. These notions still tend to linger on in our everyday language in describing each other: for example, a person who tends to be calm we describe as phlegmatic; and someone who looks on the black side of life we say is melancholic. A fifteenth century manuscript (Figure 1) provides graphic illustration of these four temperaments and, interestingly, in terms of the purposes of this book, the melancholic type is shown as featuring a musician.

The notion that everyday language embodies essential truths concerning the nature of human personality appears to have been the springboard for other early attempts at developing a systematic model. The logic of this is clear to see: if the inner predispositions of people to behave in certain ways are observable in our everyday experience and form a part of our social reality, it is reasonable to assume that they become encoded in language. Furthermore, advocates of this line of thinking would probably argue that the evolution of language reflects an ever-sharpening conceptual grasp of these observable traits. Galton (1884) was probably the first scientist to develop such a lexical hypothesis of individual differences, and he scanned the pages of *Roget's thesaurus* to extract large numbers of temperament descriptors to generate his model of personality. This set in motion a train of theoretical thought that can be traced through the work of Allport (Allport and Odbert 1936) to that of Cattell. The process was a long and laborious one: researchers like Cattell built constructs through a process of classifying these temperament descriptors, and attempted to develop a model that would embrace the total personality sphere (Cattell 1945). With the arrival of

Sanguine

Phlegmatic

Choleric

Melancholic

Figure 1 The four temperaments depicted in a fifteenth-century Zurich manuscript. (From the Bettmann archive.)

computer technology Cattell's psychometric work became l
he set about validating his dimensions using data drawn fro
ent sources: questionnaire; observation; and laboratory test
1970). In this way, the search for a definable and consistent
sonality was pursued in earnest throughout the decades tha
principal proponents being Cattell in America and Eysenck in England, both
of whom took a psychometric stance towards their work.

Alongside this research, a very different body of theory was developing
based on clinical methods. Initiated by Freud at the end of the last century,
the psychoanalytic movement gathered increasing momentum involving
other key workers such as Jung, Adler, and Erikson, to name but a few. It
would be impossible here to attempt any adequate summary of the complexity of psychoanalytic theory; nevertheless, some of its elements permeate factor theories like those of Cattell and will be described later in this
'Introduction'.

In many ways the history of the development of personality theory is similar to that of intelligence theory. Neither is a concrete phenomenon—nor are
they directly observable—and both lack physical and objective reality.
Whilst we might maintain that we can observe these dimensions in people's
everyday behaviour patterns, it is frequently suggested that they exist more
in the perceptions of the observer than in any objective sense. Whilst this
kind of suspicion permeates these fields, lending support to those who dismiss them as dangerous abstractions, nevertheless, day to day experience
frequently suggests that the concept of personality traits is of major significance to, say the careers counsellor, just as intelligence is to the educator.

Thorndike maintained that whatever is seen to exist can, theoretically, be
measured (Thorndike and Hagen 1955). In taking this line also, Cattell
(1973), who worked with Thorndike for a short period, argued that those
who maintain that trait structures are too intangible for measurement reveal
their inconsistency each time they pronounce someone as being 'highly
intelligent' or 'not very sensitive'. Cattell (1981) regards traits as real in that
they are, he maintains, determiners of behaviour. Kline (1993), in arguing the
case for 'real' traits, uses the analogy of 'dog' as a concept that is well-
defined and upon which there is general agreement. However, he argues,
the construct 'dog' cannot be observed, and such a notion exists only in the
minds of those who use the term. That there is no observable object does not
affect its conceptual status.

There are two principal ways of looking at personality. One approaches
the topic from the point of view of *traits*, which its proponents such as
Cattell claim to be the smallest units that are consistent and reliable. The second relates to *types*; the most celebrated treatment is the work of Jung (1923)
and is exemplified in the inventory known as the Myers–Briggs Type
Indicator (MBTI; Myers and McCaulley 1985). Trait theory and type theory
must not be seen as being in opposition. Traits are derived by abstracting

particular qualities in our everyday experience of perceiving types; our understanding of a type is dependent upon a knowledge of those aspects of which it is comprised, in other words, clusters of traits.

If a conflict exists between the two views, it relates to disagreements about the internal consistency of traits and, indeed, about how many there are and whether they have been correctly identified. Much has been written about this, and there is a large body of literature concerning issues relating to the complexities of factor analysis, the details of which do not need our attention here.

Another controversy relates to exactly what constitutes the personality domain and what might be viewed as lying outside this domain. Allport (1960), taking a very broad stance, considered that personality involves intellectual capacities, special abilities, temperament, and unconscious drives, as well as pathological characteristics. Guilford was similarly eclectic and considered that personality should embrace not only intelligence but also people's interests and values (Guilford 1959). On the other hand, Cattell took a more focused view and, although he incorporated an intelligence scale into his inventories, believed that personality was essentially non-cognitive. He further clarified his position on this by developing the notion that personality, abilities, and motivation constituted three separate 'modalities' (Cattell 1973). Much of the work of Cattell and his co-workers focused upon the nature of the interrelationships between these modalities and the ways in which they may possibly exercise influence upon their mutual development (see, for example, Cattell and Butcher 1968; Cattell 1971; Cattell and Child 1975).

Much play has been made of the public discussions and disagreements between Eysenck and Cattell that found their way into the literature in the 1970s. Both worked psychometrically, adopting factorial methods to clarify and validate their theoretical positions. Their main differences lie in their research intentions: whereas Cattell wished to construct a global model of the whole personality, Eysenck restricted his main focus of interest to the dimensions of extraversion and neuroticism and, later, psychoticism. However, because Cattell's primary factors overlap, they cluster to form larger 'second-order' factors, which in many ways are not dissimilar to those of Eysenck. Whilst the two systems appear, then, to correspond, the main disagreement that remains appears to relate to the consistency of primary factors, which Cattell maintains reflect crucial information in clinical and research work and which Eysenck considers to be too unstable and unreliable. In other words, we might perceive Cattell as essentially emphasizing traits and Eysenck, a more restricted number of broad types.

It is not the aim of this book to provide a composite review of the multiplicity of personality inventories that have appeared within the last 40 years, several of which have long ceased to be used. The purpose here is to provide the reader with appropriate and helpful insights into those particular inventories that tend to recur in the literature, particularly those that we shall encounter in research into musicians' personalities.

Cattell's factors

From the outset, Cattell's preoccupation lay in identifying the full range of unitary traits that could describe the structure of the total personality (Cattell 1956). Initially, his model was derived from 'life data' adopting similar methods to those of Allport (1960). Having set out to identify 4000 or so observable behavioural characteristics, he reduced these to 171 bi-polar scales. Using these, he obtained ratings from groups of subjects allowing him to develop a matrix of intercorrelations that, in turn, revealed 36 clusters. These, Cattell factored to produce the 12 primaries that have become the basis of much of his subsequent work (Cattell 1945, 1947). The foundation of his system laid, Cattell proceeded to identify these factors in a questionnaire approach that revealed four additional factors (the Q factors) that emerged from the questionnaire realm alone.

Cattell's principal personality inventory is the *Sixteen Personality Factor Questionnaire* (16PF, Cattell *et al.* 1970) designed for adult populations. It has been adopted as a research tool in a variety of fields, in predictive and diagnostic work in education, industrial psychology, and vocational guidance as well as in clinical diagnosis. Cattell maintains that the 16 primary factors represent the universal traits of the total personality, but nevertheless concedes that there may be others that are yet to be identified (Cattell 1973). These factors, to which he assigned letter labels, are shown in Table 1, along with their bi-polar general descriptions. Another of Cattell's inventories, the *High School Personality Questionnaire* (HSPQ; Cattell and Cattell 1969) was developed for school-age pupils. This measures the same collection of primary factors, although two are peculiar to the HSPQ, and there are four others that are only featured in the 16PF. The low scoring end of each factor is indicated by the minus symbol and the high end by the positive symbol. For example, a person's low score on factor A, interpreted as aloofness, is indicated by the A– symbol; a high scoring outgoing person is classified as A+. Although Cattell is well known for his adoption of neologisms to describe his factors, the reader should note that I have chosen to adopt the more familiar names throughout this book.

Three of Cattell's primary factors relate closely in terms of theoretical underpinning to Freud's *id, ego, superego* typology which Freud (1949) referred to as 'regions of mental life'. Stated briefly, the id is the inherited and instinctive, and thus obscure part of the personality: it has no direct relations to the outside world, knows no precautions to ensure survival, and, in its desire for pleasure, knows no anxiety. The ego is the part that we know best and in which we recognize our sense of 'self': it strives for safety, deals

Table 1 Cattell's first-order factors *

A–	ALOOFNESS Reserved, detached, critical, stiff	A+	OUTGOINGNESS Warmhearted, easygoing, participating
B–	LOW INTELLIGENCE Dull	B+	HIGH INTELLIGENCE Bright
C–	LOW EGO STRENGTH At mercy of feelings, emotionally less stable, easily upset, changeable	C+	HIGH EGO STRENGTH Emotionally stable, mature, faces reality, calm
D–	PHLEGMATIC Undemonstrative, deliberate, inactive, stodgy	D+	EXCITABILITY Excitable, over-active, unrestrained
E–	SUBMISSIVENESS Humble, mild, easily led, docile, accommodating	E+	DOMINANCE Assertive, aggressive, competitive, stubborn
F–	DESURGENCY Sober, taciturn, serious	F+	SURGENCY Happy-go-lucky, enthusiastic
G–	EXPEDIENCY Disregards rules, self-indulgent	G+	CONSCIENTIOUSNESS Persevering, moralistic, responsible
H–	SHYNESS Timid, threat-sensitive	H+	ADVENTUROUSNESS Uninhibited, socially bold
I–	TOUGH-MINDEDNESS Self-reliant	I+	SENSITIVITY Tender-minded, clinging
J–	ZESTFUL Likes group action, vigorous	J+	INDIVIDUALISTIC Internally restrained, wrapped up in self
L–	TRUSTING Accepting conditions, tolerant	L+	SUSPICIOUS Hard to fool, jealous
M–	PRACTICAL Down-to-earth, concerned	M+	IMAGINATIVE Bohemian, absent-minded
N–	NAIVETÉ Forthright, unpretentious, genuine, but socially clumsy	N+	SHREWDNESS Astute, polished, socially aware
O–	SELF-ASSURED Placid, secure, complacent, serene	O+	GUILT PRONENESS Apprehensive, self-reproaching, insecure, worrying, troubled
Q1–	CONSERVATISM Conservative, respecting traditional ideas	Q1+	RADICALISM Experimenting, liberal, free-thinking
Q2–	GROUP DEPENDENT A joiner and sound follower, sociable	Q2+	SELF-SUFFICIENCY Resourceful, prefers own decisions
Q3–	LOW SELF-SENTIMENT Undisciplined, self-conflict, follows own urges, careless of social rules	Q3+	HIGH SELF-SENTIMENT Controlled, exacting will power, socially precise, compulsive following self-image
Q4–	LOW ERGIC TENSION Relaxed, tranquil, torpid, unfrustrated, composed	Q4+	HIGH ERGIC TENSION Tense, frustrated, driven, overwrought

*Adapted from Cattell and Kline (1977, pp. 44–5).

with the external world, and helps develop our sense of reality. The super-ego, like the id, is a part of our internal world: it controls the ego in the form of conscience and serves to correct or punish, like an internalized parent.

Freud's notions of id, ego, and superego can be seen to underlie Cattell's factors of ergic tension (Q4+), ego strength (C+), and conscientiousness (G+), respectively, shown in Table 1. Unlike Eysenck, Cattell maintained that it would be foolish to dismiss psychoanalytic work on the grounds of its methodology. The scientific method ensures accuracy, but, nevertheless, it is possible that insightful clinicians such as Freud and Jung hit upon the truth. Although their work lacked quantification, they 'had access to data that few others have bothered to study. Their attempts to understand personality are not purely speculation but rest on data (however tenuous the connection)' (Cattell and Kline 1977, p. 3).

As already mentioned, Cattell's primary traits cluster to form a series of larger second-order factors; these are shown in Table 2. However, because children's personality structure varies from that of adults in terms of their constituent primary factors, the clusters of primary factors at the second-order level also differ. Table 2 shows these differences, and in studying this table the reader should bear in mind that the poles of the contributory primary factors relate to the second-named pole. Thus, to obtain a description of the first-mentioned pole, the plus and minus designations of all the contributory primary factors have to be changed.

Eysenck's types

Eysenck's contribution to personality theory has been as monumental as that of Cattell. Both have approached their research psychostatistically, but they differ principally in Eysenck's parsimonious approach as opposed to Cattell's more all-embracing stance, as we have already observed. Initially, Eysenck maintained that the two dimensions, extraversion and neuroticism, would describe the most essential aspects of personality, but he later added psychoticism (Eysenck and Eysenck 1976). He does not believe, however, that these three dimensions account for the whole of human personality (Eysenck 1976), and, although he has chosen to focus principally upon these superfactors, this does not indicate any denial of the existence of primary factors. However, he does maintain that his factors are of greater importance, not least because source traits are still subject to criticism due to what he believes to be their poor record of replicability.

Eysenck's work reveals his general concern that personality factors should be integrated into general psychology. For example, the areas of perception, memory, learning, and so on, he maintains, should reflect the interactive effects of personality (Eysenck 1976). This reveals itself in his characteristic multivariable approach, frequently including self and observer

Table 2 Cattell's second-order factors and their contributory primary traits *

Second-order factors †			Chief primary factors involved	
			16PF	HSPQ
Introversion	vs.	Extraversion	A+ F+ H+ Q2−	A+ F+ H+ J− Q2−
Adjustment	vs.	Anxiety	C− H− L+ O+ Q3− Q4+	C− D+ H− O+ Q3− Q4+
Pathemia	vs.	Cortertia	A− I− M−	A− E+ I−
Subduedness	vs.	Independence	E+ F+ H+ M+ L+	E+ F+ H+
Naturalness	vs.	Discreetness	N+ A+	⎫ Not found
Cool realism	vs.	Subjectivity	M+ Q1+	⎭
Low intelligence	vs.	High intelligence	B+	B+
Negative upbringing	vs.	Positive upbringing	E− F− G+ Q3+	F− G+ Q3+

* Adapted from Cattell (1973, pp. 116, 120).

† Constituent primary factors relate to the second-named term.

ratings, body measurements, galvanic skin and other physiological responses, and biographical data. As a result, one finds in Eysenck's literature and
that of his co-workers a preoccupation with correlations between personality dimensions and all manner of psychological phenomena such as arousal,
perception, memory, aesthetic preferences, and response to drug treatments.

Eysenck's early test instrument was the *Maudsley Personality Inventory*
(MPI; Eysenck 1959) and this was followed in due course by the appearance
of its improved form, the Eysenck Personality Inventory (EPI; Eysenck and
Eysenck 1964). Both were designed to measure the dimensions of extraversion and neuroticism, but the EPI contains a lie scale that allows the
researcher to make allowances for patterns of distortion due to particular
individuals' more socially desirable responses. Extraversion and neuroticism were arrived at through a process of factor analysis that would result
in factors that were totally independent. A fourfold typology therefore
emerges from the MPI and EPI: stable extravert; unstable extravert; stable
introvert; and unstable introvert. Eysenck's well-known model, comprising
four quadrants and their respective trait adjectives as well as, rather

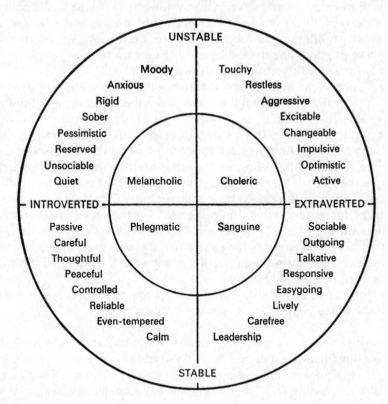

Figure 2 Eysenck's two-dimensional model of personality. From Eysenck and
Eysenck (1965, p. 54).

curiously, the Hippocratic types, is shown in Figure 2. The third dimension, psychoticism, which appeared in the *Eysenck Personality Questionnaire* (EPQ; Eysenck and Eysenck 1975), can be imagined as standing vertically away from the page from the point of intersection.

Jung's psychological types

In common with Freud, several aspects of Jung's theories appear to be based upon the dynamics of opposites such as good and bad; right and wrong; male and female; life and death; and internal and external. Human attempts to find resolutions of these conflicts in everyday life lay at the heart of their clinical work. In the case of Jung, his exploration of these opposites led him to develop his model of psychological types (Jung 1923). Although Cattell and, particularly, Eysenck were critical of clinical theorizing that was devoid, in their view, of an empirical base, both have to concede their indebtedness to Jung's pioneer work, especially in developing the notions of introversion–extraversion, referred to by Jung as 'attitudes'. According to Jung, extraverts direct their energies outwards towards other people, and live their lives adopting an objective stance. Conversely, introverts direct their energies into themselves, moving naturally away from people, choosing to operate in a subjective internal world.

In addition to the introversion–extraversion attitudes, Jung (1928) identified two pairs of fundamental functions: sensation–intuition, and thinking–feeling. Sensation relates to the process of perception through the use of the senses; intuition involves the use of the person's unconscious in perceiving objects. By thinking, Jung referred to the more cognitive processes of forming logical conclusions; feeling, on the other hand, involves the tendency of some people to evaluate subjectively. Jung maintained that these functions are never uniformly developed in people, but, rather, that one function operates in the foreground while the rest remain in the background relatively undifferentiated. *The Myers–Briggs Type Indicator* (MBTI; Myers and McCaulley 1985) arose out of Jung's theories, and was devised specifically to measure these dimensions empirically, resulting in a model that differentiates between 16 personality types.

For the sake of clarity this differentiation can be approached in a stepwise fashion (see Figure 3).

1. There are two ways of *perceiving* information about the world we live in: by sensing (S) or through intuition (N). In addition, there are two ways of *judging* this information and coming to decisions about it: by thinking (T) or through feeling (F). These preferences, or tendencies, result in four types.

a. *Sensing plus thinking (ST).* People interested in collecting facts that are verified through the senses. Decisions are made through impersonal analysis. ST types are practical, matter-of-fact types.

b. *Sensing plus feeling (SF).* Similarly, this type of person relies on a process of perception through their senses. However, they approach the evaluation of facts through their feelings. SF types tend to be sociable and friendly.

c. *Intuition plus feeling (NF).* These people also rely on feeling for the purposes of judgement, but do not centre their attention on concrete situations, but rather on possibilities and new truths. NF types are often insightful.

d. *Intuition plus thinking (NT).* These types are also intuitive but, whilst focusing their attention on possibilities, approach them with impersonal analysis. NT types are frequently good at problem-solving.

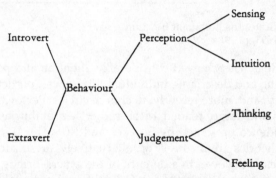

Figure 3 Jung's four sets of preferences. From Goldsmith and Wharton (1993, p. 16).

2. The four types of persons described above are further differentiated according to whether they have a basic preference for judgement (J) or perception (P). Most people use both, but not at the same time, and almost all people prefer one function over the other. The judger is characterized by organizational ability; the perceiver by adaptability. Thus, the JP dimension helps to identify the *dominant* function, as opposed to the *auxiliary* function. For example, ST types who prefer to judge (STJ) will exhibit the dominant function of thinking and the auxiliary one of sensing. On the other hand, ST individuals who prefer to perceive (STP) will exhibit the dominant function of sensing and the auxiliary one of thinking.

3. Finally, the eight types are further refined by adding the introverted (I) or extraverted (E) attitudes: the introverted attitude being characterized by

depth and concentration, and the extraverted one by ease with the environment. These interact with the above functions to produce a typology of 16 personality descriptions. Together they represent a model of personality that incorporates aspects of both conscious and unconscious functioning (see Table 3).

Table 3 Myers–Briggs Indicator types *

| | | Sensing types | | Intuitive types | |
		Thinking – S T –	Feeling – S F –	Feeling – N F –	Thinking – N T –
Introvert {	I – – J	I S T J	I S F J	I N F J	I N T J
	I – – P	I S T P	I S F P	I N F P	I N T P
Extravert {	E – – P	E S T P	E S F P	E N F P	E N T P
	E – – J	E S T J	E S F J	E N F J	E N T J

Underlining indicates the dominant function.
* From Myers (1993, p. 29).

The Myers–Briggs has achieved considerable attention and popularity as a test for assessing and describing individual differences, particularly in education, industry, and, more recently, in church circles. Personality psychologists have, by and large, tended to be rather less enthusiastic about the inventory. Evidence presented by Stricker and Ross (1964) suggested that either Jung's theories are incorrect or, alternatively, are inadequately measured by the test. However, in a defence of the Myers–Briggs, Bayne (1994) has claimed that it is probably the most widely used personality measure in occupational and counselling psychology. He also maintains that the inventory bears a consistent relationship with four of the 'big five' factors (McCrae and Costa 1989a) which are discussed in more detail on pages 15–17.

Measuring personality by questionnaire

The majority of inventories are of the self-report type. They consist of a number of statements that have been researched through processes of item and factor analysis and that have been demonstrated as representing a sufficiently high loading on a particular criterion or trait. Questionnaire items frequently relate to individual preferences for activities and interests, as well as attitudes to various phenomena or beliefs. Usually they take the form of statements to which participants are required to respond by selecting one of, usually, three given answers. For example, the *Maudsley Personality Inventory* contains items that require individuals to register responses to questions such as:

Are you inclined to keep in the background on
social occasions?   Yes   ?   No

Do you have frequent ups and downs in mood,
either with or without apparent cause?   Yes   ?   No

Here, Eysenck provides the middle option '?' for those situations where it was absolutely impossible for the respondent to make a clear decision, adding that this category should not be checked except very occasionally. Interestingly, the EPI and the EPQ both omit the middle, 'uncertain' category and force a straight 'yes' or 'no' response.

Cattell's inventories tend to be significantly longer due to the necessity of measuring 16 factors. His items also offer three alternatives which may either be similar to those of Eysenck or, alternatively, require 'true', 'uncertain', or 'false'; or 'always', 'sometimes', or 'hardly ever' kinds of response. As in Eysenck's MPI, Cattell asks his subjects to avoid the middle answers wherever possible. Some of Cattell's items take the form of a choice between qualitatively different answers, for example:

Prosecuting lawyers are mainly interested in:

(a)   making convictions, regardless of the person
(b)   uncertain
(c)   protecting the innocent

The following types of item relate to the intelligence scale:

Which of the following numbers does not belong with the others:

   (a)   7
   (b)   9
   (c)   13

Is 'lose' a better opposite to 'reveal' than 'hide'?

   (a)   yes
   (b)   uncertain
   (c)   no

As with the EPI, the Myers–Briggs also forces respondents to make a clear choice between two alternatives; for example, the two following items relate to the judging–perceiving scale:

Do you like:

   (a)   to arrange your dates and parties some distance ahead
   (b)   to be free to do whatever looks like fun at the time

When you start a big project that is due in a week, do you

(a)   take time to list the separate things to be done and the order of doing them
(b)   plunge in

Other items require subjects to select one of two words (a or b) that appeals
to them more:

(a) firm-minded   (b) warm-hearted
(a) sensible   (b) fascinating

Both Eysenck and Cattell encourage respondents to work through the test
items as quickly as possible, and certainly do not wish them to ponder at
length over a particular answer. In their view it is the first, impulsive reaction that is likely to be the most accurate response and to contain the least
distortion.

As already mentioned, each question in an inventory relates to a particular scale on which individuals may score relatively high or low. These factors are said to be *bi-polar*: each pole being assigned a trait label possessing
psychological significance. For example, in Cattell's and Eysenck's introver-
sion/extraversion scales, items build up scores towards the extraversion
pole; a low score indicates that the individual is introverted. However, this
does not mean that test items relating to this scale are all extraversion items,
merely that positive responses on extraversion items will score and that positive responses on introversion items will not. It is usually immaterial which
end of a bi-polar scale is designated high or low; this depends on how the
items have been constructed and how they are scored. Thus, what may be
designated as high scoring on one inventory may conceivably be low on
another.

Some tests containing items with three response levels may allow two levels of scoring; some answers being awarded two points, others one, the
remainder none. Cattell's inventories are of this type; Eysenck's ascribe one
mark to all questions. The Myers–Briggs features some items that have been
given double weighting and score two points.

Trait theory controversy

During the last two decades or so, a debate has ensued concerning whether
behaviour is driven by people's internal predispositions, which are measurable in the form of traits, or whether the whole notion of traits is illusory. The
debate is commonly regarded as having had its roots in Mischel's (1968) celebrated critique, which for a long period threatened to demolish the whole
edifice of personality trait theory in one single act. The central feature of the
controversy related to whether personality traits adequately predict behaviour, or whether changes in environment may exert so much variance as to
render the notion of traits more or less meaningless. The 'person–situation
debate', as it is commonly called (see, for example, Kenrick and Funder 1988;

Deary and Matthews 1993), focused attention on a polarized argument as to whether people possess unmodulated consistencies in their behaviour, regardless of their situations, or whether our behaviour is far more power-fully determined by the wide range of types of situation and circumstances that we encounter in the process of daily living.

Mischel's criticism principally related to what he believed to be the emergence of far too small correlations in research that sought causal links between trait scores and behaviour. His research subsequently received heavy criticism, due to his adoption of data that comprised unreliable single units of behaviour, made by observers who were strangers to those being observed. It was argued that behaviour ratings need to be made by those who are able to observe subjects across a variety of circumstances. The consensus that appears to have emerged since takes the view that single behavioural acts are notoriously unreliable and that, in real-life situations, judgements are made on aggregates of behaviour that enjoy considerably higher levels of reliability (see Deary and Matthews 1993). Another view that has been expressed, and one very much in line with that of Cattell, is that even quite modest correlations may be of theoretical and practical importance (Kenrick and Funder 1988).

The upshot of the person–situation debate appears to be a form of truce between the personality theorists and those psychologists who wish to take a more sociological stance towards the influences of the environment on individual behaviour. The emerging agreement between these parties takes the form of a consensus that 'behaviour depends on an interaction between qualities of the person and qualities of the physical and social environment' (Deary and Matthews 1993, pp. 299–300). Certainly, I wish to take the view here that the musician's development is a product of the kind of person that he or she is, as well as the prevailing environment in which the development of musical talent is allowed to take place and flourish.

Perhaps the most problematic issue and the one that has proved most destructive to personality trait theory relates to the lack of agreement concerning the accurate identification of traits. This certainly has added fuel to the debate insofar that, for every originator of an inventory, there appears to emerge a different set of dimensions. Personality literature contains an abundance of papers relating to issues concerning the identification of traits and the use of particular statistical techniques in order to arrive at accurate and reliable solutions (see, for example, H. J. Eysenck and Eysenck 1969; Howarth and Brown 1971; Howarth 1976; Cattell 1972a; Adcock *et al.* 1974).

The 'big five' dimensions

The above debate has resulted in the gradual emergence of some degree of consensus in the form of what are known as the 'big five' dimensions,

claimed by their proponents to be totally independent higher-order personality factors. In fact, the movement towards consensus can be traced as far
back as the work of Norman (1963) who first suggested that most of the traits
identified by most personality researchers relate to a simpler five-factor
model. After several years of similar efforts Costa and McCrae (1985) eventually also settled on a five-factor model comprising the dimensions of neuroticism, extraversion, openness, agreeableness, and conscientiousness.
These dimensions, shown in Table 4 with their respective facet scales, are
measured by the inventory known as the NEO-PI-R (Costa and McCrae
1992a).

Table 4 The 'big five' factors *

Dimensions	Facet scales
Neuroticism	Anxiety
	Angry hostility
	Depression
	Self-consciousness
	Impulsiveness
	Vulnerability
Extraversion	Warmth
	Gregariousness
	Assertiveness
	Activity
	Excitement seeking
	Positive emotions
Openness	Fantasy
	Aesthetics
	Feelings
	Actions
	Ideas
	Values
Agreeableness	Trust
	Straightforwardness
	Altruism
	Compliance
	Modesty
	Tender-mindedness
Conscientiousness	Competence
	Order
	Dutifulness
	Achievement striving
	Self-discipline
	Deliberation

* From Costa and McCrae (1992b, p. 654).

A glance at Table 4 offers the reader some insights into the nature of these dimensions, and particularly of the three factors that Costa and McCrae have added to those of extraversion and neuroticism already familiar to us. Certain pieces of research have attempted to study how the five factors relate to existing personality tests (see for example Noller *et al.* 1987; McCrae and Costa 1989a). This kind of work will not only help us understand the nature of the less familiar factors but also demonstrates how the different tests relate to one another .

Firstly, 'openness to experience' appears to be related to a proactive seeking out of experience for its own sake, and it will not come as a surprise to us to find that it relates well with the Myers–Briggs Type Indicator preferences for intuition and also with Cattell's imagination (M+), and radicalism (Q1+) factors. The 'agreeableness' dimension can be seen to relate to social attitudes, a good-natured, trusting, and helpful disposition. It has been shown to link fairly strongly with the Myers–Briggs preference for feeling, and it is easy to see why it should relate to Cattell's sensitivity (I+) and outgoingness (A+) factors. Thirdly, the conscientiousness factor speaks for itself, and describes the well-organized, self-disciplined, and persevering person. McCrae and Costa (1989a) claim that the Myers–Briggs judging preference is positively related to this dimension, and it will not come as a surprise to the reader to find that Cattell's conscientiousness (G+) and self-sentiment (Q3+) factors are also linked very strongly with it.

There still remains, however, some dissension amongst the ranks of personality theorists. For example, Eysenck (1992a) has challenged Costa and McCrae's (1992b) assertion about the reality of their five basic dimensions, maintaining that their claims are premature and that the debate needs to continue. Cattell (1995) takes an even more challenging stance, dismissing the five-factor structure as a fallacy and believing that at the end of the day his eight-factor theory will be vindicated. However, Eysenck and Cattell notwithstanding, a less fragmented view of the field is developing. This has provided personality trait theory with a confidence and bullishness that certainly did not characterize the personality researchers in the years immediately following Mischel's devastating attack.

A book such as this that attempts to draw together the diversity of research on the personalities of musicians is clearly dependent upon the 'state of the art' that obtains up to the point of going to press. Given the variation of approach within the field, it will not come as a surprise to find the same diversity represented in the literature on musicians. Any attempt to draw together research results from different inventories, let alone different theoretical perspectives, will be viewed by some as unscientific, if not spurious. On the other hand, the movement towards the adoption of the 'big five' provides a more comfortable and stable basis on which to proceed, albeit with a certain degree of caution.

Summary

This 'Introduction' has been restricted to those theories of personality that have generally been adopted in the field of research on musicians. A large proportion of this relates to the use of traits and dimensions, specifically of the kind developed by Cattell and Eysenck. Because there is a growing body of research with musicians that has adopted Jung's psychological typing, as measured by the Myers–Briggs, this is also described.

Cattell's attempt to measure personality in its totality led to the identification of a number of overlapping primary traits that, in turn, help to establish a structure of larger second-order factors. Thus, with Cattell's tests, people's personalities can be viewed, either at a general level, through a set of broader second-order factors, or in more detail through primary traits. Eysenck's more parsimonious approach involves three dimensions, two of which are not dissimilar to Cattell's second-order factors of extraversion and anxiety. Jung's psychological types, measured by the Myers–Briggs, also include the introversion–extraversion 'attitudes' as well as two dichotomous preferences: firstly, sensing–intuition and, secondly, thinking–feeling. A final preference, judging–perceiving, assists the researcher in identifying which one of these four preferences is dominant in a person's orientation to the world. Different combinations of these attitudes and preferences result in a structure of 16 types.

Trait theory has been the focus of much controversy during the last 20 years which has often focused on what is referred to as the 'person–situation' debate. This, put simply, relates to the question as to whether people's behaviour is governed principally by their personality dispositions or whether situational factors exert so much influence as to render any talk of traits meaningless. Resolution of this conflict has not been assisted by the fact that personality researchers, until relatively recently, have not been able to come to any real consensus about an overall structure for the human personality. However, the development of what has become known as the 'big five' model of dimensions has done something to unite those working in the field, although in some quarters the debate continues. Unfortunately, research with musicians that has adopted these new inventories is sparse at the point of going to press.

ONE

Musicianship from a different perspective

Introduction

The growth of literature in the psychology of music during the last 20 years
has been a remarkable phenomenon. Besides the appearance of several prestigious journals during this period, we have seen the publication of a growing number of influential books dealing with music psychology in all manner of different aspects. In his review of some of this published material,
Hargreaves (1986) helpfully maps out the ever-expanding territory, revealing a prevalence of interest in music cognition that places an emphasis on
'internalised rules, operations, and strategies that people employ in intelligent behaviour just as much as on the external behavioural manifestations of
these processes' (p. 15). The principal areas that can be identified most clearly in the literature relate to clusters of research focusing upon: testing and
psychometric procedures; acoustical and psychophysical approaches; developmental work, frequently relating to Piagetian theory; interrelationships
between linguistic structures and music cognition; information processing
and artificial intelligence; behavioural approaches; and instructional and
educational methods.

Much of this literature reveals an underlying belief that, by investigating
people's perceptual and cognitive processes of responding to and creating
music, music psychologists will be able to develop a clearer understanding
of the complexities of the musical phenomena themselves. Such an understanding, it might be thought, will help demystify and demythologize music
for the listener, the learner, and the practitioner. To give a few examples:
cognitive psychology will help explain the nature of musical communication
itself by investigating certain encoding and decoding processes; it might try
to map the territory of general abilities and intelligence and the ways in
which musical capacities and achievement relate to, or emerge as independent of these; it might attempt to define more precisely how the human
mind, at different stages of development, perceives and conceptualizes the
elements of music; it might attempt to establish how and why different people respond to pieces of music in characteristically different ways and, thereby, account for musical preferences. These research areas, and many more,

demonstrate a general concern of researchers to develop a deeper under-standing of how the musical mind functions and, thereby, hopefully to gain greater insights into music itself.

It is curious that a glance through the ever-growing number of books dealing with the psychology of music reveals, with only a few exceptions, a paucity of space devoted to personality and temperament. Certainly this may reflect the debunking of personality trait theory, referred to in the 'Introduction', which has tended to dominate the study of psychology and which may well have permeated the teaching of psychology at undergradu-ate level during recent years. It may, however, reveal a suspicion of theories and 'findings' that have 'proved impossible to operationalise and verify' (Hargreaves 1986, p. 5). However, with researchers' more recent and devel-oping interests in qualitative research methods, which it could be argued are particularly suited to music, it is conceivable that a different balance may obtain in the future.

In his argument for taking a broader view, adopting a more dynamic and inclusive approach to the study of abilities, occupations, and hobbies, Cattell (1971) criticized ability researchers for unduly subdividing psychology according to a traditional academic structure where, for example, percep-tion, sensation, and motor abilities are dealt with in isolation from personal-ity. The argument presented here takes the stance that, in considering a phe-nomenon like musicianship that, more or less by definition, encompasses not only perceptual, cognitive, and motor skills but also, just as importantly, an awareness of people's deeper levels of functioning, we must be allowed to explore, however speculatively, emotional and temperamental compo-nents. Such an approach will certainly incorporate personality dimensions as a matter of course.

Interestingly, in writing about music as a cognitive skill, Sloboda (1985) commences by remarking that

... music is capable of arousing in us deep and significant emotions. These emotions can range from the 'pure' aesthetic delight in a sound construction, through emotions like joy or sorrow which music sometimes evokes or enhances, to the simple relief from monotony, boredom or depression which everyday musical experiences can provide. (p. 1)

He considers that if emotional factors are fundamental to the existence of music then the question that arises is *how* people are affected by it. The human mind endows musical events, collections of sounds, with signifi-cance; 'they become symbols for something other than the pure sound, something which enables us to laugh or cry, to like or dislike, be moved or be indifferent' (p. 1). A personality researcher such as myself could not fail to be attracted to this line of thinking. It therefore comes as something of a surprise when Sloboda offers reasons why this issue leads him straight into the realms of cognitive psychology. Using the analogy of the joke, he maintains that understanding music is a necessary precursor to being moved by it. The cognitive stage involves the individual in forming an abstract or symbolic internal representation of the music—it is this internal representation that Sloboda considers is the central matter of the cognitive psychology of music.

A broader view

In the context of this book, Sloboda's analogy may be felt to be inappropriate simply because many people may not always feel the need to 'understand' music in quite the same way as one needs to grasp a joke cognitively before responding to it. And we are not necessarily talking only about the naïve listener here: in instances where people have developed considerable cognitive understanding of music there is, nevertheless, no doubt that deep, intuitive responses still operate in very powerful ways. Even the most skilled musician may be profoundly moved by a piece of music and *still not know why* (see Kemp 1992). This opens up a new area involving the vexed question relating to the nature of knowing, and particularly questions relating to the less cognitive forms of 'knowing' and their relationship with feeling particularly in the arts. Whether we view the musician from a Cattellian or Jungian position, we find clear evidence for their preference for a more feelingful and less cerebral approach to their art (see Chapter 4). Cooke (1959) took the view that music is the 'most articulate language of the unconscious' (p. x), which takes us into the study of personality as an alternative way of viewing people's predisposition to respond to art objects in very complex ways, and to pursue them as an inherent part of their value systems.

Because music is an art, it is important to develop a deeper understanding of the diversity of human nature and experience, which drives composers to create in various styles, conductors and performers to interpret pieces differently, and listeners to respond to musical works in a number of different ways. For, whilst choosing to be a musician in the first place is, in itself, an expression of individuality, it is the further encounter with music that allows composers, performers, and listeners to develop their individuality and their sense of identity. This view leads us straight into the field of personality. Certainly, if the geography of the phenomenon of musicianship is to be researched at any depth (and breadth), it is the contention of this book that personality should feature as an essential dimension.

It is often thought that people within a musical culture will generally agree on the emotional character of a piece not heard before. Nevertheless, within this general, and what might be perceived as very superficial agreement, there might well emerge a variety of responses which, it might be argued, arise from individual differences of a less cognitive origin. People perceive and come to know the world around them very differently, and this also applies to art objects, the ambiguity of which stretches our imaginations and allows us to delve deeper into our own sense of identity and well-being. It is not the intention here to polarize these issues, but merely to raise the alternative notion that human temperament might be more powerfully operative than is sometimes acknowledged in the more cognitively orientated literature.

Despite the principal thrust of his research being exclusively directed towards the testing of musical capacities, Seashore (1967), perhaps surprisingly to some readers, took a broader stance and encouraged researchers to look at musicianship more globally. We must, he maintained,

... keep in the foreground the fundamental fact that the musical mind does not consist of its dissected parts, but in an integrated personality. In its evaluation we must always have regard for the total personality as functioning in a total situation. . . What makes it (musical mind) musical is the possession, in a serviceable degree, of those capacities which are essential for the hearing, the feeling, the understanding, and, ordinarily, for some form of expression of music, with a resulting drive or urge toward music. (pp. 1–2)

The 'resulting drive or urge towards music' relates to one of the most critical questions in music, and certainly in music education. Why do some people respond to certain pieces and types of music and not to others? and why do some people appear to remain indifferent to engaging in music whilst others become totally absorbed by it? It was questions like these that stimulated the early research into standardized tests of musical abilities from Seashore onwards (see, for example, Shuter-Dyson and Gabriel 1981) and the search for insights into the structure of musical abilities. The underlying assumption made by some of these researchers was that different levels of musical response were largely due to individuals' cognitive capacities. Despite the considerable growth in music testing in the 1950s and 60s, these various tests have not been wholeheartedly accepted by either cognitive psychologists or music educationists, and even those particularly designed for school use, for example, by Bentley (1966a), have not received universal acceptance. The underlying reasons for this may be complex, and certainly some tests have received criticism due to their apparently, low face validity. In other words, some tests such as those of Seashore, for example, appeared to be so devoid of real musical value or meaning that they were dismissed as inappropriate for the purpose of identifying musicianship. In the view of such opponents to music tests, those that appeared to measure little more than a person's ability to hear and to make judgements about acoustical phenomena rather than music indicated that perhaps little more than auditory acuity was being measured.

Seashore (1967, pp. 4–5) cited the case of the brother of a famous musician who, in the opinion of his family, appeared on the face of it to possess no musical talent whatever. However, it transpired that he performed better than his musical brother on a battery of musical capacity tests, suggesting that he had extraordinary musical abilities. This caused Seashore to pose the question as to whether the man was, in fact, musical or not. The opponents of testing, preferring to be more convinced by life criteria, would probably maintain that the man was probably not musical, but was displaying a 'good ear'—one prerequisite of being a musician, but certainly not embracing all the necessary qualities. One of these qualities might well relate to the necessary drive and appropriate temperament for success in music that the other more successful brother appeared to possess in greater degree, despite exhibiting lower levels of musical capacity. These additional qualities, one might wish to speculate, allowed him to become eminently successful, despite his more modest musicianship, as measured by the music ability scales. In other words, musical ability tests may assist in identifying certain auditory capacities, but these represent only a limited part of what might be considered to be a global view of the total musician.

Interestingly, it was Wing (1968) who, being critical of Seashore's 'atomistic' approach, attempted to incorporate an 'appreciation' dimension into his test battery. On the face of it this might have led him to adopt a stance not out of line with that pursued here but, instead, he adopted the rather questionable strategies of measuring judgements concerning the appropriateness of certain harmonizations, dynamics, and phrasing. Despite what were, no doubt, good intentions, this part of his test is today considered to be the weakest part.

Howe (1990a) argued that high achievement in any field is fuelled by non-intellectual qualities. Those whom we perceive as being geniuses are clearly intelligent and clever but, in his opinion, one cannot make the assumption that the qualities possessed by these people are exclusively intellectual. 'The human intellect is neither autonomous nor self-sufficient. There is a sense in which it has to be driven into action' (p. 181). He went on to cite Shuter-Dyson's (1985) account of how a headmaster of a school for the musically gifted selected his pupils for entry. He maintained that the most promising appeared to be characterized by an appetite for music that was insatiable and so strong that without music they would feel deprived. Terman's early research into giftedness demonstrated that the main measurable differences between more and less successful groups constituted dimensions of personality and temperament and not intellectual factors (Renzulli 1986). Many a music teacher can describe instances where a student with apparently mediocre talent makes rapid strides towards a seemingly unattainable goal, leaving what appears to be a more talented student behind. As we have already seen, Howe stresses the importance of personal qualities other than abilities.

What are these qualities? They seem to be ones that are only weakly governed by abilities as such. They appear to depend more on motivation, and on temperament and personality. Gaining an all-important sense of direction or purpose seems to involve the combination of particular abilities and these other attributes. (Howe 1990b, p. 68)

This book adopts the stance that, whilst research into the musician's cognitive and psychomotor processes is important, nevertheless, on its own, it gives a one-sided and restricted picture. There is evidence of a ground-swell in recent research that suggests that the balance may be becoming redressed. However, it is the study of the *interrelationship* between these domains, as advocated by both Cattell and Eysenck, although principally lying outside the main focus of this book, that will offer the greatest insights.

In searching, then, for insights into the nature and structure of musicianship, we might well wish to consider Cattell's (1971) notion of three 'modalities' . Like Howe, he maintained that the close analysis of any ability is impossible without a thorough understanding of the psychological principles of personality and motivation. Although they may appear to be conceptually distinct, these three 'trait modalities', ability, personality, and motivation, nevertheless, interact, and Cattell refers to personality factors in this situation as 'ability factor stimulators' (p. 360). He gives a number of examples of how the development of an ability like music can be influenced by personality: levels of independence can be so intertwined with ability factors that they can frequently be mistaken for each other (p. 363); people's ego strength shows striking overlaps with their abilities, affecting their determination and speeds of decision-making in all sorts of tasks; cortical alertness, one of Cattell's second-order personality traits, aids several kinds of cognitive performances (pp. 362–4). On the other hand, ability can exercise a significant impact upon personality development. High intelligence, Cattell maintains, can help generate high levels of dominance, radicalism, imagination, and self-sufficiency. Incidentally, it was for this reason that Cattell included intelligence in his personality inventories.

Let us, then, move on to consider, albeit briefly, the second of these modalities, motivation, before proceeding to a broad overview of the musician's personality. These will be viewed principally from the Cattellian perspective, drawing in other theories and points of view as and when they are considered necessary.

Motivation and musical ability

Cattell and Child (1975) took the view that motivation, together with the two other main areas of human differences, abilities and personality, exercise an *equal* impact upon pupils' academic achievement. If they are correct, it certainly warrants our attention in developing our understanding of higher levels of achievement be it in an area of scholastic learning or adult occupations. Certainly a body of opinion is beginning to be established in which personality and motivational factors are considered to be powerful in the development of musical talent. Ericsson *et al.* (1990) have shown that the starting age for élite musical performers is around 7 years and, although they are careful to point out that, in these initial stages, motivation will be largely extrinsic, it would appear clear that, at some point, a more intrinsic form of motivation will take over when the individual must assume personal responsibility for his or her practice routines. Either this, or the child becomes disinterested, disenchanted, or rebellious and, as a result, drops out. Those children that progress to significant levels of achievement, therefore, appear frequently to be characterized by a consuming strength of interest. Recently, Sloboda *et al.* (1996) have calculated that, up to the age of 21, a talented pupil will have spent about 10 000 hours in purposeful practice. The single-mindedness of the musician's engagement in these excessive hours spent in isolated practice would appear to indicate an internal state of drive and energy taking the form of exceptionally well-developed urges and deeply held sentiments.

The point at which the changeover takes place from extrinsic to intrinsic motivation is not at all clear. Davidson *et al.* (1996) have recently suggested that the parents of high achievers may continue to give active encouragement for a period of between 12 and 15 years. There are at least two questions that require answering in relation to this: firstly, what happens to these young musicians when they enter conservatoires and are no longer subject to this form of support? and, secondly, is it not most likely that strong forms of internal drive, commitment, and motivation have to be well-developed alongside and within the context of this parental support and encouragement? Certainly, some evidence exists that tends to suggest that parental support has limited effects later when good practice habits are well in place (Kemp 1982b, 1995). Indeed, it might be suggested that those who emerge as particularly gifted show signs of being left very much to their own devices. Roe (1967) went so far as to suggest that a little neglect does not come amiss in nurturing creative talent. We shall return to these kinds of question in later chapters.

The study of motivation is not as advanced a science as that of personality, and, if anything, the field is even more fragmentary. As his starting point, Cattell adopted the early theories of the primary instinctual drives such as hunger, thirst, and sex, as highlighted in the influential work of Hull (1943). Taken at their face value, these might appear to be somewhat extraneous to our concerns here, whereas McClelland's (1961) work focused upon those needs that can be perceived as being more socially orientated, such as needs for affiliation and achievement. Maslow (1987) incorporated both types of approach into his more all-embracing model of human needs, which took the form of a triangular-shaped hierarchy (see Figure 1.1) in which he suggested that, once Hull's primary needs are met, safety and security become important. Similarly, when a person achieves these, the kind of affiliation needs referred to by McClelland can then be sought, and so on until the state of full 'self-actualization' is achieved. Whilst some might wish to question whether the satisfaction of higher needs is always dependent upon the prior satisfaction of the lower needs, there may be important insights to be gained from Maslow's theory for our closer study of the musician. If the musician is driven by the need to 'self-actualize' through music, then, according to Maslow, self-esteem, a search for meaning, and aesthetic needs appear to be inextricably bound up with this. Certainly, it has been shown in Cattell's early research that several of the dynamic components of motivation under-pin academic achievement (Cattell and Child 1975; Cattell *et al.* 1966) as well as interrelating with personality development (Cattell and Kline 1977).

Cattell and his co-workers have identified two kinds of dynamic factor: those concerned with *strength of motive*, and those that focus on *goals of action*. The first three of the strength of motive factors they identified were assigned Greek alphabetical names and relate closely to Freud's id, ego, and superego. The alpha factor, unlike Freud's id, is conscious, but bears a resemblance to the id in its irrational drives to satisfy certain wishes and desires. Freud (1964) described the id as being 'filled with energy reaching it from the instincts, but it has no organization, produces no collective will, but only a striving to bring about the satisfaction of the instinctual needs . . . ' (p. 73). The beta factor, which draws on the Freudian concept of the ego, relates to 'realized, integrated interests' acquired through habits and duty. It is also a fully conscious factor and is well-integrated into the routine of daily life; it has regard for remote but realistic rewards. Certainly, we shall observe in later chapters the extent to which musicians' drive is inherently bound up with their self-esteem. They appear to invest so much of themselves in their long-term musical goals that if, for one reason or another, these are unrealized severe personal crises can occur. This observation also relates to Cattell's third strength of motive factor, gamma, which has some of the features of the superego in that it appears to have an 'I ought to be interested' quality. It takes the form of a conscious preference for an activity, persevering for some kind of reward but lacking any real information about the activity. A fourth, more tentative factor, the delta factor, relates to autonomic physiological response which appears to link with the 'shiver down the spine' sensation experienced by listeners to certain moments in pieces of music (see Sloboda 1991). Cattell (1957) speculated that this phenomenon might be connected with the unconscious id.

Cattell and Kline (1977, pp. 173–4) offer a helpful example of the ways in which the alpha, beta, and gamma factors might manifest themselves in aspects of career choice. It relates to three surgeons, all equally interested in their work, equally hard-working, equally conscientious at keeping up with the latest developments in their profession. In spite of being equally moti-vated and successful, the three may operate with very different underlying patterns of motivation. One might be driven by his ego: his job might allow

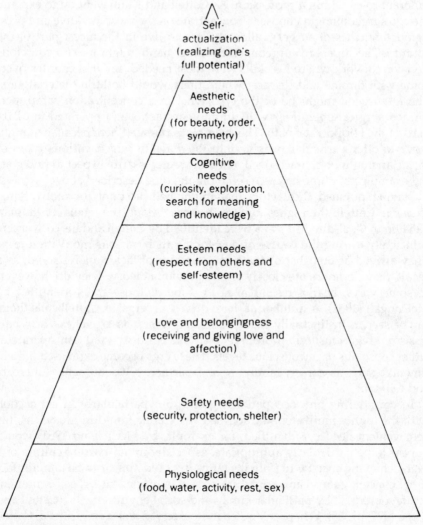

Self-
actualization
(realizing one's
full potential)

Aesthetic
needs
(for beauty, order,
symmetry)

Cognitive
needs
(curiosity, exploration,
search for meaning
and knowledge)

Esteem needs
(respect from others and
self-esteem)

Love and belongingness
(receiving and giving love and
affection)

Safety needs
(security, protection, shelter)

Physiological needs
(food, water, activity, rest, sex)

Figure 1.1 Maslow's hierarchy of human needs.

him to live well and provide for his family and to take his place in the community as a respected citizen. The second may be motivated by his superego: his interest in surgery springing from his conviction that he should alleviate human suffering and to work for the good of humanity. The third, driven by the id, might be driven by a sadistic, aggressive pleasure in cutting up bodies and the ghoulish side of surgery.

Whilst this example may not interest the reader who is more attracted to theories that help to separate the successful from the unsuccessful, it does help to explain the bases upon which people might choose to pursue different roles within a profession. As Cattell and Kline went on to explain, the ego surgeon might choose to concentrate on the most lucrative and prestigious branches of surgery, allowing him to live in the nicest part of the country. The superego surgeon, on the other hand, might make a conscious decision to work where his skills were most needed, say in a country overcome with famine and disease, where there would be little material gain. The id surgeon might be of the type who, in a concentration camp, performed surgical operations without an anaesthetic, and operated in disregard of the Hippocratic oath. The example is pursued here because it might serve to offer particular insights into the ways in which various types of musician might be characterized; not that we necessarily expect to find glaring examples of id musicians resembling the type described above!

Having pursued the factors that might help account for motivational *strength*, Cattell then goes on to theorize about the goals of human behaviour. Goal-directed traits were identified by Cattell and his co-workers principally during the course of developing their various motivation tests. They arrived at their list of traits by processes of factor analysis and, as a result, they do not relate closely to any previous theory. They do, however, in some ways, bear a resemblance to some of those traits identified by McDougall (1932). A number of these drives, or 'ergs' as Cattell calls them, can be seen as instinctually based, for example, sex, assertiveness, fear, narcissism, gregariousness, protectiveness, and curiosity, and can operate at either conscious or unconscious levels. These ergs become expressed in 'sentiments', such as career, family, sexual partner, self-sentiment, superego, and religion.

In considering any occupational group, but particularly in connection with the highly motivated and focused work ethic found in musicians, the achievement need (as identified, for example, by McClelland 1961) would appear to be particularly appropriate, especially in our current culture of a high-achieving society. In Cattell's terms it would appear to be a 'multi-factorial concept comprising a mixture of self-assertion, career, self-sentiment etc. favoured . . . by particular family and social environments' (Cattell and Kline 1977, p. 335). Whereas McClelland perceived it as a single need, Cattell and Kline have begun to clarify the achievement need as far more complex in nature. If nothing else, Cattell's work in this domain demonstrates the complexity of motivational factors, particularly manifest in his diagrammatic presentation in the form of an intricate 'lattice' that describes the complex entanglement and dynamic operation of ergs and sentiments, as well as their influences on behaviour.

It is often said that Freud placed too much emphasis on the sex erg, and, whilst this might appear to be true, it is also clear that another feature of psychoanalytic theory involving the sex erg is supported by Cattell's lattice model. As Cattell and Kline observed, Freud claimed that many apparently asexual activities actually express the sex drive and, certainly, a glance at

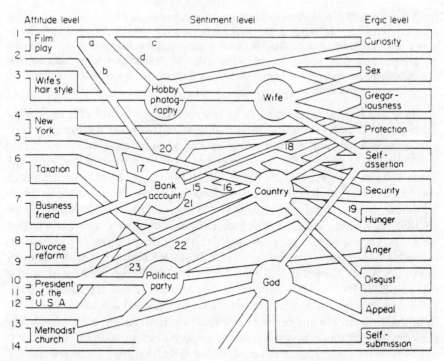

Figure 1.2 Part of a dynamic lattice. From Cattell and Kline (1977, p. 177).

Cattell's dynamic lattice (see Figure 1.2) demonstrates the ways in which many specific activities express ergs and sentiments that appear, on the face of it, to be quite remote.

To digress at this point into a lengthy discussion of sublimation would be unwarranted. However, the notion that energies such as the sex drive can be diverted away from their original objects, and become focused on cultural activities was originally developed by Freud (1925). Whilst generally supporting this view, Storr (1976) maintained that by no means do all artistic achievements have this kind of origin. He also pointed out that it may be the only defence mechanism that can be said to be employed by 'normals' (as opposed to neurotics) in a process of redirecting infantile urges into more socially acceptable channels. It is worth mentioning here that there is a small amount of empirical research that lends support to the Freudian theory of links between the mechanism of sublimation and musical response (Kline 1972). At this point, let it suffice to hold in mind, at least, the notion that creative energy may have its origins, not only in the sex drive, but in the broader set of ergs as identified by Cattell and his colleagues, which, as we have already seen, was Maslow's view. This point is also made in some work on Indian musicians by Raychaudhuri (1966) using projective-type tests, finding that the creative musician

. . . shows signs of sublimation rather than overt expressions of primitive and unconscious impulses; . . . he tends to channel aggression into socially accepted intellectu-
alised and sublimated activities; he feels challenged by frustration and anxiety-
inducing situations rather than being over-powered and crushed; he has
exhibitionistic needs to derive narcissistic satisfaction; he conceives environment to
be cold, hostile and unfriendly. (p. 119)

There are several interesting links between physiological and neurologi-
cal aspects of motivation and personality that also need mentioning here,
and to which we will be returning in future chapters. Cattell and Child
(1975) highlight the central involvement of particular areas of the hypothalamus, the lower regions of the brain, which they describe as activating each
erg. Elsewhere, Cattell (1973) has described one of his second-order factors—
'pathemia'—as a tendency towards 'living at the hypothalamic level'
(p. 185). As we shall see later, this factor appears to relate particularly to persons who choose to operate principally through their feelings and emotions
in contrast to those at the other end of the factor (cortertia) who are more
'cortically alert' (Cattell *et al*. 1970). There are two things worthy of note at
this point. Firstly, musicians appear to be particularly characterized by pathemia, and it is interesting to speculate that the implied association with the
hypothalamus might suggest a heavy reliance upon the motivating effect of
the ergs located there. Secondly, undischarged ergic tension often results in
high levels of anxiety and, as we shall see later, this may be of special significance in the personality structure of some musicians.

Another important cluster of links, to which we shall return in the next
chapter, relates to the involvement of the reticular formation in the activation of levels of arousal. Eysenck (1967) claimed that levels of arousal are
closely related to the extraversion–introversion factor. On the other hand,
Cattell challenges this and maintains that it is more closely related to his
cortertia–pathemia dimension (Cattell and Child 1975). It is Cattell's view
that arousal (excitement) and ergic tension (activation) drive behaviour
onwards and, in the normal course of events, the former transforms to the
latter, which, in turn, is continually reduced or discharged by profitable and
productive behaviour. Not only does this have relevance for theories of
structured learning (Cattell and Dreger 1975), more importantly (for our
purposes), it relates to the processes of anxiety management through purposeful activities, for example, musical endeavour.

Personality and musical ability

It must have been considerably disappointing to the early researchers, who
sought to establish links between personality and musicianship by calculating intercorrelations between music and personality tests, to end up with
largely inconclusive results. For example, Schleuter (1972), who used

Cattell's HSPQ with pupils aged 12 and 13 years, merely detected a relationship between intelligence and tonal and melodic abilities. In a very similar but more extensive study, Thayer (1972) found significant links between Cattell's factors of outgoingness, intelligence, submissiveness, and sensitivity and the composite scores on a musical aptitude test. These same factors, apart from intelligence, were also found to be linked with musical literacy and the *Seashore Measures of Musical Talents* (Seashore *et al.* 1939). In repeating the exercise with 14- and 15-year-olds, Thayer disappointingly found that only intelligence and sensitivity correlated with the music tests. A similar attempt by Shuter (1974) was no more successful: when administering Cattell's *Children's Personality Questionnaire* (CPQ; Porter and Cattell 1959) and the *Bentley Measures of Musical Abilities* (Bentley 1966b) to a group of 9- and 10-year-olds, her results indicated a relationship between the Bentley Measures and Cattell's sensitivity (I+) and self-control (Q3+).

The lack of what he considered to be convincing results from his research led Thayer to conclude, perhaps prematurely, that no systematic relationship existed between music ability factors and personality. Although the emergence of a possible relationship existing between sensitivity (I+) and auditory acuity should not be overlooked as a phenomenon worthy of further research, there may be a number of reasons for these inconclusive results. Despite warnings from Cattell *et al.* (1970) and S. B. G. Eysenck and Eysenck (1969) that gender exerts clear patterns of differences on personality data, there is no evidence that such differences were taken into account, either by adopting norms for the sexes independently, or by attempting to partial out these effects. However, the main problem courted by such research, which adopts music ability test data as the independent variable, is that such tests do not set out to measure actual real-life musical achievement. As Sloboda (1985) has suggested, music ability tests should, wherever possible, be used in conjunction with other forms of evidence. After all, on their own, aural acuity and musical memory may not be sufficiently broad prognosticators of success in musical performance, which would appear to be dependent upon a more comprehensive set of musical sensitivities, let alone factors such as musical interest and imagination. Clearly, then, given the state of the art of music ability testing, there may be few grounds for expecting data from personality and music ability tests to intercorrelate. Particularly, in taking into account Cattell's notion of modalities, it would appear appropriate to suspect that the two domains are largely independent. Such a stance would encourage the researcher to hypothesize that, together, they might mutually enhance their respective abilities to predict success in musical performance.

Certainly this was Cattell's view, not articulated specifically in terms of musicians, but in any circumstances where a special ability or occupational group was being considered. Far better that real-life criteria should be adopted when insights are being sought into the psychological aspects of a particular criterion, particularly the demands in terms of temperament of the development of a particular ability or skill (Cattell *et al.* 1970). As we have already observed, Seashore (1967) in describing the musician as living 'a life of impulse and feeling, extreme sensitivity and capacity for a high degree of specialisation' (p. 175) believed that actual life criteria linked closely with certain temperamental traits, and would have fully supported this view.

Certainly those researchers who have collected data from groups of musicians who actually display musicianship in practice have succeeded in producing rather more conclusive research findings. Even here though we find inconclusive results from some of this earlier research (Sternberg 1955; Garder 1955; Kaplan 1961; Cooley 1961). This may, in large part, have been due to a number of inherent weaknesses. Firstly, some of the personality tests adopted may have possessed dubious levels of validity. For example, Cooley used the Bernreuter Personality Inventory (BPI, Bernreuter 1933) claimed by Vernon (1953) to have serious weaknesses in this respect. Secondly, and as mentioned above, personality data are notoriously subject to the influence of a number of potential intervening variables, which were left largely unheeded in much of the earlier research. S. B. G. Eysenck and Eysenck (1969) claimed that age and gender exert clear patterns of effects upon personality data; the influence of socio-economic status and educational level is rather more obscure.

Thirdly, much early research also assumed that the musician's personality was homogeneous. Cattell *et al.* (1970) appeared to take this stance and based their personality description of the musician on a very unrepresentative sample comprising music therapists and visiting performers in hospitals (Shatin *et al.* 1968). Later research (Kemp 1971, 1979; Krueger 1974) successfully showed that there exists within the music profession a variety of profiles, which reflect the different kinds of demand made upon composers, performers, different instruments, and genres of music. Mixed or biased groups of musicians, in these respects, might well result in deviant or inconclusive profiles. Finally, research has shown that, at different developmental stages, pursuing music appears to require different combinations of what might be perceived as facilitating personality traits (Kemp 1981a, 1982b). Thus, any comparison of results drawn from groups of school pupils, fulltime music students, and professional musicians (quite apart from age differences already mentioned) are very likely to produce, not what might be perceived as tiresome inconsistencies, but patterns that may reveal important insights. It is the psychological significance of these differences and their complex interrelationships that certainly require further exploration.

Perhaps the most extensive piece of research into the personality structure of the musician was carried out at the University of Reading and reported in a series of four research papers (Kemp 1981a,b, 1982a,b). The research incorporated three very large groups of musicians: secondary school pupils, music students in higher education, and professional performers, composers, and teachers. Because of the sizes of these groups it was possible to incorporate age, sex, socio-economic status, and educational level as covariates. The results of this research will be more fully discussed throughout the chapters of this book, together with other findings that relate to the personalities of musicians at various developmental stages. What in general emerged from this research was the suggestion that there exists a set of core personality traits that can be said to characterize most groups of musicians, and other traits that appear to relate to more temporary environmental phases and needs. These second-order factors, introversion, independence, sensitivity, and anxiety, as well as androgyny, and their psychological significance within the musician's temperament will be dealt with one by one in the chapters that follow.

Summary

This chapter has taken the view that a fuller and deeper understanding of the phenomenon of 'musicality' and the nature of musical involvement is offered by incorporating the study of personality into more cognitively orientated research. Whereas cognitive psychology has been successful in making several contributions to our understanding of the conceptual aspects of musical processing, personality may offer additional insights into underlying factors relating to matters of aesthetic valuing and quality of response as well as motivation. We considered that Cattell's notion of three 'modalities' may help to broaden out our field of vision in that it stresses the equal importance of abilities, motivation, and personality in considering any special ability like music. Although musicians clearly engage in highly cognitive processes and develop skills of extraordinary levels of complexity, nevertheless, these, it is maintained here, are 'fired up' and driven by equally unusual levels and combinations of personality predispositions. Perhaps music psychologists have unwittingly subdivided their field in the way generally criticized by both Eysenck and Cattell.

In supporting this idea of taking a broader approach to the study of musicians, this chapter stressed the importance of dynamic traits that might inform our understanding of their high levels of motivation. Maslow's notion that humans are motivated to satisfy a hierarchy of needs underlies much of what is discussed in this book. In this chapter questions were raised about the need of musicians to 'self-actualize' through aesthetic experiences of the kind offered by music. The driving force may relate to a deep-seated need to develop their levels of self-esteem and personal identity. Cattell's theory of motivation was also described as offering additional insights into the complexity of drives and motives.

The chapter closed with a brief overview of research that has attempted to identify the musician's personality either through the use of music ability tests or through 'life' criteria. In doing this, it was suggested that personality research of any kind should be more vigilant about possible intervening variables such as age and gender which, if left unheeded, may result in the kind of inconclusive outcomes suffered by some of the earlier research. The more conclusive research findings suggest that musicians of any age appear to possess a set of core traits of the kind to be discussed individually in the following chapters. In addition, there are other personality factors that appear to respond to more short-term needs.

TWO

Introversion

Introduction

Of all the dimensions of personality, extraversion–introversion is perhaps the one that has attained most acceptance in psychology. Although Jung (1923) is generally considered to have been the originator of the concept, it can, in fact, be traced back to eighteenth century dictionaries. By the turn of the nineteenth century, one finds that its definition is remarkably similar to that adopted by many theorists today. However, the inevitable outcome of a psychological term entering everyday usage is that any sharpness of definition becomes eroded; certainly extraversion has suffered in this respect. Because of this kind of degeneration, in which one can find it applied to a whole range of personal qualities from sociability to emotional adjustment, Cattell adopted the neologisms 'invia' and 'exvia'. More recently, though, he has been prepared to concede that his factor is reasonably identical to that found by other researchers such as Eysenck (Cattell and Kline 1977). However, it is not only because of its long history that the trait is held to be of prime importance in personality theory: it almost invariably emerges as the most prominent factor in personality research regardless of methodology, or even, type of inventory.

Jung (1923), of course, couched his theory of introversion in psychoanalytic language, referring to the turning inwards or outwards of the libido, a notion that he developed in the course and context of his clinical work. Stated simply, extraverts direct their energies outwards towards people, and engage in a life-style of action based upon objectivity. Conversely, introverts direct their energies inwards, and tend to move naturally away from people, preferring to dwell in a personal, internal world of subjective experience. The former is characterized by quick adaptation to the environment, particularly in terms of the individual's impact upon it; the latter involves a proneness towards reflection and thoughtfulness, and a fear of unknown persons. In discussing Jung's typology, Storr (1963) expressed the view that the extraverted attitude is characterized by fear of being abandoned, whereas the introverted attitude is more likely to be characterized by a fear of being dominated.

Eysenck's definition of the dimension relates principally to processes of socialization. Extraverts like parties, need to have people around them, and seek out excitement and stimulation. They tend to be carefree, optimistic, and show their feelings freely. On the other hand, introverts are retiring and introspective, preferring a few close friends, and rarely behave in an impulsive manner. They prefer to plan well ahead; they are cautious, dislike excitement, and keep their feelings to themselves. Introverts are often thought to be more reliable, and may place greater value on the maintenance of ethical standards than do extraverts (Eysenck and Eysenck 1964).

It should also be borne in mind that, whilst Cattell was willing to concede that his definition related reasonably happily to Jung's notion of the inward-looking personality, Jung proposed a *typology* (people are either extraverts or introverts), whereas Cattell and Eysenck's factorial approach highlights the notion of *dimension*. Jung then, was proposing a bi-modal distribution on introversion–extraversion, whereas Cattell and Eysenck maintained that people can be located at any point along a continuum between two poles: thus, people can also be classed as 'ambiverts'.

Underlying factors of introversion

Eysenck's description of extraversion features five contributory traits: sociability; impulsiveness; activity; liveliness; and excitability. Of these, sociability and impulsiveness appear to be the principal components. On the other hand, Cattell's exvia is made up of four underlying traits: outgoingness (A+); surgency (F+); adventurousness (H+); and group-dependency (Q2–). Cattell's (1973) loadings for these factors on extraversion suggest that outgoingness and group-dependency are the more important.

A closer look at Cattell's contributory primaries will assist us in gaining a clearer definition of the resultant second-order factor. Since, as will be seen, our principal interests will focus upon introversion, we will concern ourselves with the primary factor descriptions that relate to that end of the dimension. Figure 2.1 shows diagrammatically the extent to which these four factors relate to introversion. Firstly, aloofness (A–) describes the individual who is reserved and detached. It is one of the largest traits in the total personality and, because Cattell's factors tend to intercorrelate or overlap, it relates to more than one second-order factor. Aloofness is commonly found in creative people of all kinds—artists, writers, and musicians—and Cattell (1973) has maintained that the factor addresses much more than merely sociability or gregariousness. In elaborating the point he suggests that

... the characteristic skeptical, critical, aloof behavior of the sizic person is thus an expression of low reward in human relations, which is due partly to rigid, ideal expectations and results in a turning to an orderly, impersonal world, such as science, logic, ideation. (p. 159)

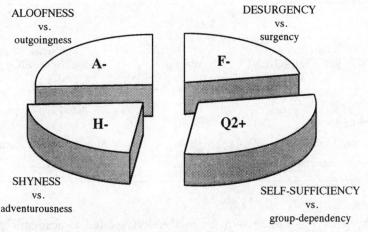

Figure 2.1 Primary factors of introversion in adults.

FACTOR A		
Low score ALOOF A–	versus	High score OUTGOING A+
Detached, reserved	vs.	Participating
Cold	vs.	Warmhearted
Critical	vs.	Easygoing
Stands by own ideas	vs.	Ready to co-operate
Cool	vs.	Attentive to people
Precise, objective	vs.	Soft-hearted, casual
Distrustful, sceptical	vs.	Trustful
Rigid	vs.	Adaptable, careless
Prone to sulk	vs.	Laughs readily

Box 2.1

The other particularly important factor that loads on introversion is self-sufficiency (Q2+). Cattell (1973) describes this trait as a predominant characteristic of artists, writers, and research scientists, and also '. . . those who were seclusive as children and stubborn in school. They developed early . . . were considered mature, and had few friends and those older. Often such people are the oldest or only children' (p. 175). Although Cattell remarked that self-sufficiency occasionally links with schizophrenia, it should normally be associated with strength of character.

FACTOR Q2		
Low score GROUP-DEPENDENT Q2–	versus	High score SELF-SUFFICIENT Q2+
Sociable	vs.	Ungregarious
A joiner	vs.	A loner
Sound follower	vs.	Makes own decisions
Conventional	vs.	Resourceful

Box 2.2

Desurgency (F–) appears to be moderately related to academic performance, to the development of strong work-habits, and to what Cattell (1973) refers to as 'deep creativity' (p. 164). Desurgent people are sober and cautious, and Cattell maintains that they have been made so by their life's experiences. As we shall see later, the fourth factor associated with introversion—shyness (H–)—appears to be less operative in the personality structure of the musician but, for completeness, let it suffice to say that it appears to be associated with strict discipline in upbringing and anxious, apprehensive mothering.

FACTOR F		
Low score DESURGENT F–	versus	High score SURGENT F+
Sober	vs.	Enthusiastic
Serious	vs.	Happy-go-lucky
Silent, introspective	vs.	Talkative
Full of cares	vs.	Cheerful
Uncommunicative	vs.	Expressive
Slow, cautious	vs.	Quick, alert

Box 2.3

At this point we should also note that the children's structure of introversion features an additional primary factor—individualism (J+). Although it appears on the surface to resemble self-sufficiency (Q2+), it is quite distinct and relates to the child's internal restraint and reflectiveness. Cattell considered that the factor is linked with laziness and non-participation in the

FACTOR H		
Low score SHY H–	versus	High score ADVENTUROUS H+
Timid	vs.	Thick-skinned
Restrained	vs.	Socially bold
Withdrawn	vs.	Likes meeting people
Retiring with opposite sex	vs.	Overt interest in opposite sex
Emotionally cautious	vs.	Responsive, genial
Apt to be embittered	vs.	Friendly
Restrained, rule-bound	vs.	Impulsive
Restricted interests	vs.	Emotional and artistic interests
Careful, considerate	vs.	Carefree

Box 2.4

classroom and with low interest in school work generally. However, he also concedes that J+ pupils do better than average in mathematics and English, and achieve good ratings in individual creativity. They also appear to have a good degree of personal confidence and a willingness to stand by their own decisions. One frequently finds that the factor is related to home background, particularly in relation to strong behavioural control by the mother and less than average by the father (Cattell 1973).

FACTOR J		
Low score ZESTFUL J–	versus	High score CIRCUMSPECT J+
Likes group action	vs.	Acts individualistically
Likes attention	vs.	Guarded, wrapped up in self
Sinks personality into group enterprise	vs.	Fastidiously obstructive
Vigorous	vs.	Fatigued
Accepts common standards	vs.	Evaluates coldly

Box 2.5

Introversion and musicianship

The notion that will be developed in this chapter is that, temperamentally, musicians are generally characterized by a distinct tendency to be introvert-ed. Bearing in mind the nature of their working environment, this is not a difficult notion to develop, although it may well have several different facets. Those whose occupations demand long periods of working in com-parative isolation, whether it be in an artist's studio, a library, or music prac-tice room, would appear likely to possess a temperament that allows such individuals to be comfortable in that kind of situation. It is also probable that such extended periods of isolation, engaged in frequently, may also exercise the effect of rendering such persons more introverted. For example, I am only too aware of the changes that have taken place in me in this connection during the process of writing this book.

In Chapter 1 we noted, in passing, the suggestion that some personality traits appear to be related to different levels of performing success in music and certainly this appears to be the case with regard to introversion. In con-nection with research that has adopted Cattell's inventories, Table 2.1 shows how some of the primary traits associated with introversion appear to be fairly consistently manifest in the profiles of all musicians (Kemp 1982b). However, as a closer study of Table 2.1 will reveal, various patterns of intro-version appear to be related to differing types of musician or to the adoption of different criteria. This is particularly revealed in respect of Martin's (1976) school pupils whose fairly modest levels of musicianship are reflected in their distinct levels of extraversion.

The personality description of American adult musicians presented by Shatin *et al.* (1968) using Cattell's 16PF also shows some deviation from the British results. This small sample of 23 musicians was employed on a regu-lar basis to perform to hospital patients, many of whom were geriatric and psychiatric patients. The results of this research, which, incidentally, Cattell seems to have adopted without question as representative of the performing musician, indicated that, amongst other things, they were surgent (F+) and adventurous (H+), although, interestingly, also self-sufficient (Q2+). It would seem reasonable to suspect that this kind of working environment and the particular demands made upon these musicians in engaging in pleasant relationships with the patients might have been responsible for the F+ and H+ indicators of extraversion.

However, some of the other American research with musicians adopting the now widely used Myers–Briggs Type Indicator has also failed to identify significant levels of introversion. Of those who have pursued groups of music majors in colleges and universities in America using the Myers–Briggs (for example, Tucker 1982; Henderson 1984; Lanning 1990; Gibbons 1990; Wubbenhorst 1994), all, save Gibbons, identified tendencies towards extraversion. For example, Wubbenhorst's results showed that, of a

Table 2.1 Summary of research on introversion in musicians

Author	Type of group	HSPQ and 16 PF primary factors †				
Martin (1976)	Secondary school pupils with various musical interests	A+			H+	Q2–
Kemp (1981a)	Secondary school instrumentalists (composite group)			J+		Q2+
Kemp (1979)	Secondary school pupils attending conservatoire junior departments			*J–	*H+	(Q2+)
Kemp (1981a)	Specialist music school pupils	*A–		*J+	*H–	(Q2+)
Kemp (1971)	Conservatoire students			—		Q2+
Martin (1976)	Conservatoire students	A–	F+	—		Q2+
Martin (1976)	Student music teachers			—		Q2+
Kemp (1981a)	Music students in higher education (composite group)	A–	F–	—		Q2+
Kemp (1981a)	Conservatoire students specializing in performance	*A–	(F–)	—		*Q2+
Shatin *et al.* (1968)	Adult performers		F+	—	H+	Q2+
Kemp (1981a)	Professionals	A–		—		Q2+

* Indicates significant differences that emerged in comparison with their respective composite group.
Other factors shown in parentheses emerged at the same level.

† A+, aloofness; A–, outgoingness; F+, surgency; F–, desurgency; J+, circumspect; J–, zestful; H+, adventurousness; H–, shyness; Q2+, self-sufficiency; Q2–, group-dependency.

Dashes indicate that factor J does not feature in the 16 PF.

group of 112 student performers and teachers, 54 per cent were extraverted. In attempting to account for results that are so inconsistent with those of British research, we might wish to enquire about the extent to which these subjects were informed of the researchers' intentions to measure personality typing. Explicit knowledge of a personality focus in the research by participants could, due to the prevailing cult of the extravert, distort responses in what were perceived to be more socially desirable directions. Such motivational distortion is quite likely to have occurred in the case of the undergraduates who were at a stage in their development when their sense of identity would not have been fully established.

The notion, pursued in later chapters, that brass players and singers display significant tendencies towards extraversion in comparison with other musicians may have a bearing on these results. Tucker's (1982) whole group, for example, constituted band members, and would certainly have reflected this tendency, but any bias towards band members and singers in any of this research would have been likely to influence significantly the results in the direction of extraversion.

MYERS–BRIGGS EXTRAVERSION–INTROVERSION PREFERENCE

Extraverts	Introverts
After-thinkers. Cannot understand life until they have lived it	Fore-thinkers. Cannot live life until they understand it
Relaxed and confident	Reserved and questioning
Mind outwardly directed, focused on people and things	Mind inwardly directed, focused on inner world of ideas and understanding
Civilizing, people of action and practical achievement	Cultural, people of ideas and abstract invention
Conduct governed by objective conditions	Conduct governed by subjective values
Understandable and accessible, sociable	Subtle and impenetrable, taciturn and shy
Expansive and less impassioned, unload emotions easily	Intense and passionate, bottle up emotions
Tendency towards intellectual superficiality	Tendency towards impracticality

Adapted from Myers (1993, p. 56)

Box 2.6

Another feasible explanation might relate to the well-documented cultural differences in extraversion levels between American and British populations. Saville and Blinkhorn (1976) showed unambiguously that both male and female American undergraduates are significantly more extraverted than their British counterparts on all four of the contributory primary factors. Admittedly, these results were drawn from 16PF test data but there is no reason to believe that the Myers–Briggs would not be sensitive to these population differences also. Certainly, the large samples of undergraduate and professional musicians whom I tested with Cattell's inventories also emerged as distinctly introverted when also tested on the Myers–Briggs although, to date, these results have remained unpublished.

Further evidence for challenging the American findings on musicians can be found in research that has attempted to identify traits that appear to be particularly linked with higher levels of musical performance (Kemp 1981a). A group of talented young performers at a specialist music school showed distinctly higher levels of introversion, particularly in terms of aloofness (A–), individualism (J+), and shyness (H–), in comparison with other musicians of the same age. Similarly, those specializing in performance at music conservatoires, compared with other music students in higher education, emerged as significantly more introverted in terms of aloofness (A–) and self-sufficiency (Q2+). It is important for the reader to bear in mind that the latter group adopted for comparison purposes was also significantly characterized by these two traits.

Taken as a whole, the results shown in Table 2.1. indicate that musicians display the two most prominent introversion traits, aloofness and self-sufficiency, throughout the whole range, and that these appear to be associated with more advanced levels of musical performance. On the other hand, desurgency (F–) is only associated with the study of music at undergraduate level, and the shyness–adventurousness (H) factor seems to bear no consistent relationship with musicianship at any level. Certainly, what we can begin to deduce from these results is the notion that musicians' introversion is less linked to timidity and shyness, and reflects far more their personal resourcefulness and sufficiency. We shall return to these notions presently.

The musician's internal life

The question to be pursued here relates to why introversion would seem to be so critical in the musician's personality. What aspects of introversion allow us to gain deeper insights into the very nature of being a musician? One answer to this question may lie in Cattell's adoption of the terms 'invia' to emphasize the central aspect of 'living inwards' (Cattell 1973, p. 182). Storr (1976) refers to the introverted, creative type as 'schizoid' and suggests that such a person is characterized by a basic mistrust of people which may have its roots in early childhood experiences. In avoiding emotional involvement with people, the schizoid type remains detached and isolated and may, as a result, find solace in things—paintings, books, and music. Storr (1976) sums up the schizoid type in this way

. . . the less satisfaction a person gains by interacting with people and things in the external world, the more will he be preoccupied with his own inner world of phantasy. This is a notable characteristic of schizoid people, who are . . . essentially introverted; preoccupied with inner, rather than with outer, reality. (p. 75)

Another important aspect of schizoid types who find their identity through artistic activity is that, in their creative work, they find their own sense of personal autonomy, they communicate on their own terms, and their art objects remain totally within their control. By these means they can retain a sense of their own omnipotence, and keep a tight hold on their sense of superiority as creators. After all, asks Storr, 'what can be more omnipotent than creating one's own world?' (p. 81). Using rather different language, Howe (1990a) suggests much the same kind of thing (although not necessarily in the context of introversion), observing that, even from early childhood, an individual can gain a sense of mastery over his or her immediate environment through creative activity. Storr (1976) presents us with something of a paradox: the essential feature of the creative person is the need for personal control which, he points out, exists alongside feelings of inadequacy.

Since most creative activity is solitary, choosing such an occupation means that the schizoid person can avoid the problems of direct relationships with others. If he writes, paints or composes, he is, of course, communicating. But it is a communication entirely on his own terms. The whole situation is within his own control. (p. 80)

Of all occupational groups, perhaps musicians would seem, by necessity, to live inwards. The main focus and material of their art, being aural and therefore lacking tangibility and visibility, has to be internalized through a process of imaging, or what Gordon (1993) referred to as 'audiation'. In one of his letters, Tchaikowsky referred to his method of composing as 'hidden utterances of my inner life', generating music 'which flows from the depths of a composer's soul' (Newmarch, in Vernon 1970, p. 58). Similarly, Schoenberg, in one of his letters, maintained that 'a real composer is not one who plays first on the piano and writes down what he has played. A real composer conceives his ideas, his entire music in his mind, in his imagination, and he does not need an instrument' (Stein, in Henson 1977, p. 240). Judd (1988) came to the conclusion that, if we wish to identify a cluster of skills important for the musician, then we need not go any further than musical memory.

But the term 'musical memory' does not capture the essential feature of what the musician must be able to do; after all, postal workers can whistle their favourite tunes on their rounds using a form of musical memory. Obviously, what the musician needs to be able to do goes far beyond mere recall. When Seashore (1967) coined the term 'mind's ear'; speculating that the links between movement and thinking were a key factor in musicianship, he appeared to be getting nearer to the essential ingredient. He summed up his views by saying that ' . . . although this has not been investigated thoroughly, case study of motor imagery will probably show that this is the outstanding characteristic of a musical temperament responsiveness to the musical situation' (p. 169). The development of this faculty was the central component in Jaques-Dalcroze's approach to the education of the musician in which he emphasized the notion of motor images in the ear, and associations between muscular and aural sensations (Bachmann 1991, p. 170). The ability to internalize sound and to develop a rich, imaginative, and comprehensive internal representation, not only of what has been previously experienced, but also for imaging new, innovative compositions and interpretations, would appear to be an essential feature of a musician's thinking. Indeed, we might want to go so far as suggesting that kinaesthetic processes lie at the heart of the compositional and interpretative processes in music (Kemp 1983, 1990).

One of the most celebrated facts in musical history relates to Beethoven's continuing ability to compose after the onset of his deafness, and this is often considered to be indicative of his single-mindedness and strength of purpose. Whilst not necessarily wanting to question this, or to minimize the feat, nevertheless, the fact that he composed some of his most enduring works during this latter period might indicate a condition that was beneficial to him and conducive to the compositional process. Once he had adjusted to his inability to hear externally, which no doubt was traumatic, his internal and personal 'soundscape' was rendered so uncontaminated by extraneous sounds that his musical imagination could operate without restrictions or external interference. So much of what musicians do in the execution of their art is bound up with, not only being comfortable in their internal imaginative lives, but also being prepared to devote sufficient 'internal space' and energy to the complex processes of creating aural and temporal artefacts. In this way they are enabled to create a safe internal haven that becomes ever richer as the individual draws new musical experiences into it and, by internalizing them, learns to preserve them and identify with them.

The notion that musicians are fundamentally different in terms of their unique auditory style has been developed by Brodsky *et al.* (1994). Musicians, they maintain, possess an auditory dominance, which is not only essential for the development of musical giftedness but may also exercise the effect of separating the musician from others from whom they feel fundamentally different. Quoting Pruett (1991), they describe how, as young children, musicians attribute intense meaning to sound, hearing and feeling something in music that they cannot articulate verbally and that they experience nowhere else (p. 103). This sense of being different gradually dawns upon them as they grow up, and, although it will be associated with feelings of being special and 'gifted', nevertheless it may be the basis of separating them off from their peers and, indeed, become the source of levels of anxiety. We shall return to this latter point later in Chapter 5 in our consideration of the role of anxiety in musicians, but here let it suffice to note that Brodsky *et al.* in their exploratory work appear to demonstrate that there is a fundamental difference between musicians and non-musicians in this respect.

This requires closer examination: certainly musicians appear to be self-contained people, but this withdrawal into an internal existence appears not to be triggered by any sense of timidity. As we have already seen, musicians do not, as a rule, demonstrate the shyness–retiring nature of Cattell's factor H– at any stage in their development. The only exception in the literature appears to be in my own work, which showed a group of able pupils at specialist music schools to be particularly shy (Kemp 1981a). However, this may have been more connected with anxiety with which the factor is also linked.

Storr's (1963) contention that the more isolated people are the less independent they will be (p. 34) may be true in clinical work with schizophrenics, but may need challenging in the case of musicians. The musician may well be identified as schizoid, but the psychological importance of this may lie in the nature of the musician's art, in other words, to exercise total control over processes that, by definition, are personal, internal, largely non-verbal, and, therefore, private. The important feature of musicians is that they emerge from their practice rooms with strength of purpose and a drive and boldness that allows them to mount the rostrum with confidence and a sense of purpose. (The notion of the musician's autonomy will be explored further in Chapter 3.) The musician must, by definition, be able to retire from human interaction and then, to use Storr's words, 'it is necessary to return to contact with humanity if the retreat is to enrich the development of the individual and those with whom he is linked' (p. 39). This is precisely what musicians engage in during the extended periods spent practising in solitude, after which they emerge with the confidence necessary for the concert platform. It is this very quality that is well-identified by the self-sufficiency (Q2+) factor.

More recently, Storr (1989) seems to have shifted his position regarding the capacity for being alone. Here, he concedes that psychotherapists may have overemphasized the capacity to form mature relationships on equal terms as the main indicator of emotional maturity. In doing this, he feels they may have failed to consider the capacity to be alone as another important indicator of emotional maturity. Storr suggested that psychoanalytic literature all too often interprets the preference for solitude as founded upon fear, and, quoting Winnicott (1965), suggests that it is through being alone that children discover their personal life (p. 34). It would seem clear from this that Storr was making the case in support of the notion that introversion, at least in the form of aloofness combined with self-sufficiency, can be interpreted as signifying a level, not only maturity, but also of strength of character. Furthermore, he considered that the 'capacity to be alone thus becomes linked with self-discovery and self-realization; with becoming aware of one's deepest needs, feeling, and impulses' (p. 21). In their study of artists and writers, Drevdahl and Cattell (1958) coined the term 'bold introvert' to describe the type of introversion displayed by the more creative—a term that seems to encapsulate precisely what Storr is suggesting here and that may fit the musician's introversion rather more comfortably than some of his earlier notions.

Arousal theory

Let us, for a moment, leave the psychoanalytical stance towards the study of introversion to explore the more biological phenomenon of arousal. Although the theory of arousal originated as a neurophysiological concept, its importance has increasingly been recognized by psychologists, particularly those who have attempted to establish causal links between personality dimensions and certain physiological factors. What requires our brief attention here is the role of the reticular activating system, a part of the mid-brain area that appears to mediate levels of alertness. Put simply, this consists of a network of ascending pathways leading up to the cortex, as well as descending pathways influencing motor functions. By means of this network, input is received from the spinal cord up through the thalamus and so on to the cerebral cortex, and controls processes relating not only to attention and arousal, but also muscular tone. Also located within this area is the hypothalamus, a very small and complex area that, as we have already observed (p. 30), controls all the basic drives, including emotional behaviour. What has interested both Eysenck and Cattell are the personality factors that appear to be linked with differences in the functioning of the reticular activating system. Unfortunately, there is some measure of disagreement between the two researchers, not about theories of arousal as such, but concerning their interrelationship with personality. For reasons that will become clear in Chapter 4, we will concentrate here on Eysenck's theories.

Eysenck (1967) has suggested that, within this region, two information-processing loops are operating: one, he maintains, is responsible for sending arousal messages to the cortex which, in turn, sends messages back, either instructing the reticular formation to continue sending arousal messages, or, to switch to 'inhibition'. These two, in many ways, opposing functions of the first loop can be seen as relating to the seeking of excitement by the extravert, and the inhibition of high levels of arousal by the introvert. The second loop, which need not occupy our attention here, involves pathways between the visceral brain and the reticular formation, and, due to its direct concern with emotional states, has in Eysenck's (1967) view, important links with levels of neuroticism (pp. 231–2).

The outcome of this research is the suggestion that tasks requiring vigilance and high levels of concentration are more suited to introverts who appear to be characterized by lower thresholds of arousal or, to put it another way, by higher levels of activity in the reticular activating system than in those of extraverts. The outcome of such differences, of particular importance for musical processing, is that introverts appear to be superior to extraverts on tasks that might be perceived as being monotonous or boring. For example, Keister and McLaughlin (1972) successfully showed that, whilst there appeared to be no differences between introverts and extraverts during the first phase of a vigilance task, towards the end of a 48-minute test the introverts emerged as significantly superior. However, although the effects of administering caffeine to the introverts had negligible effects on their performance, those extraverts given caffeine appeared to mobilize their attentive behaviour and, as a result, displayed an absence of decremental effects. Thus, these researchers concluded that their results supported

Eysenck's notion that differences in introversion–extraversion could be accounted for by these kinds of biological mechanisms and, particularly, by levels of cortical arousal.

Further, more significant findings from our point of view, in support of Eysenck's theories, were offered by Stelmack and Campbell (1974). In their study, which investigated levels of sensitivity to auditory stimuli in groups of extraverts, introverts, and ambiverts, they showed that, whilst introverts displayed greater sensitivity than extraverts and ambiverts to low auditory frequencies, no significant differences emerged between the groups at high frequencies. Whereas introverts demonstrated a progressive lowering of sensitivity with increased frequencies, the extraverts showed the opposite trend. This led them to conclude that introverts possess lower preferred frequency levels of stimulation as well as lower intensity levels. More recently Stelmack (1990) has claimed that, although introverts consistently show levels of arousal superior to those of extraverts in terms of greater physiological response to stimulation, there is no substantial difference between them in the base level of arousal prior to stimulation.

The frequently cited Yerkes–Dodson law (Broadhurst 1959) states that the level of performance on a task is an inverted-U function of level of drive or motivation, and that this is mediated by the level of task difficulty. If we apply this to the present discussion, it can be seen that introverts, who are characterized by greater levels of arousal than extraverts, will perform a moderately difficult task better than extraverts in a low-stress situation. However, introverts will perform less well under high-stress situations. In this way we can begin to speculate that there may be a direct link between arousal and neuroticism which, as we have already noted, appears to be related to Eysenck's second information-processing loop. This will be pursued further in Chapter 5 where musicianship and anxiety are considered.

Stelmack (1990) applied the Yerkes–Dodson law to what he called the 'hedonic curve' (p. 299) and suggested that the level of hedonic tone (feeling of pleasantness of arousal level) is an inverted-U function of stimulus intensity, or arousal potential of stimulation. In other words, introverts will achieve optimum levels of pleasurable arousal at lower levels of intensity of stimulation than extraverts. Some earlier research by Weisen (1965) and cited by Wilson (1977) showed the same kind of trend, in that extraverts worked hard under experimental conditions to achieve the 'reward' of loud jazz music; on the other hand, introverts made clear efforts to avoid it. Similarly, Daoussis and McKelvie (1986) found that extraverts surpassed introverts in their preference for most types of rock music, and that this preference was greatest for 'hard rock'. Taken together, these results will immediately be seen to have direct relevance to patterns of music preferences and their interrelationships with personality types, which will be discussed in Chapter 7.

Although more than 25 years have passed since Eysenck formulated his theory, and despite certain criticisms that it has received and refinements that have taken place in the meantime (Stelmack 1990), the overall theory remains remarkably intact, and would appear to offer real insights for our study of the musician as well as lines for future research.

As we have seen, the most important implication of arousal theory for the musician relates to tasks that might be perceived by more extraverted types as repetitious and boring. Kemp (1981a) showed that, at even quite modest levels of musicianship, students aged 13 and 14 demonstrated significant levels of introversion. One explanation of this must be that the practice routines demanded of even the most modest of beginners in instrumental playing require engagement in tasks that the more extraverted might find lacking in 'hedonic tone'. If we consider this further, it can be hypothesized that the length of practice that a particular instrument requires before any degree of 'initiation' is achieved or experienced will positively correlate with levels of introversion. Those instruments that provide more immediate results, that are learned in a more social context, or that can be perceived as providing high levels of arousal (that is, louder, more aggressive tone) might, it can be argued, attract more extraverted types.

Another area of enquiry of direct relevance to the musician relates to the differences between introverts and extraverts in motor activity and the acquisition of certain types of physical and technical skills. Although Eysenck *et al.* (1982) showed, as one might expect, that extraverts tend to be more involved in athletic activities than introverts, the latter seem to perform more effectively on tasks that require more refined motor control (Frith 1971). Furthermore, they were shown to make fewer errors in reaction time tests (Brebner and Flavell 1978).

By drawing together all the different facets of this research we may begin to construct a composite theory of musicians' overall introversion. However, within this overall trend we might expect to find patterns of variation dependent upon, firstly, the nature and complexity of the instrumental skill; secondly, the context in which the skill is acquired; thirdly, the tone-colours and intensity of various instruments; and, lastly, the nature of the associated repertoire. In this way we can speculate that the personality differences between, for example, string and brass players, or classical and pop musicians, might clearly be accounted for in these terms—a discussion for which we shall have to wait until later chapters.

Summary

Evidence is presented here to support the notion that introversion appears to be positively linked to levels of musical performance. In musicians, the trait appears to manifest itself particularly in a tendency to direct energy inwards, resulting in a reserved and introspective temperament. At the same time, however, it suggests considerable resourcefulness, self-sufficiency, and personal internal strength. The musician can be perceived as a 'bold introvert' who possesses the capacity to be comfortable in solitude during long periods of practice but at the same time is able to mobilize sufficient degrees of autonomy in performance. This form of introversion appears to take on aspects of the 'schizoid' personality, individuals developing their sense of control over aesthetic objects and generating a sense of their own omnipotence.

The view developed here is that this reflects musicians' very special form of auditory style, which allows them to create an internal and imaginative world of sound, rich in symbolism and indispensable for creative activity in music. It is also suggests that this aspect of musicians' temperament also links with motor imagery and refined levels of motor control, and it is speculated that this may have connections with arousal levels. Arousal theory suggests that introverts are superior at tasks that are perceived as boring and monotonous by the more extraverted. On the other hand they can suffer from overstimulation, and their performances can deteriorate more rapidly than those of extraverts under higher stress conditions.

THREE

Independence

Introduction

A description was emerging in the previous chapter of the musician as an introverted type who also displays considerable levels of inner strength and maturity, and it was felt that Drevdahl's term 'bold introvert' for creative persons was particularly appropriate in this case. Closer examination of the musician's life-style, involving as it does the two extremes of secluded practice routines and the demands of public performance, very much supports this view. In this chapter the role of independence will be pursued and, in doing so, we will find that its presence as an important part of the musician's psychological make-up will further enhance this view.

The notion that the creative person is characterized by strong independence goes back to the 1950s and 60s and the early work on the creative personality, much of it carried out in USA. For example, Drevdahl (1956) considered that individuality and non-conformity were important prerequisites for creative enterprise in both artistic and scientific fields, and similar conclusions were drawn from a parallel study of artists and writers (Drevdahl and Cattell 1958). What emerges from this work is the conclusion that creative people appear to avoid the conventional and routine ways of thinking about new projects and the processes of carrying them out. In summarizing the early work with research scientists, Roe (1961) maintained that among their chief characteristics were their independence and high dominance.

The degree of independence necessary for different forms of creative enterprise may vary however, and, as Kuhn (1963) maintained, research scientists may well have to be traditionalists before becoming revolutionaries. They must first become initiated into the body of scientific knowledge and its rule-bound systems, which, once fully internalized, can become the framework for more unconventional thinking. The same may be thought to be true in connection with the education of the musician. In music, skills and techniques have to be acquired and mastered, and the traditional approach has always required the aspiring performer or composer to pursue a route in which traditional skills were emphasized. Only after these had been taught for lengthy periods were students allowed to experiment, a regime based upon 'first learn the rules and then you can break them' routine. What remains unclear, of course, is the extent to which such modes of education and training actually discourage those very persons who are temperamentally suited to highly imaginative work. Certainly, some of the early researchers into the 'creative personality' reported a tendency for the more creative students to be disruptive, non-conforming, and frequently disliked by their teachers. More recently, however, teachers in schools and colleges have become much more aware that a subtle balance is necessary between tradition and change, discipline and freedom, and skill acquisition and imaginative exploration. We shall explore on pages 55–57 the extent to which these tensions are revealed in the personalities of musicians.

Independence as a personality dimension

Independence is claimed by some personality researchers to be another form of extraversion, and this view is held by those researchers who have developed the 'big five' factor theory (see McCrae and Costa 1989b) in which the elements of Cattell's independence appear to be totally embedded in extraversion. We can also detect in Cattell's earlier research some degree of uncertainty about the boundaries between extraversion and independence (Cattell *et al.* 1970) for we find him claiming that the most important primary factor of independence—dominance—is particularly associated (especially for males) with extraversion. However, 3 years later he had revised his factor loadings, removing dominance from extraversion, yet adding two of extraversion's contributory primaries—surgency and adventurousness—to independence (Cattell 1973). Thus, independence is now shown to be made up, principally, of dominance (E+), surgency (F+), adventurousness (H+), suspiciousness (L+), and imagination (M+). As indicated diagrammatically in Figure 3.1, of these five primary factors, dominance and suspiciousness appear to be the most powerful. Thus, the degree of continuing overlap between Cattell's second order factors will immediately be observed (see Table 2 on page 8).

The reader may well be asking at this stage 'why continue using a personality structure about which there appear to be some elements of doubt? The answer is twofold: firstly, all or most of the research reported in this book has adopted earlier factor structures; and, secondly, as we shall see presently, it appears that musicians may well split the big five notion of extraversion into two parts. By this, I mean that mature musicians may well be shown to perform at the positive end on independence, and at the negative end on extraversion. In other words, Cattell's factorization may

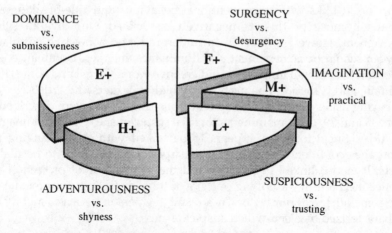

Figure 3.1 Primary factors of independence in adults.

well be of help in clarifying the musician's tendency to show a negative correlation between these two factors. And this is not the only instance where musicians appear to split a second-order factor in two: as we shall see in Chapter 4, this phenomenon also occurs on Cattell's pathemia–cortertia factor.

Let us then briefly discuss the psychological significance of the three constituent primaries involved in independence at the adult level that have not yet been described. Dominance (E+) tends to be high in first-born children and appears to be related to more authoritarian upbringing and stricter

FACTOR E		
Low score SUBMISSIVENESS E–	versus	High score DOMINANCE E+
Easily led	vs.	Assertive
Docile	vs.	Aggressive
Accommodating	vs.	Stubborn
Dependent	vs.	Independent
Considerate, diplomatic	vs.	Stern, hostile
Expressive	vs.	Solemn
Conventional, conforming	vs.	Unconventional, rebellious
Easily upset by authority	vs.	Headstrong

Box 3.1

discipline. It links with unconventional behaviour and rule-breaking and, perhaps because of this, is negatively associated with overall school achievement. However, later on in undergraduates a positive correlation between scholastic achievement and dominance emerges. Dominance is an important factor in all innovative and creative work, Cattell and Kline (1977) maintain, and is found to be particularly high in writers and artists.

Leaving aside surgency and adventurousness, which were described on pages 38 and 39, the remaining factors are suspiciousness (L+) and imagination (M+). Suspiciousness appears to be linked with an upbringing that encourages confidence and feelings of superiority; it is said to be high in artists. It is also linked to jealousy and the general use of projection as a defence mechanism—ascribing one's own traits or feelings to someone else or to some other exterior factor. As a result, the person is seen as moody and as characterized by a self-willed suspiciousness.

	FACTOR L	
Low score TRUSTINGNESS L–	versus	High score SUSPICIOUSNESS L+
Accepts personal unimportance	vs.	Jealous
Yielding to changes	vs.	Dogmatic
Unsuspecting of hostility	vs.	Suspicious of interference
Ready to forget difficulties	vs.	Dwelling on frustrations
Understanding, tolerant	vs.	Tyrannical
Conciliatory	vs.	Irritable
Conventional, conforming	vs.	Unconventional, rebellious

Box 3.2

Cattell's imagination factor (M+) is often described as the artistic/creativity factor, and tends to be linked to unconventional, 'bohemian' life-styles as well as to a liking for the world of ideas. It reflects a concern for the inner life at the expense of the real world, and Cattell (1973) has related the factor to excessive maternal affection or to a sheltered life in which demands have not been made. He claims that those who score highly on imagination enjoy college life, change jobs more frequently, and tend to have unhappy relationships.

Before moving on, it should be mentioned that, because the HSPQ does not attempt to measure the suspiciousness and imagination factors, children's independence is represented solely by the remaining three primaries.

FACTOR M		
Low score CONVENTIONAL M–	versus	High score IMAGINATIVE M+
Down to earth	vs.	Unconventional
Alert to practical needs	vs.	Absorbed in ideas
Concerned with immediate issues	vs.	Has artistic interests
Prosaic, avoids far-fetched ideas	vs.	Imaginative, engages in inner creations
Guided by objective realities	vs.	Easily seduced from practical judgement
Practical	vs.	Absent-minded

Box 3.3

Dependence and independence in musicians

Having discussed the *independence* end of the dimension, it may come as a surprise to the reader studying Table 3.1 to discover distinct suggestions of *dependence* in young musicians. For example, Thayer's (1972) intercorrelational study using a number of musical ability tests and Cattell's HSPQ with children highlighted submissiveness (E–), as did Martin (1976) with a group of 200 secondary school pupils, although, admittedly, he showed them also to be high on adventurousness (H+). The group of 496 secondary school instrumentalists that I assembled for my study (Kemp 1981a) also confirmed this by displaying significant levels of submissiveness in comparison with a control group of pupils without musical interests. This may be surprising, particularly in relation to research such as that carried out by Freeman (1979) in which she reported that gifted children were more often described by their parents as being independent than were the children in her control groups. Howe (1990a) also stresses the importance of independence and self-directedness for the development of exceptional abilities but, at the same time, concedes that it is not an 'all or nothing' situation; there must be room for people to vary on these traits.

What emerges from these personality studies with young musicians is the suggestion that, at the secondary school level, the music learner is characterized by the submissiveness that Cattell maintained is necessary for high-level achievement during this phase of education. Certainly this was confirmed by Entwistle (1972) who, citing Warburton's unpublished study, not

Table 3.1 Summary of research on independence in musicians

Author	Type of group	HSPQ and 16 PF primary factors †				
Thayer (1972)	12–13-year-olds pupils' scores on music tests	E–			—	—
Martin (1976)	Secondary school pupils with various musical interests	E–		H+	—	—
Kemp (1981a)	Secondary school instrumentalists (composite group)	E–			—	—
Kemp (1979)	Secondary school pupils attending conservatoire junior departments			H+	—	—
Kemp (1981a)	Specialist music school pupils			H–	—	—
Kemp (1971)	Conservatoire students					M+
Martin (1976)	Conservatoire students	E+	F+		L+	M+
Martin (1976)	Student music teachers	E+			L+	M+
Kemp (1981a)	Music students in higher education (composite group)		F–			M+
Kemp (1981a)	Conservatoire students specializing in performance	*E+	(F–)			*M+
Shatin *et al.* (1968)	Adult performers		F+	H+		
Kemp (1981a)	Male professionals				L+	M+
Kemp (1981a)	Female professionals	E+				M+

* Indicates significant differences that emerged in comparison with their respective composite group. The factor shown in parentheses emerged at the same level.

† E+, dominance; E–, submissiveness; F+, surgency; F–, desurgency; H+, adventurousness; H–, shyness; L+, suspiciousness; M+, imagination.

Dashes indicate that factors L and M do not feature in the HSPQ.

only identified significant levels of submissiveness in high-achievers in their early teens, but also a shift towards dominance after age 17. While submissiveness can be explained in this way, the emergence of adventurousness in my group of secondary pupils studying part-time in the music conservatoires (Kemp 1981a) requires a very different rationale. In her study of prodigies, Pruett (1991) identified a distinct tendency in the young performer to be exhibitionistic and at ease in public. However, as these children move into adolescence, this quality appears to undergo a change and become more of an act of *appearing* to be relaxed.

Table 3.1 offers evidence that the shift towards dominance in high-achievers amongst undergraduates occurs in musicians also. Martin's (1976) groups of conservatoire and student teachers were both shown to be dominant (E+) as well as suspicious (L+) and imaginative (M+), traits also associated with independence. Whilst my main sample of full-time music students displayed only imagination, the more select group of students specializing in performance (Kemp 1981a) were both dominant and imaginative in comparison with the other, more general music students. This might suggest a gradual movement towards independence as higher levels of instrumental performing skills are acquired. This phenomenon was further suggested by my specially talented school musicians who failed to display the dependence seen in the main group. In other words, those pupils who might be perceived as especially precocious musically were already outgrowing their dependence upon external support. However, the observant reader will have noted the emergence of timidity (H–) in this group: this may be better explained in terms of anxiety, which will be discussed in Chapter 5.

Turning to professional musicians we find, in common with the results of Shatin *et al.* (1968), further evidence of the link between independence and musical maturity (Kemp 1981a). However, apart from imagination, which occurred in both the men and the women, other manifestations appeared to be gender-linked. For example, the females' independence was characterized by marked levels of dominance, whereas in men it took the form of suspiciousness. It is worth noting here that these differences cannot be accounted for by general population gender differences known to exist on dominance and suspiciousness—men score higher on both dominance and suspiciousness (Saville, private communication 1976). The differences that emerged here in adult musicians occurred despite general population gender differences being eliminated through the use of separate male and female norms.

The shift from dependence to independence that appears to take place during late secondary school education and college life and continues into the professional phase may have one of two causes, or indeed a combination of both. Firstly, because my research was not longitudinal and three separate groups of musicians were adopted, the shift may have been caused by a dropping-out (or de-selection) of those who were: (1) finding it increasingly difficult to maintain motivation; (2) uncomfortable with the demands being made upon them; (3) having difficulty maintaining progress. Secondly, even if the research had had a longitudinal element, it is possible that the trend towards independence would still have emerged, reflecting not only the demands of teachers at different points, but also the different climates of the various educational institutions. In other words it may be revealing the shift of emphasis from skill acquisition routines to a more autonomous regime of personal decision-making, particularly for the more talented. Csikszentmihalyi and Robinson (1986) appear to support this kind of observation: the development of talent appears to be dependent upon different personal capacities as well as upon environmental factors at different stages within the life-span. While the point is clearly relevant to our observations concerning independence in musicians, as we have already seen, it appears to apply in the case of introversion also.

Field-dependence/independence

One of the 'big five' factors that may well warrant mention in this chapter is 'openness'. McCrae and Costa (1985) maintained that this dimension, which identifies the imaginative, creative, curious, independent, and analytical person, is distinct from their other four major personality factors. The dimension of openness appears to interconnect not only with aspects of independence but also with a whole cluster of phenomena that feature in the literature relating to the perceptual style of creative persons. Amongst these notions we find 'field dependence–independence', 'preference for complexity', 'tolerance of ambiguity', and 'non-conformity', all of which may have significance in our attempts to understand the nature of musicianship.

Firstly, let us take a look at Witkin's theory of field dependence–independence which is sometimes referred to as 'psychological differentiation' (Witkin *et al.* 1975). Although Witkin presented it as a personality theory approached through the study of individual differences in perception, he himself did not relate it to any of the personality trait theories, preferring the more projective-type approaches. However, this has not prevented Cattell (1973) from maintaining that field-independence forms a part of his independence factor.

Basically, Witkin's theory maintains that people show characteristic, self-consistent ways of perceptual functioning that pervade the processes of memorizing and problem-solving. The field-dependent person is dominated by the overall organization of the field; the parts are perceived as being fused together. The field-independent person, on the other hand, is able to perceive the different parts as discrete units, and separate from their background. The perceptual style of the field-dependent individual involves the need to use external cues, whereas the field-independent person mobilizes his or her own *internal* perceptual processes. One method of measuring psychological differentiation involves the 'rod and frame' test, which requires subjects to place a rod in a vertical position within a frame placed at differing angles. Testing is carried out in a darkened room and the person is denied any other vertical referents, and, under these conditions, field-independent types demonstrate more success.

Another, rather similar procedure that Witkin has shown differentiates between the two types is the 'body-adjustment' test. This requires individuals to judge the vertical position of their own bodies within the confines of a room which the experimenter is able to manipulate by different degrees of tilting. Research adopting this test suggests that those with a more articulated perceptual style—the more field-independent types—have a greater awareness of needs, feelings, and attributes that they recognize as being their own. This sense of separate identity, experiencing the self as being more segregated from its environment, with less dependence upon external cues, appears to bring us very close indeed, not only to Cattell's independence, but also, in some senses, to introversion. A third test devised by Witkin that should be mentioned, not least because it is the one adopted by most of the research to be cited here, is the 'embedded figures' test (Witkin *et al.* 1971). This is a paper-and-pencil test that requires the subject to locate simple geometric figures within a larger, more complex one.

Witkin maintained that field-dependent behaviour appeared to be linked to immaturity and identified a tendency for adolescents to develop a more articulated perceptual style. This developmental trend towards adulthood would appear to tie up with Karp's (1977) observation that field-independent people tend to be more autonomous and less influenced by other people. This also appears to be supported by Lester (1974) and Loo (1976) who also demonstrated a clear link with introversion. Although not directly referring to introversion, Witkin *et al.* (1977) similarly observed that the field-independent person tends to be more impersonal, less interested in others, and to prefer non-social situations, whereas field-dependent behaviour was associated with submissiveness, a need for a supporting environment, and a denial of inner realities.

When related to musicians and musical responses, this theory suggests that those attracted to the study of music will display several of the features of field-independence. Because so much of what musicians do in pursuing their work relates to analysing, extracting, and reorganizing musical phenomena, it is reasonable to expect them to emerge with higher levels of field-independence. Not only is the aural analysis of musical elements often considered to be the ability that separates the musician from others, it is this faculty that is emphasized at every level of the education and training of musicians. In their review of the literature relating to field dependence–independence and various musical tasks, Schmidt and Lewis (1987) found clear evidence of strong links between field-independence and musicianship. For example, they cite research that indicates that aural skills and sight-reading (Schmidt 1984; King 1983) as well as musical creativity (Schmidt and Sinor 1986) and musical conservation (Matson 1978) are all positively related to field-independence. Further evidence in support of the field-independent person's superiority in aural perception has been presented by Ellis and McCoy (1990) who highlighted a consistent relationship between field-independence and the ability to identify musical forms. Similarly, Ellis (1995) observed that field-independent types are more able to make accurate judgements about musical textures.

Although a discussion of the perceptual processes in music lies beyond the scope of this book, a musical example will serve to demonstrate how field independence might operate in a musical situation where aural analysis is necessary to appreciate fully the composer's intentions. The example in Figure 3.2 has been taken from a collection of small pieces (Shaw undated) especially devised to help pupils develop a greater facility to analyse aurally. It presents the first part of the folk-song, 'Early one morning', embedded

Figure 3.2 Example of an embedded melody in an accompaniment. From *A book of hidden tunes*. G. Shaw (undated).

in the middle of an accompaniment that tends to disguise its identity. On hearing this performed (and it should be emphasized that this is an aural, not a visual task), the field-independent person would be more able to take an analytical stance, and to hear the melody as distinct from its context. On the other hand a field-dependent individual would more likely be defeated by its embeddedness, and hear the piece as a complete *Gestalt*.

The notion that field-independence bears a clear, unambiguous relationship with musical ability may prove to be an oversimplification. Schmidt (1985), in reviewing research in this area, suggested that field-independent types possess a better facility to dis-embed and analyse in musical tasks. On the other hand, because of their more global perceptual style, field-dependent persons would have a more developed sensitivity to the expressive and stylistic qualities of music. Certainly this raises an important question for music education where it might be thought important to retain some kind of balance between both kinds of task, thereby relating to students of both types. We shall return to this question later in Chapter 7.

Tolerance of ambiguity and preference for complexity

Barron's (1963) research with creative groups adopted the well-known Asch experimental techniques: the use of stooges to challenge subjects' correct judgements in order to pressurize them into making erroneous judgements. (In passing we might note that Witkin carried out some of his early research in collaboration with Asch.) What Barron found was that 75 per cent of his subjects yielded to such pressure and that the remaining group of non-yielders were identifiable by their higher originality and creativity. He also found that his non-yielders were also characterized, if not by their preference for complex and apparently contradictory phenomena, at least by their ability to deal with it more comfortably. There is much in Barron's work that corresponds with Festinger's (1957) theory of cognitive dissonance, which maintained that authoritarian personalities are particularly unable to withstand highly dissonant cognitions. People of this type tend to adapt their perceptions to assimilate only those facts that are consonant with their conceptual framework. Barron maintained that these people make a decision to favour order and reject everything that might bring disequilibrium. For these people, 'equilibrium depends essentially upon exclusion, a kind of perceptual distortion which consists in refusing to see parts of reality that cannot be assimilated to some preconceived system' (Barron 1963, p. 199). Witkin (1965) suggested that this was very much a feature of the more field-dependent person who uses repression and denial as a form of defence in blocking out conflicting experiences. Conversely, the field-independent person is able to operate more comfortably with thoughts, feelings, and ideas that are in conflict.

As we have already seen, the openness factor of the big five, as described by McCrae and Costa (1985), although couched in more cautious language, paints the picture of the 'open type', amongst other things, as 'original, imaginative . . . complex, curious, daring . . . independent, analytical . . . untraditional'. At the other end of the dimension the 'closed type' is 'conventional . . . uncreative . . . simple, uncurious, unadventurous . . . conforming, unanalytical, conservative and traditional' (p. 166).

The preference for complexity was also found by Myers and McCaulley (1985), the originators of the Myers–Briggs Type Indicator, to be linked to the perceiving preference. They considered that the person whose attitude was principally one of judging would be prone to lead an orderly, controlled, and carefully planned life, whereas the person who prefers to perceive lives a life that is more open to experience, and is characterized by flexibility and spontaneity. The influential work of MacKinnon, who did much to establish the use of the Myers–Briggs in the USA, invariably showed that this preference successfully separated artistic people from scientists (MacKinnon 1962), but that in both groups the preference for perception was directly linked with levels of creativity. Furthermore, he also showed that the Myers–Briggs preference for intuition (as opposed to sensing) was strongly linked with all creative types. More recently, in a discussion of the Myers–Briggs in the context of the 'big five', Bayne (1994), citing McCrae and Costa (1989b), showed a strong correlation between intuition, as measured by the Myers–Briggs, and the openness factor and showed that perceiving was, in fact, far more strongly associated with a lack of conscientiousness. This last point may appear rather curious to the reader, but Myers and McCaulley (1985) help to

---

MYERS–BRIGGS JUDGING–PERCEIVING PREFERENCE

Judging types	Perceptive types
More decisive than curious	More curious than decisive
Live according to plans, standards, and customs not easily cast aside	Live according to the present moment and adjust easily to the unexpected
Make definite choices among possibilities; dislike unexpected happenings	Frequently masterful in handling unexpected happenings
Being rational, depend on reasoned judgements; protect themselves from unnecessary experiences	Being empirical, depend on anything that offers a flow of new experiences
Prefer matters to be settled promptly in order to be prepared for what is going to happen	Like to keep decisions open for as long as possible before doing anything irrevocable
Think or feel what other people ought to do and are not averse to telling them	Know what other people are doing and are interested to see what happens
Take pleasure in getting things finished, out of the way, and out of mind	Take pleasure in starting new things, until newness wears off
Are self-regimented, purposeful, and exacting	Are flexible, adaptable, and tolerant

Adapted from Myers (1993, p. 75)

Box 3.4

explain this by suggesting that perceptive types are more spontaneous and adaptable in their behaviour whereas judging types are more decisive and organized.

Research with musicians that has adopted the Myers–Briggs has, in fact, demonstrated this tendency towards intuition, but the links between the perceiving preference and musicianship are more complex. Wubbenhorst (1994) found that 66 per cent of his student performers were intuitive, and, similarly, my own unpublished data show that 60 per cent of the full-time students and 71 per cent of the professional musicians were intuitive. However, whereas Wubbenhorst reported that 57 per cent of his student performers were judging types, 53 per cent of my student performers were perceptive. However, the professional musicians in my research indeed emerged as 61 per cent judging types. The question that , of course, arises in this context is whether the rank and file musician can be viewed as a creative type. Certainly, the disciplined and repetitious nature of much of the musician's working life, particularly as a professional performer, would seem to suggest an orientation towards judgement. However, when we come to study the more creative musician—the composer—we might expect to find a distinct move towards perception. We shall return to a further discussion of the Myers–Briggs preferences in the next chapter in the context of musicians' sensitivity.

Conformity and control

The degree to which people observe social norms may be governed by their responsiveness to external pressures to conform or, on the other hand, their rejection of these. Individual differences in this respect may relate to aspects of conscientiousness, superego strength, and thus of self-concept formation. Basically, these factors relate to whether the person feels subject to control imposed by others, for example, by parents or teachers, or whether the individual chooses to operate with a more personal and autonomous approach to 'morality' in which he or she refuses to be rule-bound. We now come to yet another manifestation of changeover in the development of the musician from childhood, through studenthood, to professional life.

In a similar way to independence, a curious transformation takes place in factors relating to conscientiousness and self-sentiment. Conscientiousness, Cattell's factor G+, sometimes referred to as superego strength, is very much related to home background, warmth of upbringing, and a high regard for parents. The factor describes the person who is persevering and determined, who engages in responsible forms of behaviour, and has experienced the kind of upbringing based upon reasoning rather than punishment and coercion. The high self-sentiment factor, Q3+ relates to personal control with the person always being socially correct and possessing a strong self-image to which he or she rigidly adheres. It describes the person who is prone to compulsive behaviour patterns and, like conscientiousness, is linked with warmth of upbringing and parental affection. These factors are described further on pages 88–9 and 239–40.

In young musicians of secondary school age, strong evidence is found for high levels of both conscientiousness and self-sentiment (Kemp 1981a). Whilst this same level was shared by the talented pupils at special music schools, those of the same age studying part-time as junior exhibitioners at music conservatoires emerged with even higher levels on both traits. The main difference between the group from special schools and the junior exhibitioners was that the former were living in boarding schools away from their parents (and thus more independent of them), whereas the latter were probably very much dependent upon their parents for a continuing environment of support and encouragement (Kemp 1995).

When we turn to the full-time music students, a transition appears to be taking place, for, whilst conscientiousness is still seen to be in evidence, the high self-sentiment is no longer apparent. Interestingly, amongst those specializing in performance, neither trait emerges but, instead, a significant level of low superego strength (G−) (Kemp 1981a), indicating a propensity to disregard rules. Martin's (1976) results were even more convincing: a group of 78 conservatoire students emerged with significant levels of low self-sentiment—a tendency to follow their own urges—and, amongst his group of student music teachers, he identified both low self-sentiment and a lack of conscientiousness. Finally, at the professional level, whereas the women were average on both traits, I found the men displaying significant levels of low self-sentiment.

There is much here that needs considering. The gradual shift away from conscientiousness and control towards a disregard for externally imposed rules combined with tendencies to be governed by personal urges fits comfortably with the move from dependence to independence. Myers (1993) put it rather succinctly in describing introverted-feeling types (who appear to characterize British musicians) as people who 'maintain independence from the judgement of others, being bound by inner moral law' (p. 95). Certainly, these characteristics were identified in large numbers of creative groups in early research and, in reviewing much of this material, Chambers (1969) came to the conclusion that these types were

. . . independent non-conformers, relatively unconcerned with group approval of their actions, and relatively uninterested in socialization. On the whole they . . . have chosen not to conform to a given mould but rather to express their sensitivities and other characteristics through their creative abilities. (pp. 791–2)

What can be seen here has perhaps less to do with a lack of morality than a reflection of developing levels of personal autonomy necessary for mature artistic existence. Certainly, Myers (1993) described the introverted-feeling type (as measured on the Myers–Briggs), which characterizes most musicians, as maintaining an independence from the judgements of others, being subject to an 'inner moral law' (p. 95). This can be seen particularly as a need to break away from imposed, well-worn, and orthodox work patterns, skills, and disciplines, which, whilst they appear to have their place in the earlier developmental stages, exercise diminishing returns later.

Whilst we must wait until Chapter 13 for a fuller discussion of the whole question of the education and upbringing of musicians, key elements of this topic require to be raised at this point simply because they relate to the processes whereby the young musician is allowed and encouraged to develop his or her independence as a creative artist. The research into the developmental trends of musicians' personalities discussed in this chapter reflects, in a fairly graphic way, their dependence upon a supportive environment in the early stages during which techniques, knowledge, and good working habits are acquired. Throughout childhood and studenthood, and particularly in the case of the more talented, we can perceive the gradual disappearance of this dependence and the eventual emergence of independence in the professional musician. As we have seen, the discussion here relates, not only to the emergence of a general personal autonomy, but also to questions concerning locus of control.

This research challenges the myth of the child prodigy in which cases of young precocious composers and performers are cited in support of the romantic view that such children are endowed with such innate gifts and high levels of personal autonomy that, regardless of environment, they would have emerged as pre-eminent anyway. When such talent appears to emerge at very young ages, we almost invariably find that it has occurred within a musical environment—instruments were at hand and parental, or other encouragement in evidence. In some of these cases we may find suggestions of such levels of support involving considerable parental sacrifice. On the other hand we can find cases in which child prodigies have not maintained their early promise—the two Wesleys, for example, where we may suspect that this was perhaps due to a lack of parental encouragement and support (Shuter-Dyson 1985, p. 163).

Recently, much research effort has focused upon the whole question of nurturing musical talent and the emerging conclusion appears to highlight the importance of a musical environment, parental support, the encouragement of a warm encouraging teacher with whom the child closely identifies, and the need to acquire good practice habits and routines (Davidson *et al.* 1996; Howe *et al.* 1995; Sloboda *et al.* 1996).

Leaving any detailed discussion of this research aside for the moment, the more relevant question here relates to the location of the particular point at which the process of transition from the supporting-encouraging environment to more self-directed and independent existence might occur. Howe (1990) cites the cases of Newton, Einstein, and Shaw as examples of thinkers who were exceptionally independent-minded and self-directed and who, in his view, rarely received intensive day-to-day parental supervision of their learning activities beyond childhood. Furthermore, presenting Ruskin as an example, Howe suggests that tight parental control may lead to some form of crisis later on in adolescence or adulthood (pp. 194–5). This was very much the view of Keniston (1968) who believed that it was the warmth and encouragement within the family that not only offered the security from which to break away but also the impetus to do so.

Paradoxically, those who come from what to an outside observer would appear to be the best families often underwent a severe struggle to emancipate themselves from these families. It may be that the very closeness, warmth, and encouragement toward independence in some of these families were what made adolescence both possible and necessary . . . Put differently, many of these families seem to have given their children the strength and the need to challenge, reexamine, and partially reassimilate their parents' values, and eventually to achieve an unusual degree of individuality for themselves. (Keniston 1968, pp. 102–3)

Thus this chapter ends where it began with a clear picture of the mature, creative person as independent-minded and autonomous in his or her working patterns and personal life. The dilemma for parents and teachers relates to the styles and methods of upbringing that instil the appropriate working routines, the necessary technical auditory and performing skills, and the acquisition of relevant bodies of knowledge to ensure that this process occurs in a climate that allows sufficient freedom for self-motivation, commitment, and individuality to develop alongside. It is the apparent conflict between these two equally important processes that has for so long haunted music teachers concerned with the disproportionately large numbers of drop-outs from their instrumental teaching programmes.

Summary

This chapter has further developed the view that, whilst musicians are distinctly introverted, there is also a 'boldness' which arises not only from their considerable inner strengths but also from their sense of independence. Musicians tend to share these qualities with several other creative types. We have explored the evidence that suggests that, whereas young musicians tend to be somewhat dependent, those who proceed into music in higher education and professional life are characterized by distinct independence.

Another aspect of this factor that is particularly relevant to the musician is Witkin's theory of field-dependence/independence. The field-independent type is seen as more autonomous and less influenced by other people and, in terms of perceptual style, describes the individual who is more able to take an analytical stance to musical and other phenomena. For the musician, this more articulated perceptual style and ability to 'disembed' particularly manifests themselves in a number of musical tasks and processes such as aural work, musical creativity, sight reading, and the perception of form.

Independence is also strongly linked to the 'openness' dimension of the 'big five', which involves personal qualities such as originality, imagination, and a preference for complex ideas. In addition, the intuition and perception preferences of the Myers–Briggs, shown by MacKinnon as key characteristics of creative types, also bear strong interrelationships with these qualities. In the context of our concern with musicians, it appears that, whereas intuition is consistently linked to musicianship, the involvement of perception is a little more obscure.

Finally, the notions of conformity and control also have relevance to this area of concern. Evidence from the use of Cattell's tests suggests that, whereas conscientiousness and strong self-concept were in evidence in young musicians, this tendency was actually reversed in more mature musicians. This phenomenon is interpreted as the young musicians' need to respond positively to the regular practice routines, which are inculcated through encouragement by parents and teachers. Later, in the more professionally orientated musician, these work habits are more 'owned' and internalized and, as a result, they become more autonomous and internally controlled.

FOUR

Sensitivity

❧

Introduction

As with other personality factor labels that have suffered from imprecise usage in everyday language, we can find 'sensitivity' being used in all sorts of circumstances ranging from a loose sensuousness through to various manifestations of perceptiveness. Even within the field of psychology the term can be applied to a number of phenomena, for example, general susceptibility to stimulation, responsiveness to weak stimuli (having a low threshold), and even to a degree of vulnerability in which a person is easily upset or offended (Reber 1985, pp. 684–5). Thus, on the one hand we find Freeman (1979) reporting high levels of 'sensitivity' amongst creative children who, in their earlier development, were often troubled by television and radio news reporting and who demonstrated a concern and understanding well beyond their years (p. 240). On the other hand, we find Seashore (1967) referring to sensitivity in terms of 'sensory capacities' (pp. 2–5) and, whilst receptivity to the elements of music such as pitch, dynamics, tempo, and timbre are clearly of fundamental importance to musical development, they are essentially *perceptual* abilities.

As we saw in connection with field-independence in Chapter 3, perceptual capacities may help inform our understanding of a person's temperamental predisposition to respond to events in particular ways but, nevertheless, the two aspects should remain separate as far as possible. In our consideration of the musician, the dividing line may prove to be problematic, not only because a musician's level of sensitivity may influence his or her ability to perceive elements and changes in music, but also because it may affect the predisposition to perceive these in a number of different ways. It might be thought that the direction of influence could also work in reverse. After all, if a person's perceptual abilities remain undeveloped for any particular reason, to the extent that sensory input is impeded or limited, this may clearly influence his or her capacity to respond sensitively. However, a sufficient number of examples of successful deaf musicians come to mind to cause us to be cautious about this: Evelyn Glennie, the percussionist; Elizabeth Barlow, viola player in the London Symphony Orchestra; and Paul

Whittaker, ex-organ scholar at Wadham College, Oxford. That these and other deaf musicians can operate successfully at high levels of musicianship suggests that the musician's sensitivity, of the kind we need to discuss here, has much more than a purely auditory basis.

Although it is entitled 'Sensitivity', I ought to make it clear to the reader that this chapter intends to focus on Cattell's wider concept of 'pathemia'. Indeed some people who have adopted Cattell's inventories in their research refer to his second-order factor as sensitivity but it is important to bear in mind that sensitivity is a *primary* factor, which forms an important part, but only a part, of the broader higher-order factor of pathemia along with imagination and outgoingness. Let us take a closer look at the construct of pathemia (as opposed to cortertia) in order to develop insights into its nature and the ways in which it might assist us in our study of the musician.

Cattell's 'pathemia' as a personality dimension

Cattell (1973) maintained that the antithesis of the poles on pathemia is more subtle than on his other second-order factors. This view may relate to its being less observable than those dimensions already described. On the surface, pathemia might be associated with a relaxed and even indulgent life of feeling, the individual appearing warm, sentimental, and prone to daydreaming and living through sensitive emotions. At the contrasting pole, cortertia, the individual operates in an alert and realistic fashion; feelings are cool and well under control. To form a better grasp of the construct we need to take a look at the primary factors that make up this 'emotion–coolness' dimension, which, on the face of it, we might well expect to be operative in the musician's personality.

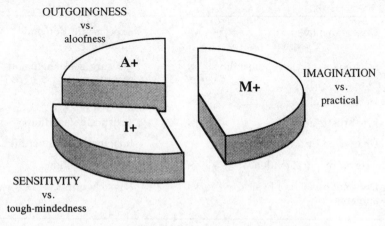

Figure 4.1 Primary factors of pathemia in adults.

The three primary factors that relate to pathemia are sensitivity (I+), imagination (M+), and outgoingness (A+).These are shown diagrammatically in Figure 4.1 indicating their relative strength of importance in overall pathemia. Sensitivity is an exceptionally strong trait in children in so far as it occupies a considerable amount of variance in their personalities. Its importance, though, is found to decline to more modest levels in adulthood, although there is a detectable upturn in middle-aged men (Cattell 1973, p. 168). In Cattell's view, sensitivity tends to be associated with a highly protected upbringing and parental control through reasoning rather than punishment; it appears to be linked positively to performance in language and the arts, but negatively with mathematics. People who are high on this factor tend to live by their feelings and intuition, whereas, at the opposite pole, they rely more upon logic and facts. Cattell observes that, when sensitivity is linked to intelligence, the individual frequently finds him or herself taking up an occupation where 'cultural myths' abound (p. 169) rather than working in a more emotionless and mechanical world. The reader might agree that the musical world offers plenty of variety in terms of its cultural myths!

Imagination (M+) has already been described (pages 54–5) in connection with the independence dimension with which it has a weaker association than with pathemia. However, whilst this is true in adult personality, imagination does not feature as a stable trait in children but, instead, submissiveness (E–) takes on a moderate loading. The third factor of outgoingness (A+)

FACTOR I		
Low score TOUGH-MINDEDNESS I–	versus	High score SENSITIVITY I+
Unsentimental	vs.	Expects affection and attention
Self-reliant, takes responsibility	vs.	Insecure, seeks help and security
Hard, cynical	vs.	Kind, gentle
Few artistic interests	vs.	Artistically fastidious
Unaffected by 'fancies'	vs.	Imaginative in inner life
Acts on practical evidence	vs.	Acts on intuition
Does not dwell on physical ailments	vs.	Hypochondriacal

Box 4.1

as opposed to aloofness (A–), which was described on pages 36–7 in connection with our discussions about introversion, can also be seen as having a modest involvement in pathemia. Thus, due to this common element, there is a minor degree of overlap between the two second-order factors (Table 2, p. 8). However, as we have already discovered, musicians tend to be introverted, and, because of this common component, introversion sits less happily with any disposition towards pathemia. An alternative way of viewing it is that the musician's introversion is tugging against pathemia as far as aloofness is concerned, or, expressed in a different way, the musician's pathemia is of a slightly different type than that found in general populations. We shall return to this a little later in the following sections of this chapter.

In an attempt to describe the dimension more fully, Cattell (1973) claimed that pathemia has particular biological connotations. He maintained that it emerges as a result of 'living at the hypothalamic level', making maximum use of the lower regions of the brain (p. 185), whereas cortertia is dependent upon a predominating tendency to function at the higher levels of the cerebral cortex. Although this factor originally resulted from questionnaire data, Cattell maintained that a good deal of additional understanding has emerged from laboratory tests. The research resulting from this very different source of information has demonstrated strong links existing between cortertia and phenomena such as 'rapid reaction time, ideomotor speed, endurance of difficulty, less fluency on emotional than unemotional themes' (p. 186). Thus, as we noted in Chapter 2 in connection with Eysenck's theories of the biological bases of introversion–extraversion, particularly in terms of levels of arousal, we find Cattell making the same kinds of links with pathemia–cortertia. In fact, Cattell (1971) went further than this: he maintained that the factor is explicitly a temperamental expression of cortical alertness, a perceptual processing dependent upon different levels of arousal or activation (p. 65). The essential quality of this dimension is therefore one that describes a temperamental predisposition to adopt an alert, cognitive thinking style as opposed to dealing with life's issues in a more feelingful and impressionistic way. We shall return to a discussion of this later on in the chapter.

Jungian preferences

At this point we may begin to perceive some similarities of language with Jung's theory of psychological types that underlie the Myers–Briggs Type Indicator, particularly in respect of the thinking–feeling preference. Myers (1993) describes how there are two quite distinct and contrasting ways of making judgements and coming to decisions: the logical process of thinking, resulting in an impersonal conclusion; and the process of feelingful appreciation, projecting upon things a personal and subjective value (p. 3). Thus the two types of person develop along very different lines, each more comfortable in habitually using and trusting one or other of these processes and ready to obey its dictates. The person will tend to leave the other process as a kind of minority opinion that is barely listened to and often wholly disregarded. The thinking type of person is more concerned about whether something is true or untrue; the 'feeler' responds on the basis of liking or disliking.

Myers and McCaulley (1985) present data concerning the intercorrelations between the Myers–Briggs and the 16PF, showing not only a strong statistical interrelationship between the feeling preference and Cattell's sensitivity factor, but also that the latter relates just as strongly to two other preferences: intuition and perception (p. 185). Furthermore, they also show significant interrelationships between both these Jungian preferences and Cattell's imagination factor. Thus we may assume that some direct relationship exists between Cattell's pathemia and the Myers–Briggs intuitive-feeling-perceptive (NFP) combination and that both inventories have located an important aspect of personality that is, perhaps, particularly

---

MYERS–BRIGGS THINKING–FEELING PREFERENCE

Thinking types	Feeling types
Value logic above sentiment	Value sentiment above logic
Impersonal, interested in things	Personal, interested in people
Tend to choose truthfulness before tactfulness	Tend to choose tactfulness before truthfulness
Stronger in executive ability than social arts	Stronger in social arts then executive ability
More likely to question people's conclusions on principle believing them to be wrong	More likely to agree with those around them believing them to be right
Brief and businesslike; appear to lack friendliness	Naturally friendly, find it difficult to be businesslike
Able to organize facts and ideas into logical sequences	Have difficulty organizing ideas; tend to ramble and repeat
Suppress, undervalue, and ignore feelings that are incompatible with thinking judgements	Suppress, undervalue, and ignore thinking that is offensive to feelings

Adapted from Myers (1993, p. 68)

Box 4.2

relevant to creative people. Before moving on then, we ought to take a closer look at these additional preferences.

Intuitive people appear to perceive possibilities, meanings, and relationships by way of insight, and Jung considered that the process was dependent upon the unconscious mind giving rise to divergent thoughts and feelings. As Myers and McCaulley (1985) suggest

. . . intuition permits perception beyond what is visible to the senses, including possible future events. Thus, persons orientated toward intuitive perception may become so intent on pursuing possibilities that they may overlook actualities. They may become . . . imaginative, theoretical, abstract, future orientated, or creative. (p. 12)

The outcome of this is that persons who use intuitive perception appear to have little capacity for living in the present, they are restless, often indifferent to what other people do or want, preferring to face life expectantly

---

MYERS–BRIGGS SENSING–INTUITION PREFERENCE

Sensing types	Intuitive types
Face life observantly, craving enjoyment	Face life expectantly, craving inspiration
Admit to consciousness every sense impression; aware of external environment	Admit to consciousness only those related to current sense impressions related to current inspiration
Observant at expense of imagination	Imaginative at expense of observation
Pleasure lovers and consumers	Initiators, inventors, and promoters
Great capacity for enjoyment	Small capacity for living in the present
Imitative, wanting what other people have, and do what they do	Desire opportunities and possibilities; inventive and original
Dependent upon physical surroundings	Independent of physical surroundings
Always in danger of being frivolous	Always in danger of being fickle; lacking persistence

Adapted from Myers (1993, p. 63)

Box 4.3

and seeking new enterprises and achievements. In this way the link with Cattell's imagination (M+) factor is clear to see.

Let us now turn to the judging–perceiving preference that was briefly referred to in Chapter 3. It ought to be explained to the reader at this point that this preference was not fully worked through by Jung and that, in the course of operationalizing his theory in the form of the Myers–Briggs Type Indicator, Briggs extended the theory beyond the point where Jung was content to stop (Myers 1993, pp. 23–4). The judging–perception process relates to people's overall attitude towards dealing with the outer world. As we have already seen, individuals make a choice between two ways of judging—thinking and feeling—and two ways of perceiving—sensing and intuition. It is the judging–perceiving preference that identifies which of the these is a person's *dominant* process. For example, if a person is extravert, intuitive, and thinking (ENT), and intuition is trusted more than the thinking process (relegating the latter to a kind of consultation process when it does not conflict with his or her intuition), the person can be seen to prefer judgement. In this case the *dominant* process is intuition and the *auxiliary* process is thinking. Such a person is said to be ENTJ. Alternatively, if he or she relies on thinking more than intuition, the dominant and auxiliary process would be reversed and the typing would be ENTP.

In the case of introverts slight additional complexity occurs and, since we have come to recognize that most musicians (amongst British groups at least) have a distinct tendency towards introversion, this requires particular consideration here. As Myers (1993) explains, because extraverts live outwards they use their dominant process to understand the outer world of people and things; their auxiliary process is more focused on their inner lives. On the other hand, because they live inwards, introverts use the energies of their dominant process internally and are reluctant to use it to process the outer world. This leaves the introvert to mobilize the auxiliary process as best as he or she can in everyday dealings with people and events. If the auxiliary process is not developed in any real sense, the introvert will appear awkward and uncomfortable in social situations. Take myself as an example. Tested on the Myers–Briggs, I emerge as INFP. If I were extraverted my dominant function would be the intuitive form of perception, but because of my introversion, this is kept well hidden and used in my internal life. As a result, my auxiliary process lies in the feeling form of judgement, and this I mobilize as best I can in my daily dealings with the external world.

Space does not allow us to get into a deeper discussion of the Jungian theories and how they led Myers to develop the underlying rationale of her test. A useful discussion of the issues can be found in her book *Gifts differing* (1993) to which the reader is encouraged to refer. We shall need to return to some of these issues when discussing the musicians' results on the Myers–Briggs in a later section of this chapter.

Tender- versus tough-mindedness

Myers and McCaulley (1985) also suggest that their feeling–thinking preference relates to psychology's classical distinction between tender-minded
versus tough-minded individuals, and it may be thought that Eysenck's psychoticism dimension would be pertinent to this discussion. 'Psychoticism'
does not appear to be a particularly appropriate term to use with normal
populations and, perhaps because of these persecutory and depressive connotations, it sometimes has been referred to as a 'tough-mindedness' factor.
As tough-mindedness is the description that Cattell has given to the negative pole of his sensitivity factor, it would seem reasonable to speculate that
'psychoticism' might offer yet another slant on the pathemia dimension.
However, it needs pointing out that, whilst there is a reasonably normal distribution for general populations on Cattell's sensitivity, Eysenck's psychoticism shows a substantial bias towards the negative pole (perhaps
emphasizing its clinical connections) thus suggesting that it is somewhat
unidimensional. The outcome of this is a suspicion that psychoticism does
not bear a consistent relationship with the traits that principally interest us
here. This view appears to be borne out by Myers and McCaulley's conclusion that there appears to be no link between Eysenck's EPQ psychoticism
factor and any of the Jungian preferences (p. 179).

Musicians viewed from Cattellian and Jungian perspectives

The evidence shown in Table 4.1, drawn from several studies, supports conclusively the notion that pathemia is a reasonably stable feature of the musician's personality insofar as sensitivity and imagination, its two principal
components, repeatedly emerge in groups of performers. In his study of 12-
and 13-year-olds, Thayer (1972) found all three factors (A+, I+, and M+) positively related to composite scores on three music tests. In retrospect, perhaps Thayer was a little too hasty in concluding that there was no systematic relationship to be found between personality and musicianship. However,
in his defence, it must be admitted that these results were not replicated in a
similar exercise with 14- and 15-year-olds, except in the case of sensitivity.
Similarly, Shuter (1974) had also found a similar connection between sensitivity and the Bentley Measures. That sensitivity emerged in correlational
studies with music tests would certainly support Seashore's notion, alluded
to earlier, that the musician's sensitivity might have a particular relationship
with sensory-perceptual capacities important in musicianship.

Table 4.1 also shows the results of the other type of research with musicians who had demonstrated moderately high levels of musical ability in
real-life situations. As mentioned earlier, in many ways groups of musicians
who display proven levels of performing ability form somewhat more valid

Table 4.1 Summary of research results on pathemia in musicians

Author	Type of group	HSPQ and 16 PF primary factors †			
Thayer (1972)	12–13-year-olds measured on music tests	A+	E–	I+	—
Thayer (1972)	14–15-year-olds measured on music tests			I+	—
Shuter (1974)	9–10-year-olds measured on a music test			I+	—
Martin (1976)	Secondary school pupils with various musical interests	A+	E–	I+	—
Kemp (1981a)	Secondary school instrumentalists (composite group)		E–	I+	—
Kemp (1981a)	Specialist music school pupils	A–*	(E–)	(I+)	—
Kemp (1971)	Conservatoire students		—	I+	M+
Martin (1976)	Conservatoire students	A–	—	I+	M+
Martin (1976)	Student music teachers		—	I+	M+
Kemp (1981a)	Music students in higher education (composite group)	A–	—	I+	M+
Kemp (1981a)	Conservatiore students specializing in performance	A–*	—	(I+)	M+*
Shatin *et al.* (1968)	Adult performers		—	I+	
Kemp (1981a)	Professionals	A–	—	I+	M+

* Indicates significant differences that emerged in comparison with the immediately preceding group. Other factors shown in parentheses emerged at the same level.

† A+, outgoingness; A–, aloofness; E–, submissiveness; I+, sensitivity; M+, imagination.

Dashes indicate that factor M does not feature in the HSPQ or that factor E does not occur in adult pathemia.

criterion groups than those measured on musical ability tests. The only departures from a fairly conclusive pattern of sensitivity (I+) and imagination (M+) (sensitivity and submissiveness in children) emerged in the results of Shatin *et al.*(1968) which we earlier considered as pertaining to a non-typical group of performing musicians (p. 40). As previously observed

(p. 41), the aloofness factor appears to have a link with musical maturity, appearing as it does at the opposite pole in children (apart from the especially talented) and occurring particularly strongly in the full-time students specializing in performance. Interestingly, this latter group also emerged with significantly higher levels of imagination in comparison to a group already high on this trait. Finally, as if to add final confirmation of the foregoing pattern, my own groups of male and female professional musicians together displayed reasonably consistent results across these factors.

Turning to the profiles of musicians on the Myers–Briggs, evidence of the importance of feelingfulness is equally persuasive. Invariably, the preference for feeling over thinking emerges in earlier studies of performers in higher education (Lanning 1990; Gibbons 1990). Fifty-seven per cent of Wubbenhorst's (1994) student performers were found to express a preference for feeling, and further evidence is presented by Myers and McCaulley (1985) who claimed that the same was true of 63 per cent of a group of 136 musicians. My unpublished data showed that 76 per cent of the students and 84 per cent of the professional musicians expressed the preference for feeling, and Table 4.2 shows the distribution of the students and professional musicians across the 16 types. What emerges from this table is the clear pattern of distribution down the 'intuitive types with feeling' column. Both groups of musicians appear to be fairly equally distributed across those types who use intuition as their dominant function and those who use feeling. It will also be apparent that there is some minor 'pull' towards sensing in both the professionals and the students. We might wish to speculate whether this might reflect the more technical orientation of some performers.

The view developed here is that the thinking–feeling preference is a factor closely related to cognitive style, and this notion is certainly supported by the research carried out by McCrae and Costa (1989a). However, since a large proportion of musicians combine the feeling preference with that of Jungian intuition (as opposed to sensing) for their perceptive processing of the world around them, it would appear appropriate to speculate as to how this intuition might influence the nature of this cognitive style. The tendency towards intuition that musicians demonstrate appears to reinforce the levels of imagination that we have already noted. This helps describe their cognitive style as embracing the seeking out of possibilities through insight rather than focusing upon particular concrete experiences of the here and now. For example, we might expect intuitive–feelingful types always to be on the lookout for new experiences, to look for underlying, hidden, and symbolic patterns in events, and to reveal interests in the complexities of communication (Myers and McCaulley 1985, p. 35). These qualities might well be of the kind we would expect to find in performing musicians.

The question that arises from this persuasive picture is what exactly is the psychological importance of these characteristics that make up pathemia?

Table 4.2 Dispersion * of student and professional musicians amongst the Jungian types

Musician	Sensing (S) types (%)		Intuitive (N) types (%)	
	Thinking (T)	Feeling (F)	Thinking (T)	Feeling (F)
Introverts (I)				
With a preference for judging (J)	ISTJ	ISFJ	INTJ	INFJ
Students	6.5	11.2	4.0	9.4
Professionals	4.9	12.8	2.4	20.7
With a preference for perception (P)	ISTP	ISFP	INTP	INFP
Students	2.0	6.8	3.4	20.6
Professionals	2.4	3.7	3.0	12.8
Extraverts (E)				
With a preference for perception (P)	ESTP	ESFP	ENTP	ENFP
Students	1.2	4.3	2.9	11.8
Professionals	1.2	1.2	0.6	12.2
With a preference for judging (J)	ESTJ	ESFJ	ENTJ	ENFJ
Students	1.8	6.1	2.0	6.0
Professionals	1.8	5.5	0.6	15.9

Jungian type	Students (%)	Professionals (%)	Jungian type	Students (%)	Professionals (%)
E	36	36	TJ	14	10
I	**64**	**64**	TP	10	7
S	40	29	FP	**43**	31
N	**60**	**71**	FJ	33	**52**
T	24	16	IN	**37**	**44**
F	**76**	**84**	EN	23	27
J	47	**61**	IS	26	20
P	**53**	39	ES	14	9
IJ	31	**40**			
IP	33	24			
EP	20	15			
EJ	16	21			
ST	12	9			
SF	28	20			
NF	**48**	**63**			
NT	12	8			
SJ	26	20			
SP	14	9			
NP	**39**	30			
NJ	21	**41**			

* Unpublished data relating to groups of musicians also tested on Cattell's 16PF (Kemp 1981a).

At this point we must not overlook two important issues. First, as already indicated, we should not neglect the imagination factor, which, although not featuring as strongly as sensitivity in Cattell's factorizations, remains an important aspect. The second relates to the fact that musicians tend to depart from Cattell's factor structure in displaying aloofness (more associated with cortertia) alongside the other pathemia factors. In other words, musicians appear to be producing a factor structure different from that of general populations in a similar way to what was discussed in connection with extraversion (pp. 43, 52–3). These instances of significant departures from accepted factor structures amongst specialized occupational groups is a fundamental principle, not only in careers advisory work, but also in gaining a deeper understanding of any specialism. It may also help explain, amongst other things, underlying reasons for large drop-out rates at various points in the education and training of musicians. After all, if the most highly skilled of musicians display a fundamentally distinct combination of personality characteristics that we interpret as significant in the development and maintenance of those skills, it is reasonable to expect that those who are not endowed with these more unusual combinations of traits and are uncomfortable in developing them will drop out as a matter of course. Whilst we shall need to return to this point in later chapters when educational issues are pursued, the more relevant and immediate issue relates to the actual musical processes that might be thought to depend upon these more 'deviant' trait combinations.

The musician's pathemia then comprises sensitivity and imagination combined with, or at least tolerant of, strong aloofness, which can be viewed as 'tugging in the opposite direction'. Whatever warmheartedness brings to pathemia in general populations (and let us remember that the association is a minor one), it is unimportant in musicians, in the sense that it does not feature here except, possibly, at the earlier stages of development. On the other hand, it *is* important because the trait appears at significant levels in its opposite direction. This may be explicable purely in terms of the musician's introversion, in which case we might be tempted to ignore it here. Alternatively, we can interpret it as contributing to a special form of pathemia that might be considered to be peculiar to musicians.

Whichever way we view this, one key principle is of fundamental importance. Although the chapters in the first part of this book focus upon separate key factors in the musician's temperament, it would be very wrong to view each one in isolation. No one person's personality is compartmentalized in this fashion: all salient features interact in a dynamic fashion; all contribute in an interactive way to the whole being. Thus, these chapters should be seen at least as cumulative and, just as we noted the interrelationship between independence and introversion, there are many insights to be gained by linking pathemia to both of these.

In Chapter 2 we began to build up a picture of musicians' personal and internal world rooted in introversion and characterized by the thing that they cherish most—their music and its repertoire. All this exists internally, hidden from view but exerting a powerful motivating force on much of what they do, think, and feel. In referring to the introverted-feeling type, Myers (1993) described them as having 'feelings that are deep but seldom expressed, because inner tenderness and passionate conviction are both masked by reserve and repose' (p. 95). Thus when we combine the introverted attitude with the elements of feelingfulness and imagination we may begin to develop a much clearer picture of the form that the musician's internal life takes. Seashore (1967) refers to 'esthetic attitude', 'poetic intuition', 'life of feeling', and 'life of isolation' (pp. 173–5), and each of these expressions captures an important aspect of the musician's priorities, personality, and way of being.

The fact that they possess this rich inner life is taken for granted by most musicians, and it may only become apparent to them in their dealings with those with whom they attempt to share their enthusiasms, say in the classroom or studio. Only in these kinds of situation do they discover that many others do not possess this 'storehouse of experience', as Seashore (1967, p. 180) described it, to the same degree. The feature that makes the musician unique, perhaps, is that the elements of pathemia are not projected outwards towards other people, which is the common pattern when it occurs in extraverts, but are internalized, and kept largely private. The aloofness (A–) factor *is* significant because, in combination with the other introversion factors, it helps clarify the kind of internal world we are talking about. In other words, it allows the person to retain, not only a degree of detachment, but a sense of distance, cool critical objectivity, and even a sceptical attitude towards what is and what is not valued, imagined, and internalized. Over and above this, musicians' independence allows them to adopt this detached stance within the world around them with the manifest confidence and autonomy we have already considered.

Arousal

If we refer back to Chapter 2 to the discussion concerning arousal, it will be recalled that Eysenck developed the notion of its direct link with introversion–extraversion. Cattell, on the other hand and as we have already mentioned briefly, placed more emphasis on his theory that alertness and arousal are related to cortertia. In other words, arousal is directly linked to tough-mindedness, a concern for practicalities, and aloofness. Apart from this difference in emphasis, there appears to be a certain degree of compatibility between the theories of Eysenck and Cattell. Both agree that there are two information-processing loops operating: one dealing with levels of sensory stimulation, intellectual and symbolic processes of a cortical nature; and the other involving the visceral brain and reticular formation that are responsible for emotional expression via the limbic system (Cattell and Child 1975, p. 150). Eysenck has argued that the terms 'arousal' and 'activation' should be adopted for these two separate processes, one relating to introversion and the other to neuroticism. We shall return to this issue again in Chapter 5.

It will not have escaped the reader's attention that, at least in one respect, this leaves us in something of a dilemma. We are left with Eysenck's explanation that musicians' introversion interconnects with their higher levels of arousal and sensitivity in situations of low stimulus intensity—an explanation which well fits the work ethic and life-style of the musician at all levels. On the other hand, Cattell's concept of pathemia suggests that musicians are characterized by a functioning that is less cortically based, involving a tendency to feel rather than to think and to operate more at the 'mood' level. Whether or not this paradox can be explained in terms of Eysenck's two separate loops is a question that we shall have to leave obscure. As Gale (1987) has remarked, arousal theory has attracted considerable controversy during the last 20 years and may well not be a unitary trait. As we have seen earlier, the musicians' highly specific combination of skills appears to involve particular clusters of personality traits, even if they contravene Cattell's more usual structure of second-order factors.

There may be many readers who will wish to challenge any suggestion that the musician somehow lacks cognitive precision. We might wish to speculate that, whilst those who proceed to academic studies and research may demonstrate a greater proclivity towards cortical functioning, other musicians may be different in this respect. Conservatoire professors who teach performing musicians may vouch for certain elements of truth in the notion that the musician's strength lies in his or her more cautious, assimilative perceptual style and a disposition that resists making swift and more superficial judgements. On the other hand, this may go unnoticed if the professors themselves share these same characteristics.

'Inferior' functions

There is one further subtlety embedded within Myers–Briggs theory that requires mentioning at this point. This relates to the *inferior* function. Whether the person is extravert or introvert the inferior function is invariably the *opposite* of the first function. In other words, in ENFP and INFJ types the inferior function is sensing; in ENFJ and INFP individuals, I hesitate to tell you, it is thinking! The effect of this on these musicians' processing of events is that they may tend to gloss over facts and details and approach things more emotionally. They have a desire for broad experience, but their need to understand it in any detailed sense may be less important.

However, to prevent the writer of this book being dismissed and written off before the end of Chapter 4, let it be said that Myers (1993) claimed that INFP and INFJ types show some of the highest scores on conventional intelligence tests. As she suggests,

... the mark of a thinker is not so much the possession of greater mental powers but having them run on a different track . . . Thinking is not always first-class thinking. Its product is no better than the facts it started with . . . and no better than the logic employed . . . When feeling types . . . value a course of action, a thinker's argument designed to confute that value leaves them cold . . . Thinkers often contradict each other, each one claiming 'This is truth'. The feeling type need only say, 'This is valuable to me'. (p. 67)

That we are not discussing intelligence levels here is borne out by my results achieved with the use of Cattell's inventories, which incorporate an intelligence scale. Despite the musicians' pathemia, they also emerged as being significantly *more* intelligent than those students who were pursuing other disciplines and who emerged as higher on cortertia (Kemp 1981a). Admittedly, this was somewhat surprising particularly as 71 per cent of the full-time music students did not possess the necessary number of 'A' levels that most of the non-music students would have gained for university entrance. Whilst the more modest performance of the musicians in terms of 'A' level examination results may reflect little more than where their priorities lie, their particular form of pathemia may be suggesting a cognitive style that operates more flexibly across *both* lower brain and cortical functioning than is normally the case in other students. In discussing the connection between musical performance and the importance of feeling life, Gardner (1983) sums up the point well in suggesting that music

... can serve as a way of capturing feelings, knowledge about feelings, or knowledge about the forms of feelings, communicating them from the performer or the creator to the attentive listener. The neurology that permits or facilitates this association has by no means been worked out. Still, it is perhaps worth speculating that musical competence depends not upon cortical analytic mechanisms alone, but also upon those subcortical structures deemed central to feeling and motivation. (p. 124)

Thus we might wish to ruminate further about the musician's pathemia. Certainly, some readers might have expected musicians to be more characterized by cortertia. After all, musicians appear to be required to think quickly and to make swift judgements in performance. However, research might well show that these kinds of movements and decisions are actually too fast to be under the direct control of the brain. Expressed in another way, cortical functioning on its own may not help the musician to operate in the performing mode; performance *by necessity* involves pathemia. We speculated in Chapter 2 that a key aspect of the musician's thinking was kinaesthetic, a form of muscular 'thinking' in which 'decisions' are taken more feelingfully.

Elsewhere (Kemp 1990) I have described this kind of process by way of an example of a pupil with a beater, poised over a suspended cymbal, preparing to strike it. In moving the arm in an arc-like gesture, the child develops an intention to create a sound. The qualities of the sound, of course, are determined by the velocity of the beater and the size of the arc. The kinaesthetic sensations of the moving arm evoke images of the intended sound as well as stimulating images of previous similar experiences. In this way the pupil's imaginative intention is actively stimulated and 'informed' by the gesture itself. The key point being made here is that this highly complex 'decision-making' is essentially body-thinking. It arises out of a pupil's sensitive and feelingful impulse in which lower brain activity is heavily engaged.

Continuing this line of thinking in terms of skilled musicians, it may well be true that their far more refined movements, developed over long hours of practice, are less 'cognitive' than we sometimes suppose. Their levels of pathemia linked to this kind of kinaesthetic functioning allow them, during a performance, to engage in decision-making of a specially sensitive, emotional, and imaginative kind through the activation of viscerally based operations. Certainly, what we have observed by means of a Cattellian and Jungian interpretation of the musician well supports this kind of position.

Summary

Sensitivity features within a wider cluster of personality traits for which Cattell has adopted the term 'pathemia'. This second-order factor comprises two other primary factors, imagination and outgoingness, that appear to exercise an important role in musical processes. This conclusion is well supported by the research cited in this chapter, which involves musicians of different ages. The concept of musicians' pathemia, characterized by high levels of sensitivity and imagination (its most prevalent components), is well supported by other research using the Myers–Briggs Type Indicator, particularly in connection with the preferences for feeling and intuition.

Taken together, this research suggests that pathemia, intuition, and feeling converge in identifying a fundamental quality of musicians' personalities. This relates to their characteristic stance of seeking out complex and symbolic possibilities in aesthetic objects and events, particularly mobilizing their high levels of sensitivity, imagination, and intuition. This perceptual mode of operating is in direct contrast to its opposite manifestation in which individuals engage in a cerebral, cortically alert manner enabling them to focus on factual realities and logic in an emotionally cool fashion.

Viewed within the context of introversion, musicians' pathemia takes on an important feature. The qualities outlined above tend to be internalized and kept well hidden from others. In doing this, musicians often conceal the very thing that motivates them most highly, thus obscuring their raison d'être and rendering them somewhat enigmatic to others, particularly of another type. Another important feature of the pathemia–introversion combination relates to our speculations about the involvement of kinaesthetic sensation in musical performance, offering support to the notion that visceral brain activity is of fundamental importance.

Cattell's theory concerning the connection between higher levels of arousal and cortertia appears to be at odds with Eysenck's tendency to link arousal with introversion. In this chapter pathemia is interpreted as a distinct tendency for musicians to *feel* their way intuitively through the process of making judgements. Earlier, in Chapter 2, musicians' introversion was interpreted as connected with higher arousal levels in tasks perceived to be monotonous by more extraverted types. This dilemma cannot be resolved here, particularly as more recent research has suggested that arousal is unlikely be a unitary concept.

FIVE

Anxiety

❦❧

Introduction

Of all the personality factors that are to be discussed in the context of the musician, anxiety is the one that has most penetrated the literature on musicians and their training, professional work, and life-styles. This is, in part, due to its multi-faceted nature, and only a small proportion of these aspects can be strictly viewed as personality orientated. Much of the remainder deals with issues relating to behavioural and cognitive aspects of performance stress as well as coping strategies, therapies, and treatments, and therefore will not directly concern us. But wending our way through the field, with our particular concern for personality in mind, will not be a straightforward task. As has already been seen in the context of other key personality factors in musicians, the interrelationships between personality and other phenomena relevant to the musician require us to make connections with other theoretical areas. After all, it is the links with these associated fields that allow us to develop more penetrating insights into the very nature of and the reasons for the emergence of these factors in musicians. There will be places where studies that tend to lie outside our domain of interest have, nevertheless, a specific contribution to make. These will assist in developing our understanding of the different ways in which the presence of anxiety may influence how the musician responds to, and operates in, different circumstances. Although several of these cannot be dealt with in detail here, there are often important findings and insights embedded within them that need to be extracted for our particular purposes. This has been inevitable for, although the boundaries between personality, cognitive, and psycho-physiological aspects are not always clear, a major concern has been to keep this chapter focused and of a reasonable length.

Trait and state anxiety

At the outset it is important to make a distinction between two aspects of anxiety. One relates to 'trait' anxiety, that aspect of an individual's general predisposition to be anxious, and the second to 'state' anxiety, which is a description of how a person's anxiety levels are affected in a more transitory fashion by particular situations.

As one might imagine, in reality, the distinction between these may not be quite so clear. The two aspects may interact insofar as a person's proneness to anxiety will directly influence his or her level of response to what is perceived to be dangerous. The problem that presents itself, of course, relates to any attempt to separate out what can be viewed as permanent traits from the more transitory states and moods. In a sense this brings us back to the 'person–situation' debate and our discussion of Mischel's (1968, 1973) criticisms touched on in the 'Introduction', which highlighted two extreme positions. One emphasizes the consistency of traits, and the other stresses the impact of particular circumstances that so influence a person's behaviour that any consideration of stable traits is dismissed as fanciful. Cattell and others have rebutted this latter view, and clearly the contribution of Spielberger *et al.* (1970) in developing the State–Trait Anxiety Inventory (STAI) in a sense satisfies both positions.

In his attempt to develop a working definition, Spielberger (1966) suggests that state anxiety is characterized by 'subjective, consciously perceived feelings of apprehension and tension, accompanied by or associated with activation or arousal of the autonomic nervous system' (pp. 16–17). On the other hand, trait anxiety is frequently seen as reflecting residues of earlier experiences, and, presently, we shall observe how frequently the primary factors associated with anxiety have been linked to childhood experiences, particularly those relating to parent–child relationships and to styles of control and punishment.

It may be thought, of course, that we would want to focus principally upon trait anxiety, simply because a trait can be understood as belonging more comfortably to the realm of personality than perhaps does a transient state. However, as state anxiety may well prove to be an important feature of the musician's response to certain kinds of performing situations, it also requires pursuing here. Certainly, the exact relationship between the trait levels of musicians and susceptibility to performance stress requires close examination. However, whilst trait levels may help reveal the lifelong and continuing impact of music upon the developing personality, state levels should help us identify the more transient effects of various performing conditions and demands made upon different kinds of musicians.

Cattell's theories of anxiety

Since there is a body of research with musicians that has adopted the Cattellian inventories, let us start with an analysis of Cattell's second-order factor of anxiety. Very early on he claimed to have identified a cluster of six primary factors contributing in a dynamic way to trait anxiety, these being: low ego strength (C–); shyness (H–); suspiciousness (L+); guilt proneness (O+); low self-sentiment (Q3–); and ergic tension (Q4+) (Cattell *et al.* 1970, p. 118). As Figure 5.1 shows, ergic tension, guilt-proneness, and low ego strength are the three strongest factors; low self-sentiment and shyness are the weakest (Cattell 1973, p. 116). The shyness factor was described on pages 38 and 39 in connection with its far higher loading on introversion, and a description of suspiciousness, in the context of independence, can be found on page 54.

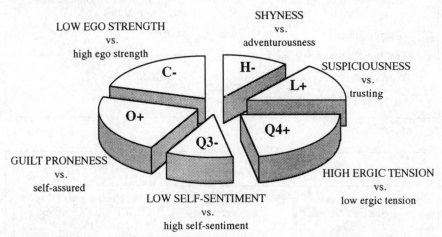

Figure 5.1 Primary factors of anxiety in adults.

With regard to the four remaining primaries, Cattell describes low ego strength (C–) as a general emotionality factor that highlights tendencies towards disorganization and frustration. The C– person may get annoyed by things and people, appears generally to be dissatisfied with life, and often reveals feelings about being unable to cope. The trait is linked with the appearance of phobias, psychosomatic disorders, sleep disturbance, and hysterical and obsessional behaviour. It has been found to be associated with dominant mothers, and with those occupations where individuals can set their own pace. In Cattell and Kline's (1977) view, it is one of the more significant characteristics of academics, artists, and writers.

The guilt proneness factor (O+) relates to a worrying, insecure, depressive disposition in which the individual is prone to overfatigue and feelings of inadequacy and unworthiness. It features heavily in the profiles of artists and priests, for example, and appears linked to less than average participation at school, but not necessarily to low achievement. Cattell (1973) suggests that, in terms of home background, guilt proneness is associated with physical punishment, less overall behavioural guidance and control, and patriarchal rather than matriarchal regimes (p. 173).

FACTOR C		
Low score LOW EGO STRENGTH C–	versus	High score HIGH EGO STRENGTH C+
Emotionally less stable	vs.	Emotionally stable
Easily upset	vs.	Calm
Evasive of responsibilities, tends to give up	vs.	Does not let emotional needs obscure realities
Changeable	vs.	Mature
Emotional when frustrated	vs.	Emotionally mature
Worrying	vs.	Unruffled
Gets into problem situations	vs.	Avoids difficulties

Box 5.1

FACTOR O		
Low score SELF-ASSURED O–	versus	High score GUILT PRONENESS O+
Placid	vs.	Worrying
Complacent	vs.	Apprehensive
Secure	vs.	Insecure
Self-confident	vs.	Anxious
Cheerful, resilient	vs.	Depressed, cries easily
Insensitive to people's approval or disapproval	vs.	Sensitive to people's approval or disapproval
Does not care	vs.	Scrupulous, fussy
No fears	vs.	Phobic symptoms
Given to simple action	vs.	Lonely, brooding

Box 5.2

The self-sentiment factor (Q3–) reveals people's self-image and the strength of their resolve to adhere to it in their daily living. It appears to reduce markedly in adolescence, reflecting the notion of loss of identity during this particular phase, but builds up gradually in the maturing adult. Like

FACTOR Q3		
Low score LOW SELF-SENTIMENT Q3–	versus	High score HIGH SELF-SENTIMENT Q3+
Uncontrolled	vs.	Controlled
Lax	vs.	Exacting will power
Follows own urges	vs.	Conforming
Careless of social rules	vs.	Socially precise

Box 5.3

FACTOR Q4		
Low score LOW ERGIC TENSION Q4–	versus	High score HIGH ERGIC TENSION Q4+
Relaxed	vs.	Tense
Tranquil	vs.	Overwrought
Torpid	vs.	Driven
Unfrustrated	vs.	Frustrated
Composed	vs.	Fretful

Box 5.4

guilt proneness, low self-sentiment is associated with parental control by punishment as well as lack of affection. Again, it is associated with artistic occupations and priestly vocations.

Finally, ergic tension (Q4+) relates in some ways to Freud's id, and also to McDougall's notion of 'total instinctual energy' (Cattell 1973, p. 177). Cattell has suggested that the trait describes energy of this kind that is undischarged, and that frustrations and deprivations of all kinds increase its magnitude. This is supported by evidence that shows the factor to be linked with poor academic performance, bereavements, and with unhappy love affairs. Interestingly, Cattell maintains that the trait is associated with jobs that have high stimulation, excessive demands, and uncertainties as well as with a poor ability to perform under stress. It has also been shown to be linked to a susceptibility to high blood pressure. In terms of family background, it is associated with a lack of demonstrated affection, with unstructured behavioural control, and punishment that is inconsistent. Before moving on I

FACTOR D		
Low score PHLEGMATIC D–	versus	High score EXCITABLE D+
Inactive	vs.	Overactive
Undemonstrative	vs.	Unrestrained
Stoical	vs.	Demanding, impatient
Complacent	vs.	Attention-seeking, showing off
Deliberate	vs.	Excitable
Not easily jealous	vs.	Prone to jealousy
Self-effacing	vs.	Self-assertive, egotistical

Box 5.5

should mention that an additional anxiety factor, excitability (D+), features in children's personalities in place of suspiciousness (L+). This manifests itself in overactive and unrestrained behaviour in which children may be demanding and attention-seeking, egotistical, and prone to jealousy.

It is important for us to pull together what may appear to be a rather disparate group of factors so that we can begin to interpret the anxiety factor as a composite psychological syndrome. It is now accepted that Cattell's anxiety is more or less equivalent to Eysenck's neuroticism, although Cattell and Kline (1977) maintain that the latter term is inappropriate. The grounds for this view relate to the fact that neurotics have been shown to differ substantially from normals on more factors than merely anxiety (p. 121). However, they stress the importance of the anxiety factor within the broader syndrome of neuroticism. The definition that they give to the overall factor describes the anxious person as 'easily perturbed, worrying, emotional when frustrated, lax, uncontrolled, depressed, moody, hypochondriacal, shy, embittered and of restricted interests' (pp. 121–2).

As we have observed previously, one can perceive underlying threads of psychoanalytic theory in Cattell's terminology for his primary factors. We can, if we wish, speculate in Freudian terms about the interaction between some of the anxiety factors. For example, Freud maintained that the ego and the id (ego strength and ergic tension) interact dynamically. In addition to defending itself against the external world, the ego has to contend with the demands of the instinctual id which it must energetically hold in check. Any serious conflict between the ego and id, Freud considered, may create neurosis, and a disturbance between the ego and the external world, psychosis. Any involvement of Cattell's conscientiousness factor (G+) (superego) in anxiety is far less clear, but the high levels of guilt proneness (O+) found in anxious individuals may well be interpretable by the punishing effects of the superego with which the ego also has to deal.

Although Cattell concedes that a person's performance on all his factors will fluctuate from situation to situation, nevertheless he maintains that, generally, they should be viewed as traits. However, some second-order factors possess varying levels of state influence; this applies particularly to anxiety, but also, incidentally, to a much lesser extent to extraversion. When we take a look at the primary factors in the light of state and mood variation, Cattell (1973) appears to suggest that there is a tendency for low ego strength, guilt proneness, and ergic tension to show more bias towards state anxiety (p. 185). Interestingly, these are the very traits that we noted earlier as being particularly interpretable in terms of Freudian theories. On reflection, of course, this is not altogether surprising, for one would expect state anxiety to be more manifest in clinically based theory. However, the knowledge of the association of these primaries with state anxiety may be useful when we arrive at the point of attempting to interpret the results of personality research with groups of musicians.

Trait anxiety in musicians as measured by Cattell's inventories

Research undertaken with musical pupils of school age, regardless of whether life or ability test criteria have been adopted, has indicated definite signs of adjustment (the opposite pole of anxiety). Table 5.1 shows this to be the case, particularly in Martin's (1976) results with secondary school pupils. The results of Shuter (1974) and Kemp (1981a), in highlighting the single factor of self-sentiment (Q3+), may be showing nothing more than a slight manifestation of another second-order factor—superego strength. However, when we turn to Kemp's two subgroups (the conservatoire exhibitioners and the more gifted pupils at the specialist music schools), we begin to perceive phenomena that may relate to the two very different climates in which the education and training of young musicians take place. First of all, the exhibitioners (those attending conservatoire junior departments on Saturdays) demonstrate unequivocal adjustment, possibly reflecting the strong parental support system already discussed in Chapter 3. Secondly, what emerges in connection with the specialist music school group is a persuasive profile of anxiety-related factors. We might wish to interpret these in terms of the 'hot house' effect (Howe 1989) in which undue acceleration and pressure can generate anxiety. This issue will be discussed more fully in Chapter 13. An alternative view might suggest that what we observed before in connection with introversion (Chapter 2) might be recurring here—the phenomenon of the more precocious pupils anticipating the characteristics of full-time music students. What is certainly clear is that, once selected for

Table 5.1 Summary of research on anxiety in musicians

Author	Type of group	HSPQ and 16 PF primary factors †						
Shuter (1974)	9–10-year-olds' measured on a music test				—		Q3+	
Martin (1976)	Secondary school pupils with various musical interests		D–	H+	—	O–		
Kemp (1981a)	Secondary school instrumentalists (composite group)				—		Q3+	
Kemp (1979)	Secondary school pupils attending conservatoire junoir departments	*C+		*H+	—	*O–	*Q3+	*Q4–
Kemp (1981a)	Specialist music school pupils		*D+	*H–	—	*O+	(Q3+)	
Kemp (1971)	Conservatoire students		—					Q4+
Martin (1976)	Conservatoire students	C–	—		L+		Q3–	Q4+
Martin (1976)	Student music teachers	C–	—		L+		Q3–	Q4+
Kemp (1981a)	Music students in higher education (composite group)	C–	—			O+		Q4+
Shatin et al. (1968)	Adults performers		—	H+				
Kemp (1981a)	Male professionals	C–	—		L+	O+	Q3–	
Kemp (1981a)	Female professionals		—					Q4+

* Indicates significant differences that emerged in comparison with their respective composite group. The factor shown in parentheses emerged at the same level.

† C+, high ego strength; C–, low ego strength; D+, excitability; D–, phlegmatic; H+, adventurous; H–, shyness; L+, suspiciousness; O+, guilt-proneness; O–, self-assurance; Q3+, high self-sentiment; Q3–, low self-sentiment; Q4+, high ergic tension; Q4– low ergic tension.

Dashes indicate that factor L does not feature in the HSPQ or that factor D does not occur in the 16 PF.

and receiving full time music tuition, students show a strong disposition towards anxiety, and the lower part of Table 5.1 unambiguously demonstrates this.

Turning to the professional musician, we can observe distinct suggestions of a continuing pattern of anxiety. The profile produced by Shatin *et al*. (1968) appears in Table 5.1 for the purpose of completeness, but we may agree to disregard it for reasons presented in Chapter 2, namely that the group was working in a safe and caring environment, and may not have been particularly representative of the professional performing musician.

The more complex pattern of my results with professional musicians showed gender-linked results. These appeared in spite of the use of separate sex norms, and tend to suggest that a different form of anxiety is involved in male and female musicianship. However, it should be noted that no gender by group interactions emerged on anxiety primary traits in my group of students. Looking at the whole picture of these results there appears to be a reasonably consistent pattern of low ego strength (C–), suspiciousness (L+), low self-sentiment (Q3–), and ergic tension (Q4+) in adult musicians, although, as we have seen, some gender-linked differences emerged in the professional group. In addition, there is some evidence here to suggest that the guilt proneness displayed by young gifted performers and students specializing in performance as well as by the male professional musicians indicates a possible direct link with performance demands or stress. There is some evidence here to suggest, also, that full-time music students display the highest levels of anxiety, a finding also confirmed by Steptoe and Fidler (1987). Also, it is perhaps significant that the three factors more related to state anxiety (C–, O+, and Q4+) appear with some degree of consistency in the adult performers.

Anxiety in musicians as measured by other inventories

It is reasonable to expect that the adoption of Spielberger's State–Trait Anxiety Inventory would allow researchers the opportunity to further clarify some of the findings described above. After all, if it measures what it purports to measure, it should be effective in helping us separate out the state and trait characteristics of the performing musician measured under differing conditions of stress. The kinds of question that we still wish to clarify are: are musicians as a group generally characterized by a predisposition towards anxiety; or are they more prone to fluctuations generated by the various situations in which they find themselves, and the demands made upon them?

Watson and Valentine's (1987) work with members of a professional orchestra, using Spielberger's test, supported the conclusions we have already arrived at with regard to trait anxiety, showing the men and women to be significantly higher when compared to the norms. In addition, they identified significant correlations between both the state and trait scores and the Performance Anxiety Inventory (PAI; Nagel *et al.* 1989). The results also suggested that performance anxiety was negatively correlated with the length of experience as a professional musician. Whether this reduction was attributable to experience itself or to a tendency for the highly anxious to leave the profession was not clear to them. However, this finding appears to be consistent with Hamann's (1982) results, which also indicated that those student performers who had received the most years of formal training performed in a significantly superior fashion under increased anxiety conditions.

In their study that compared musicians with groups of actors, dancers, singers, and controls, Marchant-Haycox and Wilson (1992) also showed the musicians to be highly stressed when measured on the Eysenck Personality Profiler (Eysenck and Wilson 1991). They also described them as being 'cynical, resigned, and world-weary' (p. 1065) as well as inactive and unambitious. The world-weariness may well be interpretable by the sources of stress highlighted in professional musicians by Steptoe (1989) in his research into coping strategies and stage fright. Quite apart from the stresses of performance, other stressors that he reported appeared to relate to separation from their families, irregular hours, extensive travelling, and the monotony of rehearsals. A similar picture was painted by Cooper and Wills (1989) in connection with popular musicians whom they found to be high on neuroticism as well as psychoticism. In summarizing his findings, Steptoe suggested that the elements of career stress, which, incidentally, he also found in music students (although taking on different levels of importance), were not independent of manifestations of stage fright. However, this does not, of course, necessarily indicate that they have a common root or cause. Although the musician's anxiety appears to be well-identified in terms of both state and trait factors, what, of course, still remains unclear is its exact aetiology. For further insights we may have to pursue theories of anxiety further. Before attempting this, there is one aspect of the Myers–Briggs Type Indicator that requires consideration.

Although, as observed in the 'Introduction', the Myers–Briggs does not contain an anxiety scale, Quenk (1993) maintains that the various Jungian types, as measured by the Myers–Briggs, may react in their own particular ways to stressful situations. When people come under stress, it is their fourth or inferior function—the most undeveloped part of their personality—that takes over. In such situations the individual appears to fall into the grip of behaviour that 'is not them' and quite out of control, which the theory maintains relates to unconscious, regressive features. Bayne (1994) cites research findings that suggest that each of the four *inferior* functions, intuition, sensing, feeling, and thinking, has a characteristic response to stress. As we have already noted, most musicians appear to be intuitive-feeling types, and this narrows down the possibilities to two of the four: sensing in the case of INFJ and ENFP types; and thinking for those who are INFP and ENFJ. Inferior function sensing types tend to overdo something—over-organize themselves, or possibly behave obsessively, perhaps in terms of practice routines. On the other hand, inferior function thinking types will become analytical and critical, and may feel useless and incompetent. Quenk (1993) quotes the words of an INFJ person overcome with uncontrollable inferior sensing:

When I am fully 'in the grip', I don't get anything done. I try to obsessively control every detail, I notice everything that is disorganized or needs cleaning in my outer world, and I want to fix it all perfectly and immediately. I eat too much, don't enjoy it, and feel guilty about losing control.

I feel like nobody helps me; I have to do it all myself and nobody appreciates me. I can't see any possibilities or alternatives around negative facts. I *really* focus on negative facts. I feel immobilized and unproductive, and have trouble concentrating. (p. 168)

Similarly, Quenk reports an INFP person in the grip of inferior thinking as saying:

I become overwhelmed by an awareness that I am totally incompetent at everything that I do, that I always have been and always will be—and that the whole world knows it! The truth of this is beyond doubt. I am mortified at not recognizing this before, and of compounding the offense by acting as if I were incompetent. (p. 98)

Another characteristic of the INFP type in full possession of inferior thinking can be a total rejection of their typically mild and self-effacing nature in preference for an aggressive, attacking stance towards what they see as objectionable aspects of others. Again, Quenk quotes an INFP as admitting 'I tend to lash out at people with great anger. I am blaming and accusatory. I get vicious "Ben Hur"-type images with a lot of violent action' (p. 98).

As we shall see presently, these kinds of response appear to find their way into the literature in connection with musicians suffering from performance anxiety.

Facilitating and debilitating anxiety in musicians

In his various writings Cattell frequently linked anxiety and motivation but was careful to point out that the two were quite distinct. In some ways he considered that anxiety could be perceived as a degenerate form of motivation in that it was no longer fully available for motivation and could not be mobilized for this purpose (Cattell 1972b, p.176). He thought that trait anxiety could be reduced by learning that he described as 'integrated' (this is understood to mean educational as opposed to conditioning) and because of this, he considered it to be particularly motivational (p. 177).

Thus we find ourselves again considering the Yerkes–Dodson law relating to an inverted U-shaped relationship between anxiety and performance, reflecting the facilitating effects on one side and debilitating on the other. In other words, at optimum levels, anxiety may be better perceived as motivational, involving a state of activation that allows us to operate more efficiently on tasks that are well within our capabilities. This would certainly account for the higher levels of anxiety to be found in undergraduates as well as high academic achievers in secondary schools.

Powell and Enright (1990) offer a useful example of three different conditions of anxiety imposed upon a simple imaginary task of picking up individual counters from a pile and placing them into a jar. Firstly, you are told to take as long as you like, and no-one will check up on you. In the second condition, you are told that for every counter placed in the jar within 30 seconds you will receive a pound coin. In the third condition, for every counter that you fail to get into the jar within the 30 second period you are told that you will have a finger chopped off. In the first condition no anxiety will be present, and the performance is likely to be careless and slow. The second condition will generate a level of anxiety that will facilitate a fast and efficient performance. Finally, the third condition might create so much anxiety that, in a state of panic, you might fumble and perform less efficiently (pp. 64–5).

Certainly, the motivational aspects of anxiety can often be overlooked, and Hamann (1982) and Hamann and Sobaje (1983) remarked how frequently it is that researchers interested in the incidence of anxiety in musicians have focused their attention on its *negative* effects upon performance. Understandably, it is this aspect that tends to occupy the attention of musicians themselves simply because they are only too aware of how an uncontrollable attack of nerves can destroy a performance with sometimes quite disastrous effects. However, many musicians will also be aware, if called upon to give it some thought, that, in what might be perceived as extreme low stress situations, they actually find themselves artificially inducing levels of anxiety state. By 'psyching themselves up' in this way they clearly feel more highly aroused, and thus perform with heightened degrees of sensitivity and imagination. In other words, a certain amount of anxiety is not only quite normal, it is facilitative, and actually necessary to perform tasks more efficiently.

Hamann and Sobaje (1983) pursued this kind of notion, using a group of student performers under two performance situations of low and high stress, the stress being induced by the presence of a jury. An interval of five days occurred between each performance, and immediately after each the students completed the STAI and the State–Trait Personality Inventory (STPI; Spielberger *et al.* 1979). This latter inventory was adopted with the specific purpose of measuring the additional states of curiosity and anger. Each student's history of formal training provided an additional research dimension. The quality of the two recorded performances was rated by a panel of five judges. The main findings relating to notions of facilitating anxiety revealed considerable support for Spielberger's theory that state anxiety has motivational and drive properties that are beneficial to the performance of different kinds of task. Hamann and Sobaje, indeed, found evidence that increased state anxiety appeared to *facilitate* performance. Whilst state anxiety levels were found to be higher in the high-stress performing situation, the performances under these conditions were superior to those in situations of low stress. This was true for all three groups of students, grouped in terms of number of years of formal training. Whilst the difference was minimal for those with the fewer years experience, and only moderate for those with medium, those with the most experience displayed a remarkable enhancement of their performance standard under the stress condition.

More recently Hamann (1985) has returned specifically to the question of length of training and skill acquisition. Here, he states succinctly that

... individuals with high trait anxiety will experience greater increases in state anxiety than individuals with low trait anxiety. Also, individuals with high trait anxiety with high task-mastery skills actually benefit from increased anxiety states, while individuals with low task-mastery skills and high trait anxiety tend not to benefit from increased anxiety states. Thus, the higher the task-mastery level and the higher the trait and state levels of anxiety, the better an individual will perform in a stressful situation. (p. 28)

In many ways this reinforces what many teachers advise their students: if they are prone to performance nerves, they should make sure they have a good margin of safety within which to operate. In other words, they should not play pieces in public about which they have doubts concerning their technical proficiency. Clearly, length of experience allows a person to perform more technically advanced repertoire whilst still maintaining adequate safety margins. However, Hamann's assertion that the relationship between anxiety and performance is wholly positive and linear, with task-mastery operating as a mediator, is likely to be challenged by many researchers as well as performing musicians.

Although programmes of treatment for performance anxiety need not feature in this discussion, Lehrer (1987) in his review of such literature suggests that anxiety can be mobilized as a facilitator by engaging in performance frequently. Periods of lay-off can lead to an 'incubation effect' in which anxiety is allowed to build up (McAllister and McAllister 1967). As with all phobias, avoidance is the natural and understandable defence response, but is the least helpful in dealing with the problem. It may well be that the cynicism, resignation, and world-weariness identified in musicians by Marchant-Haycox and Wilson (1992) may be interpretable as various forms of avoidance strategy—defence mechanisms and denial adopted precisely in an attempt to reduce the discomfort and debilitating effects of high anxiety.

Another important finding in Hamann and Sobaje's research relates to the levels of anger amongst the students regrouped according to trait anxiety scores. Although group differences of anger levels under the low-stress performance situation were minimal, the high anxiety trait group displayed significantly more anger than the remaining two under the high-stress situation. Hamann and Sobaje interpreted this manifestation of anger under performing stress in terms of mobilizing a defence mechanism to protect the ego against threat. Put another way, the students, and particularly those with high trait anxiety, were not only attempting to protect themselves against what they perceived as negative assessments of the judges, but were perhaps demonstrating the very quality of low ego strength highlighted earlier in Table 5.1 as a characteristic of adult musicians. Another explanation of the anger response relates well to the stress reaction of the INFP types in the grip of their inferior extraverted thinking function referred to on pages 94 and 95. Certainly, anger appears to be quite an inappropriate response since, although the group was under the greatest stress, their performances were judged to be the most successful. On the other hand, the expression of anger would certainly allow undischarged ergic tension to be effectively dissipated.

Taken as a whole this research suggests that anxiety states generated by performance situations perceived as being stressful may reveal certain conflicting components. Firstly, and as Hamann's work has suggested, there certainly appears to be a facilitating component, but, secondly, whilst generating levels of drive and arousal, the anxiety levels also contain negative (debilitating) elements. The traits highlighted in Table 5.1 such as low self-sentiment, ego fragility, and apprehensiveness combine to produce low levels of self-esteem, which, if not dealt with effectively, can mobilize themselves into degenerative reactions such as panic and catastrophizing. It is interesting that Hamann and Sobaje's research does not reveal any significant manifestation of these debilitating anxiety states.

In an extensive, and in some ways similar study, Craske and Craig (1984) selected two groups of college student pianists who, whilst of equal performing attainment, were identified as 'relatively anxious' and 'relatively nonanxious' and subjected them to two performing situations: firstly, in private, and then to an audience of judges. Several tests were administered; those of more direct interest to us were the STAI, an index of performance quality, 'self-efficacy' inventories, and an index of observable behavioural anxiety. It should, perhaps, be explained that self-efficacy theory was first developed by Bandura (1977) and relates to an individual's self-perception of their capacity to perform particular tasks. What emerged from Craske and Craig's work, of particular relevance to our concerns here, were a number of trends suggesting the presence of both facilitating and debilitating anxiety. More specifically, they found that the presence of an audience had greater effect upon the anxious group in that their performance quality decreased, whereas indications of an improvement were shown by the non-anxious group. Similarly, whilst the anxious group showed signs of *observable* indications of anxiety as well as a reduction of self-efficacy scores under the audience condition as compared to playing alone, the non-anxious group indicated opposite trends on both factors.

However, it needs to be borne in mind that the inverted U relationship between anxiety and performance may not be uniform and is possibly skewed to the left. Gaudrey and Spielberger (1971), for example, raised doubts about accepting the Yerkes–Dodson law too readily as the association, as far as an academic performance is concerned, appears to be far more strongly negative than positive. However, in terms of musicianship there may be grounds (quite apart from those provided by Hamann) for speculating that, at deeper levels, anxiety is inextricably bound to various aspects of the phenomenon of being a musician. Let us briefly consider a few of these.

Arousal

We encountered the notion of arousal earlier in Chapters 2 and 4 in connection with the musician's introversion and pathemia and, in this way we can see that it appears to be fairly well-embedded within the musician's temperament and modes of functioning. In the context of this chapter, this form of arousal, autonomic nervous system activation, involves a state of readiness and attention that allows us to scan the environment in order to interpret and analyse events. These basic 'gut feeling' responses have their origins in lower brain activity that triggers messages that , in turn, activate the subcortex and cortex into a more cognitive understanding and appreciation of events. It will be recalled that earlier, in connection with introversion, we discussed two information-processing loops. According to Eysenck's (1967) theories, the first loop was related to introversion, and the second to neuroticism and emotion (see p. 47 in Chapter 2). This latter aspect can be seen to be well in line with Freud's (1964) view that overstimulation and anxiety are closely linked.

Whilst we do not need to become involved in any discussion of the brain physiology of arousal, it is important to recognize the central notion of neuroticism/anxiety links with emotion and activation. It may well be true that it is the onset of these physiological reactions that triggers the musician's kinds of perception of impending catastrophe to be discussed later. Such links certainly help explain the symptoms of stress displayed by musicians immediately before and during performance, such as shaking, sweating, fast heart rate, nausea, and so on. These can be viewed as being a direct reflection of autonomic nervous system activation, which, if not moderated, can lead to a dangerous diversion of attention if not to the disintegration of a performance. Although Eysenck's two loops both involve cortical arousal, he maintains that they are quite separate and distinct. The first, with its links with introversion, is related *principally* to high cortical arousal, but involves little autonomic activity. On the other hand, the second loop principally involves autonomic-emotional arousal, which influences the dimension of neuroticism. Cattell (1972b) also differentiates between the two, but adopts somewhat different terminology. He refers to the cortertia–pathemia dimension as a more stable trait associated with cognitive style, whereas autonomic arousal is a form of 'state arousal'.

What is important here is to appreciate that, because introverts have higher arousal states, it follows that they will reach their optimum level earlier than extraverts in situations that involve high levels of arousal. Consequently, in a demanding performing environment it is likely that introverts are more likely than extraverts to suffer from overstimulation. Thus, it would appear likely that both arousal loops might well militate in generating over-arousal and anxiety in the performing musician. In other words, both cortical alertness and autonomic nervous system activation are operative in the performing musician simply because anxious and introverted types are more likely to suffer from overstimulation of these processes in anxiety-provoking situations.

The neurobiological work of Gray (1982) has further developed this kind of notion. He suggests that, in effect, introversion and neuroticism combine to form an active and highly sensitive behavioural system that reacts to stimuli by exaggerated inhibition. This dimension is, he maintains, the biological basis of anxiety. If this notion is applied to musicians we might begin to see how, in a performing situation perceived as stressful, the behavioural inhibition system takes control, producing the kind of increased attention, vigilance, and interference with motor behaviour that Gray maintains characterizes anxiety.

Musicians' self-concept

The picture that is becoming clear is that musicians, as a group, are so profoundly committed to music that they find it difficult to separate their own personal identities from their musical ability, and thus their capacity to perform music. Pruett (1991) describes it in this way:

The young musician who chooses an anxiety-binding pattern of grandiosity and omnipotence risks his self-esteem. That self-esteem can become anchored in the possession of certain *qualities*, such as musical talent and success, instead of the more sustaining authenticity of one's own perceptions. He can become increasingly dependent upon adulation and admiration. (p. 345)

Dews and Williams (1989) supported this notion observing that 79 per cent of their student musicians claimed that a considerable amount of their self-esteem was directly related to how they performed (p. 45). The conviction that one had to be a perfectly competent musical performer in order to be a worthwhile person was the kind of irrational belief that was also identified by Tobacyk and Downs (1986).

In their work with performers of popular music Wills and Cooper (1988) constructed a questionnaire containing a checklist of high stressors. The item that attracted the highest number of responses was one that related to the 'feeling that you must reach or maintain the standards of musicianship that you set yourself' (p. 74). That over half the musicians checked this item may show graphically how musicians induce their own stress by the self-imposition of high standards. Wills and Cooper concluded that 'the popular musician appears to be a driven individual, striving towards artistic self-satisfaction and a high level of performance. In doing so, he imposes a high level of pressure upon himself' (p. 81). Wills and Cooper also linked popular musicians with 'Type A behaviour', a syndrome originally identified by cardiologists Friedman and Rosenman (1974) as being a proneness to premature coronary heart disease. Its positive aspects, however, are drive, ambition, competitiveness, a willingness to take on several tasks simultaneously, and overall job-involvement. On the negative side, the Type A person suffers from aggressiveness, impatience, and feelings of being under pressure. Wills and Cooper concluded that their group of popular musicians could be characterized by their drive, striving towards artistic self-satisfaction, high levels of performance, and the imposition of a high level of pressure upon themselves.

The driving force, which may have connections with strong identification patterns between music students and teachers, appears to lead to a search for perfection that is nothing less than an extreme form of self-punishment. Whilst we might wish to take issue with Babikian's (1985) interpretation of this phenomenon as a hard and rigid superego ideal (this is certainly not supported by the evidence presented here), the effect of 'trying-too-hard', instilled into young musicians from the early stages, and discussed by Fogel (1982), would seem to add to the syndrome.

Such a degree of identification in which personal worth and musical achievement are inextricably linked would appear to be a scenario for the emergence of two kinds of behaviour patterns frequently found in music conservatoires and universities. Firstly, the 'prima donna' behaviour that can emerge in environments where interpersonal competition is rife, and can be observed in some student performers who perceive themselves to be on an upward spiral of success. In the opposite direction one witnesses a psychological disturbance in which anxious thoughts trigger autonomic reactions leading to heightened apprehension, self-criticism, and feelings of incompetence leading to increased anxiety. This also involves not only the disintegration of the performance but also severe damage to the person's sense of well-being and self-concept. In other words, one might be perceiving the outcomes of an upward spiral of increasing levels of success involving the emergence of high levels of self-esteem in one direction (facilitating anxiety), and a downward trend for those whose self-esteem is fading due to a progressively debilitating anxiety and regular occurrences of performances perceived as catastrophic.

Musicians' search for perfection may well be inextricably bound up with their upbringing. There is an unusually high incidence of first-born and only children in groups of musicians, which often results in the early acquisition of adult standards of behaviour and expectation. So called 'hothousing' in which children can be pressured into high levels of achievement sometimes exercises the same effects in which children take on the physical, psychological, and social trappings of adulthood before they are ready (Elkind 1981). Bound up with this is a chronic fear of failure, and a mode of thinking in which the individual believes that nothing lies between total success and abject failure (Burns 1980).

The personal investment that musicians make in music, which is inimical to feelings of personal esteem, appears to be intertwined with the manifestation of competition at every level. Quite apart from the interpersonal rivalry often found in full-time music students already referred to, competition also manifests itself in professional orchestras. Piperek (1981) reported that 60 per cent of the members of the Vienna Symphony orchestra believed that 'envy is an integral part of the musician's profession' (p. 50). This manifested itself in 36 per cent of the orchestra reporting difficulties in personal contact with their colleagues. Steptoe (1989) also reported concerns about interpersonal competition and back-stabbing in members of two London symphony orchestras. Interestingly, the reported levels on these two aspects were even higher for music students at one of the London conservatoires (p. 7).

Certainly the direct links between low self-concept and high anxiety have been well-established empirically, and Cattell's factoring of self-esteem as a component of anxiety appears to confirm this. Burns (1979) presented evidence that suggests that the connection is causal in both directions: anxiety generates low self-esteem; and low self-esteem renders a person sensitive to evidence that confirms inadequacy, thus provoking anxiety (p. 259). This form of interactive relationship was also claimed by Krug *et al.* (1976) who also speculated that low self-esteem and anxiety were fundamentally and dynamically linked. As Burns points out, it is quite easy to see how, by a classical conditioning process, negative and maladaptive thoughts about oneself can generate anxiety as part of a continuous loop. In the context of musical performance this kind of degenerative spiral may involve what some of the literature refers to as 'catastrophizing'.

Catastrophizing

An important element in the downward spiral effect appears to be the notion of 'catastrophizing', feelings of vulnerability that involve fear of reaching a point of no return when total disintegration of a performance becomes inevitable. Steptoe and Fidler (1987) found that all three of their groups of professional, amateur, and student musicians reported a tendency to imagine catastrophes, and exaggerated feelings of the consequences arising out of a minor mishap. The kinds of sentiment that appeared to feature heavily in these fantasies were 'I'm almost sure to make a dreadful mistake, and that will ruin everything'; 'I don't think that I will be able to get through to the end without cracking up'; and 'I think I'm going to faint' (p. 245).

An important finding in Steptoe and Fidler's research was that, whilst the tendency to catastrophize was strongly related to state anxiety levels, it appeared to be independent of neuroticism, as measured by Eysenck's EPI. In other words we might be forgiven for suspecting that the phenomenon is a product of generating high anxiety states rather than more inherent levels of trait anxiety.

However, this finding appears to be in conflict with Gaudrey and Spielberger's (1971) view that a person who is high on trait anxiety, brought about perhaps through earlier stressful experiences, is more likely to perceive situations as threatening. Such persons, they believe, would respond with higher anxiety states, triggering fear reactions about failure and accompanied by self-depreciating tendencies. Similarly, Marchant-Haycox and Wilson (1992) claimed that tendencies towards emotional instability significantly predispose performing artists to symptoms of panic in situations perceived as threatening.

Much of the evidence, however, points to the conclusion that catastrophizing belongs to a network of what we might call secondary anxiety or 'worry about anxiety' (Powell and Enright 1990). Irrational thoughts and fears will tend to increase physiological arousal and the likelihood that these physical symptoms will recur in the future. As Steptoe (1989) remarks, besides being maladaptive, such off-task behaviour and a diversion of attention away from the complex matters of the performance in hand in themselves significantly increase the danger of committing errors.

Earlier, on page 101, in connection with Wills and Cooper's (1988) research with popular musicians, we discussed the notion that the musician might be characterized by 'type A' behaviour . However, Scheier *et al.* (1983) maintain that type As are *more* likely to focus their attention on the task at hand and less on information about physical states. If this is true, then it introduces a new complexity into our discussion. If the introverted, self-focused musician actually attempts to focus upon the task at hand—the music being performed—to the exclusion of everything else (including self and psychological state), this disregard for personal well-being may involve the kind of denial and avoidance behaviour that has already been noted. This notion may also lead us to a sharper definition of the musician's introversion, possibly as being less tied up with notions of self-absorption and more with total involvement with musical performance. Certainly, this is in accordance with the kinds of observation we have already made in connection with the musician's self-concept.

However, it has to be conceded that this picture does not, on the face of it, sit happily with the phenomenon of catastrophizing. Catastrophizing by definition involves a shift of attention away from the actual concerns of performance and towards self-conscious concerns about physical states, which are far more appropriately associated with type B behaviour. We must bear in mind, of course, that Wills and Cooper were studying popular musicians and, even then, their group was exactly 50 per cent equally distributed between type A and B behaviours. Furthermore, they showed that the distribution of type A behaviour was very unevenly distributed between different kinds of instrumentalists (p. 91), a notion we shall return to in Chapter 8.

Thus the phenomenon of catastrophizing needs to be viewed rather more widely than merely in terms of anxiety. Certainly more research is required to clarify the interrelationships between degrees of self-focusing, anxiety, and introversion and to clarify the extent to which these are deeply embedded in the musician's temperament. Of course, we must also bear in mind that any tendencies towards self-focused attention and sensitivity to internal states will, in themselves, result in high scores on anxiety scales (Storr 1976). In other words, musicians, by their very nature, may respond to questionnaire items with greater levels of personal insights than general populations, thus increasing anxiety scores.

Auditory style

Finally, in our discussion of the musician's anxiety, we ought to consider again here an issue that was first raised in Chapter 2. As we observed, the musician's introversion incorporates aspects of a particular type of internalized musical life. This may be of relevance to our deliberations here concerning the role of anxiety in musicianship in that we may wish to link this with the notion of auditory style of a kind highly developed in musicians. As the environment becomes more heavily polluted by noise it is reasonable to suspect that the general population may be developing lower levels of auditory sensitivity, depending more heavily on the visual—television, video, magazines, and so on. Brodsky *et al.* (1994) suggest that, in the case of musicians, their primary sensory mode, their special 'gift', amounted to a predisposition to perceive the world more aurally than visually. Citing the psychoanalytic work of Nass (1971, 1975) in which he argued that this sensory style is adopted as a means of adapting to and mastering reality, they consider that it might be something of a curse rather than a blessing. After all, might it not be conceivable that such a difference in perceptual style might prove to be the root of feelings of being different and of separation, and thus generate higher levels of anxiety?

Suggesting that highly developed auditory style might not only prove to be the motivator towards music but also the generator of anxiety, Brodsky *et al.* proceeded to explore possible links between the dimension, state anxiety, and music performance anxiety in a group of professional musicians. Preliminary analyses showed that, although the musicians were significantly higher on trait anxiety than a control group of non-musicians, this did not apply to state anxiety. Taken as a whole the results indicated that certain factors that emerged from a factor analysis were successful in differentiating between musicians and non-musicians. However, the only interpretable factor that significantly separated the musicians from the non-musicians, whilst also loading on state and trait anxiety, was the first to be extracted and which attracted over 20 per cent of the variance. This factor appeared to relate to an acute sensitivity to music, which had developed continuously throughout their childhood and adolescence. It had somatic as well as auditory aspects, involved a feeling that music was 'in the mind', and resulted in feelings of being special or different. It should be added that only the musicians demonstrated any association between this factor and state and trait anxiety, confirming Brodsky's conclusion that the associations between auditory style and the anxiety factors are qualitatively different for musicians and non-musicians. When the musicians were classified into low, medium, and high auditory style groups, this last group emerged with significantly higher levels of state anxiety. In addition, the high state anxiety group scored highly on factors associated with avoidance of performance stress, more extensive practice, and with a higher incidence of symptoms related to misuse or overuse. Clearly, this exploratory research warrants further investigation, particularly if the notion of auditory style operating as a motivator as well as debilitator can be shown to have credence.

The view presented here is that anxiety appears to be inextricably bound up with certain physiological, emotional, and cognitive aspects of human functioning. These have been shown to interrelate with personality factors, particularly those that appear to characterize the musician. This should not come as a surprise to us, simply because, by viewing the nature of musicianship and musical performance in its full complexity, we identify a discipline that integrates all the aspects of what it is to be fully human, the development of interacting functions and skills of physical, emotional, and cognitive kinds.

In a sense the preceding four chapters have come full circle, finishing with the identification of strong theoretical links, not only between introversion and anxiety, but also between sensitivity and independence. These have been shown to characterize musicians as a special occupational group. As we have already seen, personality traits do not exist in isolation; they combine and interact dynamically in characteristically different ways according to chosen life-styles, values, abilities, and skills. In the following chapters these notions will undergo further refinement, allowing us to develop deeper understandings of musical processes and, ultimately, insights into the educational and training processes most beneficial for musicians.

Summary

Anxiety appears to take two forms: *trait anxiety*, which refers to a reasonably consistent aspect of people's personality; and *state anxiety*, a more transient state that fluctuates according to particular situations. Cattell's model embraces a broad collection of factors, which he maintains are principally trait-based. Musicians' anxiety appears to manifest itself particularly in emotional instability and a form of frustrated tension, but suspiciousness and low self-sentiment also feature as important components. These traits are revealed as an inherent part of the psychological makeup of most musicians and tend to become first manifest during higher education and, thereafter, continue to be apparent in professional life. There is some evidence, however, that high levels of anxiety also emerge in younger, particularly talented musicians attending special music schools. This may reflect the 'hothousing' syndrome of pressure and interpersonal competition or, alternatively, the outcome of a too early adoption of the social and psychological trappings of adulthood.

Although the Myers–Briggs Type Indicator does not contain an anxiety scale, its theory offers some insights into certain behaviour responses of the different types under conditions of stress. This relates to the 'inferior' function which, in the case of musicians, may well manifest itself either in states of immobilization and lack of concentration or, alternatively, in feelings of total incompetence and aggressive anger. Other researchers have stressed the psychologically unhealthy degree to which musicians' self-esteem is intertwined with their levels of success as performers. This strong identification can lead to excessive forms of self-punishment and high anxiety particularly in situations where performance standards appear to slip and catastrophe seems to be inevitable.

The more physiological view of anxiety as proposed by Eysenck should not be overlooked in any discussion of the musician. Apart from the interconnection between arousal and introversion, he suggests that a second feedback loop involves neuroticism which is more strongly related to autonomic arousal and emotion. If this theory is correct, it may well account for the apparent close interrelationships between manifestations of stress in aesthetic performances and tendencies to 'catastrophize', which may be caused by 'overload'. Musicians' high levels of auditory style may well also prove to be inextricably bound up with Eysenck's second arousal loop.

The theory may well also contribute to the concept of facilitating anxiety in performance. Contrary to what is often stressed about anxiety in musicians, there is a body of research that suggests that, for some, anxiety can *facilitate* higher levels of standards of musical performance. This facilitative role appears to be particularly manifest in more experienced performers who may have learned to control the more debilitating effects of anxiety.

SIX

Gender role adaptability

Introduction

That men and women reveal significant differences in most aspects of personality is well documented in the literature, and these appear to be reasonably consistent throughout the whole developmental range from childhood to adult life (Saville 1972; Saville and Finlayson 1973; Saville and Blinkhorn 1976). Although there are minor disparities between the British research and Cattell's American standardizations (Cattell *et al.* 1970), we can identify a reasonable correspondence between the two cultures in terms of gender-linked differences. Of particular interest in the context of our previous chapters is that men invariably score higher on introversion and some aspects of independence than women within general populations. On the other hand, women tend to be more sensitive and anxious than men. It is patterns of gender-linked traits such as these that contribute to what we perceive as 'la différence', not only in more abstract personality terms, but in our predispositions to behave in certain ways and to respond to circumstances in characteristic fashions.

Such behavioural patterns and responses, of course, are engendered from birth onwards: mothers are often perceived as the carers in the home, and traditionally fathers are seen as more distanced and independent. Until relatively recently, fathers were invariably seen as the ones who return home after a day's work to discipline the children on a 'wait until your father gets home' basis. Perhaps by a process of identification with their same-sex parent, children become socialized into predominantly masculine or feminine behaviour patterns. Certainly, research suggests that the more strongly gender-stereotyped parents are, the more stereotyped their children will be also. From birth onwards, gender identity is reinforced by the selection of toys—cars and guns as opposed to dolls and furry animals—but also in more subtle ways relating to the ways in which parents and others touch, caress, and console young children. These patterns clearly become further developed and reinforced during the period of statutory education. Later, at secondary level, pupils' preferences for teachers and subjects may, to some extent, be the outcome of an unconscious process of matching in terms of the degree to which they are gender-stereotyped. Despite several attempts to bring about changes in the school curriculum and in teaching styles that equally benefit girls and boys, old stereotypes die hard and still operate in society at large. Certainly, what influences upbringing and educational practices in these respects is a certain fear of nurturing a boy who turns out to be effeminate.

Some personality tests actually contain a masculinity–femininity scale, and these help identify whether a person is strongly or weakly gender-stereotyped or, indeed, is characterized by a temperament more associated with the opposite sex. It was in the use of such tests that researchers into creativity, way back in the 1950s and 60s, began to show empirically that certain groups of creative adults did, in fact, tend to display more characteristics of the opposite sex than was generally considered to be 'normal' (Barron 1957; MacKinnon 1962; Hall and MacKinnon 1969). However, Bem (1974) subsequently claimed, along with several others, that this kind of bi-polar scale is an oversimplification of a far more complex phenomenon. She suggested that masculinity and femininity could be viewed as independent dimensions that were not inextricably and inversely related. Her pioneer work in this field initially generated the gender-role theory frequently referred to as 'psychological androgyny'.

Bem's theory of psychological androgyny

Theories of androgyny, the word being derived from the Greek *andros* (man) and *gyne* (woman), pursue the notion that masculinity and femininity do *not* lie at the opposite ends of one dimension. It develops the notion that a person's gender identity can be measured on these aspects as two quite independent dimensions: certain people can be both or, indeed, neither. Thus, the *Bem Sex Role Inventory* (BSRI; Bem 1974), allows individuals to be identified as one of four types: high masculine and high feminine; high masculine and low feminine; low masculine and high feminine; and finally, low masculine and low feminine. These types can then be referred to as androgynous; masculine; feminine; undifferentiated, respectively, and allow the researcher to approach the phenomenon of opposite sex-typing in a more sophisticated manner. A number of different methods of calculating the typology have been discussed and devised, but these need not concern us here.

Persons, identified as androgynous, regardless of their biological gender, can be regarded as possessing predispositions to respond to different situations using either male- or female-associated behaviours that they perceive as appropriate. For example, an androgynous person would be equally as comfortable fussing over a baby or stooping to smell a flower arrangement as in dealing assertively with an intruder into his or her home. On the other hand, an undifferentiated person might well not react to these situations with what are considered to be appropriate responses.

Later, Bem (1981) extended her work in gender-role stereotyping by attempting to explain the theory in social learning terms, placing more emphasis on the processes of socialization by which children develop their gender-linked self-concepts. She is at pains to explain how the child's learning in this area ranges far and wide from the more specific anatomical and reproductive functions to a whole heterogeneous network of sex-related associations. In her view, this whole complex cognitive structure operates as an individual's personal gender schema, and it is within the context of this that he or she searches for and assimilates incoming information that is felt to be consonant with it. The child's self-concept itself gets assimilated into this gender schema, and in early life an infant may learn that some attributes do not normally relate to their gender. For example, girls may learn that strength is more often attributed to boys, and boys observe that, in the usual run of things, nurturance is something rarely attributed to them. Gradually children evaluate their adequacy as people in these terms and learn to control and direct their lives accordingly; their personal gender schema becomes their prescriptive standard and guide. It is within the context of such gender schema that individuals respond to most items in personality inventories, and thus we find gender influencing most, if not all, factors.

By developing her gender schema theory, Bem has, in effect, moved away somewhat from the theory of androgyny. Rather than maintaining the notion that there is a masculine and a feminine in each one of us as independent and palpable realities, she now sees these as cognitive constructs, socially generated and maintained. In developing a position more conducive to a feminist perspective, Bem now places less emphasis upon the notion of an individual as androgynous and more on the need for society to be aschematic (Bem 1981, p. 363). However, whilst noting this preferred position, there are particular insights to be gleaned from the results of earlier research, which had either adopted personality inventories, masculinity–femininity scales, or Bem's inventory. These research findings can be viewed, if the reader prefers, as outcomes of a society that remains essentially schematic in Bem's terms. In other words, those persons who emerge from research as 'androgynous' may be individuals who possess certain capacities to disregard quite powerful sociocultural influences. As we saw in Chapter 3, both male and female musicians certainly possess the introversion, independence, and personal autonomy to direct their lives according to a well internalized and idiosyncratic self-concept.

Gender role stereotyping in musicians

We have already noted that gender-linked personality differences in general populations tend to suggest that patterns of upbringing and processes of socialization encourage men to perceive themselves as more independent than women. By similar processes and from an early age, women are generally allowed to display greater levels of sensitivity than men. These two temperamental characteristics, generally perceived as predominant aspects of stereotypical male and female schema, may have subtle connections with a third feature, the frequently claimed predisposition of women to be more anxious than men.

Very much in line with research with other creative groups, musicians are generally observed to show tendencies towards certain characteristics of the opposite sex. For example, Garder (1955) was one of the first to report that a group of male high-school instrumentalists appeared less masculine than non-instrumentalists. Similarly, Sample and Hotchkiss (1971) found that those young people who played in bands displayed more sensitivity than those who did not. More convincingly, Martin (1976), in his research with music students, showed the women to be more independent than the men, and the men to be more sensitive than the women. However, because Martin used single sex norms in his research, his male and female profiles would have accentuated these particular features. Expressed another way, his profiles for male and female musicians were revealing more about their respective comparisons with men and women in the general population than *real* differences between them.

In Martin's defence, of course, it can be argued that so-called 'real' differences are themselves more like statistical artefacts, and that population norms are precisely what they say they are—norms. In other words, a man and a woman in our society, sharing the same 'real' level of measured sensitivity, say, on the 16PF, might well be considered oversensitive and insensitive, respectively. Such patterns of interaction on gender-related traits between male and female musicians and non-musicians were also identified in my own research, which entered gender as an experimental variable (Kemp 1982a). The point needs to be made in passing that all the differences between musicians and other groups in my research, and reported in earlier chapters, took account of the effects of gender by correcting the data. In this research, then, any gender differences in musicians that emerged as having characteristically different trends from those in comparison groups would be highlighted in the form of interactions of the kind shown in Figure 6.1.

The results of my own research with the three main groups of secondary school pupils, full-time music students, and professional musicians revealed a consistent pattern of gender differences in musicians differing from those found in the comparison groups of non-musicians (Kemp 1982a). Those traits where these interactions took place most consistently and that are most

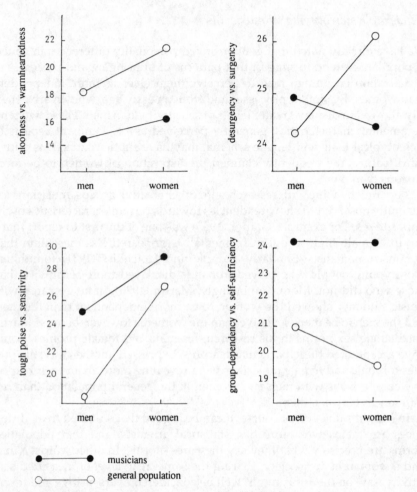

Figure 6.1 Gender differences on aloofness, surgency, sensitivity, and self-sufficiency, for professional musicians and general population.

significant for this discussion were aloofness (A–), surgency (F+), sensitivity (I+), and self-sufficiency (Q2+). In studying these in Figure 6.1, it can be seen that, in professional musicians, for example, the male and female musicians invariably show a tendency to minimize the differences shown by the non-musicians. Whilst, as we would expect, both men and women show a distinct trend towards musicianship linked traits, the gender that might be perceived as 'deficient' on any specific trait moves further towards what we might view as an optimum level. However, it will be noticed that an actual inversion took place on surgency (also confirmed by the pupils) in which the strong tendency of female non-musicians towards this trait was reversed in male musicians.

A most important finding in respect of the group of secondary school pupils requires highlighting at this point. Although the whole group of nearly 500 pupils showed the above interactions at highly significant levels, when the group was divided into two halves—those under 15 years and those over—only the second group revealed these interactions. In other words, it was only the musicians in middle and late adolescence who showed tendencies towards androgyny.

The above findings prompted me to adopt the BSRI with a small number of musicians to help clarify some of the issues raised above (Kemp 1985). If we are correct in maintaining that both male and female musicians reveal characteristics of the opposite sex, it follows that they are, by Bem's definition, androgynous. The research investigated a group of 80 music students and compared them with a similar group of non-music students; each group contained an equal distribution of men and women. The results showed that, whilst the women were indeed both more masculine and feminine than the non-musicians, the male musicians were found to be more feminine and less masculine than their comparison groups. Whilst this pattern of androgyny in the women clearly confirms earlier findings, it is possible that the men's femininity minus masculinity may have been due to sampling error. The fact that the musicians were recruited from one institution that may, possibly, have reflected a particular ethos could have influenced the results. Certainly, in a more recent study, Wubbenhorst (1994) showed his groups of student music teachers and performers both to be predominantly androgynous (48 and 38 per cent, respectively), the other members of the groups being distributed fairly evenly over the remaining three types.

The importance of these findings relates to two issues. Firstly, the demands that music makes upon the developing person appear to exert an influence that can be interpreted as a temperamental requirement, all those having ambitions to become musicians needing to aspire to optimum levels on particular key traits. These are interpretable as task-linked characteristics of the kind identified by Csikszentmihalyi and Getzels (1973) in their research with creative people. They maintained that the temperament of more creative types 'can be explained in terms of a task requirement . . . to use a full range of cognitive and emotional responses *regardless of sex-linked socio-cultural expectations*' (my italics) (p. 102). The second issue relates to certain outcomes of the first: namely that, as a result of these task-required temperaments being sex-linked in general populations, creative people will, as a natural outcome, be perceived as more sex-typed in the opposite direction, and thus, 'abnormal'.

Much of this is directly in line with MacKinnon's (1962) findings with creative men, which concluded that

. . . the more creative a person is the more he reveals an openness to his own feelings and emotions, a sensitive intellect and understanding self-awareness, wide-ranging interests including many which in the American culture are thought of as feminine.

In the realm of sexual identification and interests, our creative subjects appear to give more expression to the feminine side of their nature than do less creative persons. (p. 488)

We should, perhaps, return to the observation made in connection with the personalities of young musicians (Kemp 1981a). We noted that it was only those who were aged 15 years and over who demonstrated any suggestion of androgyny. If we speculate about this, it would appear likely that any study of musical populations in ordinary secondary schools, as opposed to schools for the musically gifted, is likely to reveal a significant change at this point due to high drop-out rates. For many pupils, the uncertainties of pubertal changes, the search for a new identity and wider interests, and rejection of certain aspects of parental values, quite apart from increasing academic pressures, might lead to discontinuing music and instrumental lessons. We might wish to speculate further concerning those who drop out as possibly constituting a group made up of the more heavily sex-stereo-typed characters. Not only might these types find it most difficult to resist peer group pressures, they may also prove to be the most ill-equipped tem-peramentally to pursue music at more advanced levels. What would also influence them, significantly, would be any suggestion or observation that the older musical pupils were inappropriate role-models due to their devia-tion from generally accepted personality norms.

In her work on the BSRI, Ruch (1984) investigated its underlying factor structure and identified some important differences between the masculin-ity and femininity scales. For example, she showed that, whereas the femininity scale was made up of a fairly loosely structured and diffuse set of factors, the factors associated with masculinity were far more tightly clus-tered. This might suggest to us that, not only does society perhaps view these gender roles differently, but also that to be described as feminine a per-son may not need to display all the various femininity traits. On the other hand, to be described as masculine, a person must adhere to a much more rigidly defined set of attributes. There may be two outcomes of this finding that are of importance to us. Firstly, it may be easier for a man to be identi-fied in these terms as feminine than for a woman to be perceived as mascu-line. Secondly, it may well suggest that society imposes a far stricter view of what are perceived as masculine behaviours than it does for feminine behaviour. In other words, for a man to continue to be typed as masculine requires him to adhere rigidly to a tightly defined set of attributes and, at the same time, he may feel constrained to view manifestations of the creative person's flexibility with disdain.

As Bem (1981) remarks, because of society's strong attachment to the male and female prototypes, individuals generally are highly motivated to be especially vigilant about manifesting any behaviour that might be thought to be cross-gender related. Thus, for the majority, an individual's gender makes a fundamental difference in virtually every aspect of his or her daily existence. In this way we might begin to see how, in certain circumstances, boys may choose to resist any activities in the school curriculum that their gender-schema indicates are effeminate. One aspect of this that appears to be particularly powerful in school life relates to people's perceptions of particular musical instruments as being endowed with gender-related connotations. These are discussed more fully in Chapter 8, but let it suffice to say here that these beliefs and attitudes appear to be well in place in primary school children and right up into adult life. They will certainly influence the patterns of children's instrumental choice, and instruments such as the violin and flute may, as a result, be avoided by boys, and trumpets and trombones by girls.

As we observed earlier, the musician's self-concept is so powerfully tied up with that of being a musician that the maintenance of a rigid gender role stereotype may be felt to be unimportant. Musicians may be so used to making decisions and valuing artefacts that can be seen as being dissonant with matters relating to social desirability that a few additional factors that relate directly to their gender identity may be of little consequence. For example, a boy who is seen regularly carrying his violin case to school each day may be so distanced from the usual norms of school behaviour and thus from his peer group that the prevailing view of violin playing as effeminate may not present him with very much additional conflict. On the other hand, a boy carrying a trombone or trumpet to school may not be quite so infra dig. Chapter 8 suggests that certain groups of instrumentalists, for example, brass players and some woodwind are, in fact, able to retain particular elements of gender stereotyping. At the critical age of 15, players of certain instruments may have to choose to brazenly disregard pressures to conform to stereotyped gender schema in preference for the kind of individualism discussed in previous chapters. Howe and Sloboda (1992) cite cases of pupils at a school for the musically gifted being made to feel different and uncomfortable in their former schools. For example, one boy was heard to say

I remember on occasions thinking, oh I'd really like to stop the violin, because there was a lot of pressure in my old school to stop because it wasn't a musical school, and they thought it was a bit iffy and strange. So there was a lot of pressure from them, and then I didn't want to be weird, and different I suppose, so I did occasionally think, oh, I don't want to carry on. (p. 17)

Such levels of discomfort experienced, as in this case, by a presumably highly motivated and gifted child have to be viewed with concern, and certainly help account for the drop out rates from instrumental tuition in many ordinary schools. The solution, of course, is that a more agreeable environment, conducive to music-making, needs to be established that can offer musical children a haven that insulates them from such difficulties as well as providing mutual support. They may well be already sensitive to feelings of being different on account of their androgyny; any additional discomfort experienced will exercise the effect of generating and clarifying the changeover pattern at age 15.

We are left, therefore, with something of a paradox. One picture has been painted of the musician as an independent, self-sufficient, autonomous individual; the other is very different, someone very vulnerable and sensitive to pressure and abuse by peers. It may, of course, be the outcome of the latter that helps establish the former at such significant levels. Storr (1976) discusses the vulnerable side of creative people particularly in terms of their gender schema suggesting that their 'contra-sexual side is close to the surface, more in evidence, and less shunned than is the case amongst the average' (p. 243). He speculates that this may in part be due to the creative person's more tenuous sense of identity, whereas, in most other people, the feeling of being unequivocally masculine or feminine is an important and central part of their self-concept.

Music may provide a kind of haven for those creative types who can take an independent attitude to directing their lives according to their own inner standards. As Storr (1976) points out, this will involve much conflict, complexity, and anxiety (p. 238), and artistic pursuits can be a forum for reconciling these in a socially acceptable symbolic from. This process can apply just as much to gender identity as to any other felt conflict. After all, the arts, including music, allow us to work through many of life's issues and conflicts in symbolic yet real ways (Kemp 1992). Classical sonata form can, itself, be frequently viewed as a symbolic working out of inner conflicts and opposites within ourselves. For example, the reader will be able to think of several first movements (more or less any classical symphony will do) where the composer firstly introduces a dominant and what might be viewed as a masculine theme only to follow it up with the presentation of a more lyrical and, possibly, feminine one . During the development section that follows we may perceive something of a consummation taking place between these contrasting elements in which they are brought closer together, worked through, and sometimes united. The recapitulation may present the listener with certain feelings of reconciliation, due to, if nothing more, than the unity offered by the shared tonic tonality. We shall return to notions such as this later in Chapter 11.

Gender orientation

An inherent danger in any discussion that focuses on gender role identity issues in artists and musicians is that the adoption of the term psychological androgyny is perceived automatically as a euphemism for homosexuality. In reviewing research into sex roles and sexual behaviour, Howells (1986) concludes that, generally, there may be some relationship between the two. However, this relationship, which is certainly not upheld by all research, evades any identification of causal direction. Furthermore, there is one attendant problem in becoming drawn into this field of research, and this relates to shifting definitions of what constitutes sex-role identity. Certainly, the manner in which we have approached the topic in this chapter, via the study of personality traits, may be significantly removed from what Howells refers to as 'sex-role inversion' (p. 274). As we have seen, the notion of psychological androgyny presents us with a complex personality-type structure in which *separate* clusters of personality characteristics are associated with masculinity and femininity, allowing a person to be mobile across a wide repertoire of perceptual and conceptual schemata.

On the other hand, much of the research investigating the links between gender roles and gender orientation tends to view the latter more dichotomously and in terms of overt behavioural indicators. For example, Howells cites the work of Van Wyk and Geist (1984) who showed that a child's choice of opposite-sex playmates at about the age of 10 was positively associated with homosexual preferences in adulthood. This kind of behavioural approach may be unhelpful in our discussion here simply because, as we have already recognized, there appears to be a greater subtlety in the musician's gender schema. For example, it is possible that younger children will choose playmates on the basis of the kinds of games that they play: certain boys may choose more 'aesthetic' games often played by girls; some girls may wish to engage in more aggressive activities perceived as more appropriate for boys. Such choices may be made quite independently of the participants' gender, and this would appear to be well in line with the view that we are taking here. Musicians, as we have identified them here, will reveal a propensity and inclination to engage in a wide range of gender-related activities and an independent-mindedness that allows them to do so without undue discomfort.

In the same way as Bem constructed a fourfold typology for masculinity and femininity, Storms (1980) speculated that perhaps sex orientation might be similarly structured. In pursuing this notion, he administered the *Personal Attributes Questionnaire* (PAQ; Spence and Helmreich 1978) to mixed-sex groups of heterosexuals, bisexuals, and homosexuals. His results showed no significant differences between the three groups on the masculinity and femininity measures. A second hypothesis, relating to Tripp's (1975) suggestion that male homosexuals were of two distinct types, high masculinity and low masculinity, was also tested. Storms' results showed unambiguously that this hypothesis could not be upheld; homosexuals as a group appear reasonably heterogeneous in terms of gender role identity. On the basis of, admittedly, these few pieces of research, we might conclude that there appears to be little correspondence between gender role and gender-orientation, and that the musicians' androgyny appears to relate much more closely to the musical tasks required of them than to mere patterns of sexual attraction. Clearly, it is in the seriously stereotyped nature of social perception that these two very different issues tend to become confused.

Although well-known examples of homosexual composers, conductors, and performers can be cited, there appear to be sufficiently large numbers of heterosexual musicians to challenge any theory of a direct causal connection. Post's (1994) study of biographical accounts of 291 eminently creative men tends to support this view, showing that amongst the 52 composers, only 3.8 per cent were homosexual. In terms of his groups of artists and writers there was no reported incidence of homosexuality at all. As Post comments, the above figure is exactly half the rate shown in a recent survey of the incidence of homosexuality in the general population.

Apart from the stereotyped nature of people's perceptions of gender identity, mentioned above, another reason for confusion might be attributed to the greater ease with which the artist can 'come out' in professions that supposedly tolerate homosexuality rather more than, say politics or sport. The ease with which they may be able to do so not only reflects people's acceptance of a perceived norm (all artists and musicians are queer), but also, of course, helps to perpetuate the stereotype. An important feature, already mentioned, relates to the musician's independence and general disregard for society's imposed rules and standards. These features of the autonomous person, remaining independent from the judgement of others and possessing an individualistic moral law, might well allow him or her to 'out' with a greater sense of confidence and disregard for the outcomes.

In summary, the point should perhaps be reiterated that, because we are all conditioned, to some extent, to perceive masculine and feminine behaviour patterns as two separate clusters, we see the musician's androgyny as taking the form of two independent and contrary dispositions. The first one, more commonly associated with femininity, concerns a cluster of traits that involves the predisposition of a person to respond to musical experiences with sensitivity, feelingfulness, insight, and intuition. The second cluster of traits relates to introversion and independence, autonomy, and the motivation necessary for musical progress to be made, and which can be viewed in Ruch's (1984) terms as being masculine. In other words, we might wish to speculate that these two groups of attributes, so frequently perceived as opposites, are task requirements of being a successful musician of either gender. Both are requirements for satisfactory levels of progress in music throughout education and later on in the profession. Clearly, this is a somewhat theoretical abstraction, and, in reality, the two clusters of attributes may not be as distinct as this. In artists, and in musicians in particular, we may well find that these two sides of their nature are fully reconciled. In other words, the person who has the predisposition to respond aesthetically to art objects naturally develops the necessary drive and single-mindedness to pursue what is valued and cherished.

In this kind of way we can see why Bem (1974, 1975) maintained that androgyny is the most desirable condition for both sexes in terms of psychological health and adjustment. Both men and women need the freedom to express both nurturant and reflective characteristics as well as assertive and self-sufficiency traits. Since the earliest civilizations, pursuing music has been considered to be a humanizing and educational activity, and some might wish to argue that music has precisely this kind of educational function in developing the child's personality. The continuing featuring of music within the school curriculum, however threatened its current position, might be thought to be justified in terms of its role in exercising a more comprehensive influence on the developing personality than some other disciplines that might be viewed as more in conformity with gender-stereotyping.

Summary

Research reveals significant gender differences across various cultures in connection with particular personality traits. These relate to a tendency for men to score more highly on introversion and independence, and women on sensitivity. These differences can be perceived as the outcomes of society's adoption of strong gender prototypes, first within the home and later at school. They permeate most aspects of social interaction within the family.

Bem's theory of psychological androgyny offers a way of perceiving gender role that departs from the dichotomous nature of the earlier masculinity–femininity scales by suggesting that gender roles may take the form of a fourfold typology. Thus, in addition to the usual masculine and feminine types, people can also be identified as being both masculine and feminine (androgynous), or neither (undifferentiated). Later, Bem developed her schema theory, which stresses the social learning aspects of gender role development in children. This relates to the process by which individuals learn to construct gender schemata, and in which most individuals tend to entrap themselves increasingly from early childhood onwards.

Evidence suggests that musicians generally appear able, probably quite unconsciously, to extricate themselves from the major influences of these prototypes, each gender appearing to assume certain characteristics of the other. In common with other creative groups, musicians may minimize differences on gender-related traits or, in some cases, actually reverse them. Those aspects of personality on which this occurs are connected with introversion and pathemia, women appearing to be more introverted than usual and men more sensitive. Viewed in terms of Bem's inventory, musicians appear to be more androgynous than people in general or, if one prefers, more aschematic. This phenomenon, which first manifests itself in mid-adolescent musicians, is accounted for in terms of the demands that music makes on the developing personality. It may also relate to the degree to which the person feels adjusted to the pursuit of music at ever-increasing levels.

Such levels of perceptible differences as these may well result in musicians appearing to be different from ordinary people, or even strange. This may, in turn, have the effect of marginalizing them socially, quite apart from their natural tendency to segregate themselves because of their introverted and individualistic interests. In some instances, this may account for the higher levels of anxiety in musicians. However, little evidence is forthcoming to suggest that musicians' androgyny is a manifestation of homosexuality.

SEVEN

Music preferences and listening styles

Introduction

That different kinds of people like different types of music would appear to be a truism that barely warrants utterance, but those beliefs that we commonly hold still require exploring and clarifying by empirical investigation. In this chapter we shall discuss some of the research that has attempted to explore direct relationships between certain types of people and the ways in which they are attracted to the music of particular composers, periods, and types. From our own concert-going experiences, we may well harbour a number of attitudes and beliefs about the kinds of audiences that are attracted to different types of concert programme, say, for example, a performance of the Monteverdi *Vespers* as opposed to Puccini's *Madame Butterfly*, a brass band contest, or a heavy metal concert. Quite apart from some generational and socio-economic differences, we might, on further reflection, expect these audiences to dress differently, and to engage in very different styles of conversation in the bar during the interval.

Most of the research that we shall be discussing here focuses upon the use of personality inventories to clarify issues relating to individual differences in listening to music of different kinds. Hopefully, this will lead to a better understanding of the aesthetic experience itself by clarifying for us the demands that different types and styles of music make upon listeners, and the nature of their responses.

One of the earlier researchers in the field was Cattell, but his research intentions were in some ways quite different from our principal concerns here. His main aim was to use pieces of music to create an alternative type of personality inventory that would lie half-way between more objective personality tests like the 16PF and those that adopted 'projective'-type techniques such as the Rorshach test, which requires individuals to respond to abstract ink blot-type shapes. As Cattell explained, because music satisfies deep and unconscious needs, he considered that musical preferences would open up new and effective avenues towards our understanding of the deeper aspects of personality. Because music bypasses verbal content, a test comprising purely musical items, Cattell believed, would allow people to respond without the kind of distortion that is generated by our more cognitive and conscious defences. After all, if 'music is a tonal analogue of emotive life' in the way that Langer (1953, p. 27) has suggested, and the 'most articulate language of the unconscious' (Cooke 1959, p. x), it is reasonable to view it as one of the most effective ways to approach the study of temperamental differences.

With these laudable intentions in mind, Cattell and his co-workers set out to develop the *IPAT Music Preference Test* (Cattell and Anderson 1953a). In this work they adopted 120 musical themes, each lasting about 30 seconds, and analysed the patterns of preferences of a large group of students and older adults. In their results they identified a set of 11 factors that they maintained could be interpreted as personality factors that existed at a deeper, because less cognitive, level. The test was subsequently criticized by Payne (1967) on a number of counts, but especially in connection with the performance of all its items being on the piano, their extreme brevity, and the particular choice of extracts.

These 11 factors were further explored by Cattell and Saunders (1954) in a lengthy paper that attempted to identify their psychological significance. On the face of it, it would be reasonable to expect that such an endeavour would provide us with a considerable amount of information about the interrelationships between personality and musical preferences. However, because Cattell and Anderson's interest principally lay in developing a personality instrument, it is not always clear what exactly the *musical* significance of the factors were. A glance at Cattell and Saunders' (1954) 11 factors in terms of their associated musical pieces does not always indicate any coherent underlying patterns of musical meaning (pp. 18–22). Furthermore, the factors do not always appear to bear a clear relationship with Cattell's personality factors either (Cattell and Anderson 1953b, p. 450). Much later, Kline (1973) raised more questions about the nature of the test, demonstrating a lack of interrelationship between its factors and Eysenck's EPI—rather alarming in view of the fact that Cattell had identified adjustment, self-centredness, tough sociability, introspection, and anxiety amongst his factors. This inventory, then, may have limited relevance for our discussions here in that it appears to occupy a different 'space', and appears distanced from any meaningful concepts of personality or coherent patterns of music preferences. It is only fair to note that it has been claimed to possess a high test–retest reliability. This emerged despite serious attempts by the investigator to influence the results by manipulating different mood states amongst the experimental group (Schultz and Lang 1963). However, we must always bear in mind that high reliability certainly does not imply high levels of validity.

Music preferences of Eysenck's types

Another well-known and early investigator in the field was Cyril Burt who developed a theory about personality and aesthetic preferences, not only in music, but also developing parallel hypotheses involving paintings (Burt 1939). In carrying out this work Burt attempted to show that a fourfold typology, similar to Eysenck's, was associated with specific stylistic characteristics of art objects. For obvious reasons, we shall concentrate our attention on his findings in relation to music (see Table 7.1). For example, he maintained that stable extraverts would be attracted to music that possessed dynamic equilibrium, solidity, and weight and a certain predictability, as well as balance and brightness. He considered that music that tends to evoke cognitive associations would appeal to them, mentioning the music of Handel, Verdi, Mussorgsky, and possibly Brahms. The stable introvert, on the other hand, was more likely to take an intellectual stance, valuing aspects of form rather more than emotional expression with the listener appearing to take a cold and critical stance to pieces. Stable introverts, he believed, show an attraction for pieces that reveal a feeling of unity possibly through the use of repetition in a conventional and economical way. According to Burt, the abstract nature of much of Bach's music particularly appeals to them.

Table 7.1 Personality types and music preferences *

	Extravert	Introvert
	Stable	
Preferred period	Classical/baroque	Classical/baroque
Musical characteristics	Solidity/ weight; balance/ brightness; predicatability	Absolute music; feeling for unity/form; intellectual/ cognitive
Preferred composers	Handel, Verdi, Mussorgsky, Brahms	Bach
	Neurotic/unstable	
Preferred period	Romantic	Romantic
Musical characteristics	Programmatic; vivid colours; strong contrasts; vigorous/ flowing; emotional/ sensational	impressionistic; mystical romanticism; deep, internal emotions offering escape from reality
Preferred composers	Wagner, Richard Strauss, Liszt, Berloz	Debussy, Weber, Delius, Chopin

* Based on Burt (1939)

In contrast, the unstable extravert, Burt considered, is more likely to be attracted to programme music of a more emotional and sensational kind. Particularly citing Wagner's *Meistersinger* and *The Ring*, as well as works by Richard Strauss, Liszt, and Berlioz, he maintained that it was their vivid colours, strong contrasts, and vigorous and flowing passages that attracted this type of person. Programme music appeals to them provided it is emotional rather than scenic. Finally, the unstable introvert is drawn to impressionistic pieces, particularly by composers such as Debussy, Weber, Delius, and Chopin. He viewed the unstable introvert as searching for music that possesses a mystical romanticism, and that arouses deep emotions within the listener, rather than overtly depicting them. In this sense music is used by the listener as an escape into a private dreamworld offering a refuge from reality.

Any reader who returns to Burt's work will immediately observe that, perhaps because he was more comfortable discussing paintings than music, he developed rather clearer notions about the particular characteristics of paintings that attracted his four types than he did for music. As a result, those interested in this theories in relation to the latter will, as I have done, attempt to draw several observations he made about artistic works and apply them to musical styles. This is only done here in those instances where Burt seems to be implying the same kinds of observations for both. In several ways it is easy to criticize Burt's work for his overgeneralizations concerning the style of output of the composers whom he cites. However, as we shall see, certain aspects of his findings have been supported by subsequent work, although a detailed replication of his research is not possible due to his failure to supply complete details of the works that he had used.

The preferences of neurotics and non-neurotics

Another early researcher in the field, whose work is more frequently cited than that of Cattell or Burt, is Payne (1967) who started out from a somewhat similar position to that of Burt. Initially, her hypothesis was simply that stable or non-neurotic types would show a preference for classical styles and that those attracted to romantic styles would be significantly more neurotic. Having classified a collection of 42 composers into their 'relative classicism' and 'relative romanticism' using a set of musical experts, she constructed a questionnaire in which a group of students, and a second one of older listeners, were asked to list their favourite six composers. They were also asked to complete Eysenck's personality test and three of Wing's tests of musical aptitude. Her results showed that neuroticism was indeed a powerful factor in discriminating between classical and romantic musical preferences, and also in the expected direction. In observing that neither gender nor aural ability exerted influence upon these results, she did, however, speculate that introversion/extraversion might operate as an additional factor in helping to separate out another dimension of preference that she referred to as 'introvert or extravert music' (p. 137).

What appears to emerge from the work of Burt and Payne is the suggestion that people's anxiety might be operating in a reasonably consistent fashion in determining whether they are attracted to either classical or romantic styles. However, Payne went much further than Burt in explaining how these particular terms were being used in her research.

The classical/romantic dichotomy is basically a matter of form/feeling. Form may not be lacking in romantic music, but here it is never more than a means to an end—a means to the communication of subjective emotional experience, while in classical music it is an end in itself. Similarly feeling in classical music is the by-product of form, while in romantic music it is the primary instigator of the expression. (Payne 1967, p. 134)

She was also very careful to point out that the terms 'classical' and 'romantic' can be applied to music of any period and need not be restricted to that of the eighteenth and nineteenth centuries. She also felt it necessary to clarify the terms 'form' and 'feeling', explaining that 'form' included all aspects of structure while 'feeling' was used synonymously with 'emotion'. 'This emotional subject-matter is . . . concerned specially . . . with "mystery, abnormality and conflict". The emotional element in classical music is necessarily more elusive since it is less apparent' (p. 134).

We may well wish to speculate about this connection between neuroticism and romantic styles in terms of these listeners' emotional needs. The more neurotic listeners, who may tend to feel that their lives are subject to turmoil and stress, may seek music that assists them in projecting these uncomfortable feelings on to musical pieces as a form of defence against their anxiety. Certainly romantic music, with its tendencies towards more changeable mood states, its harmonic tension and resolution, its overt emotional overtones, and its general working out of conflict, offers the listener more opportunity to engage in a process of identification with these kinds of elements.

Elsewhere, I have suggested that listeners may well identify with particular pieces of music by making deep and sometimes unconscious connections with anxiety-provoking experiences in their past (Kemp 1992). If we take, for example, the need in each one of us for 'attachment' and our deep fear of separation from loved ones, it is possible to see how these fears of separation, as well as joys of reunion, are constantly acted out in music. We only have to take an example of the composer's use of ground bass or ostinato to see just how they contribute to an underlying feeling of stability. Or, take Schubert's frequent use of repetition of a beautiful melody in which he engenders a sense of continuity and 'containment' in the listener. It is clear to see, in this context, how, in accordance with Burt's suggestion, the stable introvert would be attracted to music that possesses a certain unity, engendered by the very kind of repetition highlighted here. Similarly, it is not difficulty to see, in Burt's terms, how the stable extravert would be attracted to music that has a fair degree of predictability.

On the other hand, what about those pieces of music that cause us to be placed under different degrees of tension, possibly by dismantling a theme in variation form or during the process of development? Or what about those pieces that, without warning, deprive us of a theme or melody to which we have become closely attached, like, for example, Fauré's 'Pavane', Opus 50? Such pieces in the repertoire may well provide particularly anxious types with a scenario that is all too familiar in their lives. Music that engenders these feelings of loss may well present material on to which listeners can project their anxieties, and also an opportunity to engage in a therapeutic experience when the listener is re-united with the melody intact in the final section. Witness the feelings of relief that are practically visible in a concert hall at the end of, say the first movement of Haydn's 'London' Symphony, or the reintroduction of Purcell's theme in the final fugue of the Britten Variations.

This kind of notion is supported by a piece of research by Weaver (1991) who found that neurotics preferred popular music that was 'downbeat' rather than 'upbeat'. This classification related to the themes of the lyrics: examples of downbeat being 'If you leave me now', 'It's too late', and 'He stopped lovin''. It is interesting to observe how all these pieces refer in one way or another to various experiences of loss of the kind described above.

The preferences of introverts and extraverts

Turning to Burt's findings concerning the introversion–extraversion dimension, we can begin to perceive, as shown in Table 7.1, that it appears to suggest that the introvert is generally more prepared to 'do more work' on what he or she hears. In contrast, it appears true that the extravert chooses music that generally makes fewer demands, and offers experiences in which the 'self' is less than totally engaged. This notion is much in line with our earlier discussions in Chapter 2 in which the introvert was described as a person with a more highly developed internal life, and possessing a more self-contained mode of internalizing what is valued. The introvert delays judgement about objects and ideas, takes a more analytical stance towards them, and needs to 'live with them' before becoming committed. Extraverts, in contrast, seek their stimulus outside themselves, and will tend to pursue music that satisfies immediate needs without making too many demands.

That introversion is strongly associated with music preferences was also highlighted in the work of Keston and Pinto (1955). Interestingly, they adopted a little known personality inventory that measures 'intellectual introversion' as a separate dimension from 'social extraversion'. Whilst the former was found to bear a strong relationship with a measure of a person's preference for 'serious classical' music, as opposed to more popular styles, the latter emerged as non-significant. Their distinction between intellectual introversion and social extraversion is an important one for our discussions here and supports the notion that the kind of introversion important in musicianship appears to be related to intellect rather than sociability. Thus Drevdahl and Cattell's (1958) suggestion that creative types are introverted yet bold seems a legitimate one (see Chapter 2) in the context of this work. In discussing their findings, Keston and Pinto observe that introverts can be viewed as being particularly analytical and theoretical, focusing on their own reactions to abstract and formal elements in an aesthetic experience (p. 110). Although they offer no information about the music selected for their preference test, the 'seriousness' of the music might well relate to Burt's thoughts on the introvert's preferences, and certainly to Payne's ideas about introvert and extravert music.

Indeed, in some later work, Payne (1980) found that, amongst trained musicians and those familiar with music, introverts preferred music with a formal structure while extraverts preferred music with human emotional overtones. To be more specific, particular pieces that attracted the introverts were Stravinsky's *Le Sacre du Printemps* (Introduction, Dances des adolescents, Jeu du rapt), and Schubert's Symphony No. 9 in C (second movement). On the other hand, the extraverts were more attracted to Elgar's *Enigma Variations* (fourteenth variation) and Brahms' *Variations on a Theme by Haydn* (theme and first six variations).

Sensation-seeking and openness to experience

We should not pass on from our discussion concerning the links between introversion–extraversion and musical preferences without considering the notion of sensation-seeking. As we have observed previously, because of their higher arousal thresholds, extraverts may actively seek out situations in which they need to find higher levels of stimulation, which might prove quite uncomfortable for the more introverted. For example, Daoussis and McKelvie (1986) found that, while extraverts performed adequately on a retention test while music was being played, the performance of the introverts was negatively affected. Furthermore, under the 'no music' condition introverts were superior to the extraverts. Whilst this appears to support the notion of a lower threshold of arousal for introverts than extraverts, the expected increase in performance of the extraverts under the music condition did not occur.

The interrelationship between sensation-seeking and patterns of music preferences has been researched by Litle and Zuckerman (1986) quite independently of extraversion. Using their own music preference scale, which contained a broad spectrum of styles, they found that sensation seekers generally preferred rock music and particularly disliked soundtrack music. Litle and Zuckerman concluded from this that sensation seekers need to get involved in their music rather than merely using it as a background. Some of the subscales of their sensation-seeking inventory also showed some finer preference patterns, for example, those who showed that they were 'experience seekers' were particularly receptive to a wide variety of music, which they experienced with high levels of involvement and intensity.

Dollinger (1993) followed up Litle and Zuckerman's work adopting their music preference scale along with Costa and McCrae's (1985) personality inventory that measures the 'big five' dimensions. As Table 4 (p. 16) shows, one of these dimensions, openness to experience, can be described as a tendency to become easily absorbed and prone to fantasy. At its negative end it signifies certain authoritarian and conservative attitudes. A quite separate big five dimension, of course, is extraversion, which contains, as one of its subscales, an excitement-seeking factor. Thus, in this way, Dollinger was able to clarify whether a person's particular liking for hard rock and jazz was more linked to the broad dimension of extraversion, its subfactor of excitement seeking, or openness.

His results showed an interesting separation between a liking for hard rock and that for jazz. Whereas hard rock adherents appeared to be characterized by their excitement seeking—supporting Litle and Zuckerman's results, jazz lovers were more generally extraverted, and also open to experience. Other findings related to preferences for classical, as well as soul/rhythm and blues, which were also linked to openness. Thus, overall, extraverted types appear to be drawn to jazz whereas those who seek out excitement in their lives tend to be attracted to hard rock. That a preference for most other styles of music is unrelated to extraversion will not come as a particular surprise to us.

Analytic and holistic listening strategies

In their work on people's aesthetic reactions to music, Hargreaves and Coleman (1981) attempted to identify different types of listening strategies in a group drawn from various adult education classes. It should be noted that only about a quarter of the group was studying music. Using a variety of extracts in a range of styles they discovered that, by and large, two principal listening strategies emerged: one which might be called 'objective-analytic' and the other 'affective'. The first was considered to involve objective or technical reactions to the music and was adopted by those individuals who were musically experienced. Those who used the 'affective' strategy responded more emotionally, and were found to be more musically naive. Interestingly, a third strategy, 'associative' (extramusical associations), shown in a pilot study to be operative in young children, did not emerge in any significant way.

Hedden's (1973) research was similar, in that it attempted to identify a number of listening factors, but went on to explore their interrelationships with personality traits, and other factors such as musicality and background. Initially, working with five types of musical response, not unlike those of Hargreaves and Coleman, Hedden assigned a number of non-music undergraduates to different groups according to these response styles. The results that eventually emerged after a number of research procedures relate well with Hargreaves and Coleman's objective-analytic and affective strategies. Two groups of students emerged with particular characteristic response styles, one related to a 'cognitive' stance, the other distinctly more 'associative'.

That the listening strategies of musically trained groups responding to a music preference test might be qualitatively different from those of the less initiated is of importance to our concerns here. Clearly, one can imagine how different kinds of groups might seriously influence the results on a test like that of Cattell and Anderson (1953a). In his key work in this area, Smith (1987) has shown that music experts and novices do, indeed, respond to different *aspects* of a piece of music, rather than the same ones at different levels of efficiency. He suggests that 'syntactic' pleasure is of the kind that is gained through an acquaintance with a composer's music. It involves an ability to 'go along' with a composer, to engage vicariously in his or her craft—posing a problem, solving it, denying expectations and then fulfilling them, and so on. In syntactic listening the process is one in which 'the delicate syntactic teasing by the composer evokes emotions of forepleasure, anticipation, and restful satisfaction' (p. 374).

Non-syntactic listening, on the other hand, may be referential, emotional, or sensual, and of the kind typically depreciated, indeed, if not dismissed by a number of musicologists. Smith invited a group of musicologists to rate the musical idioms of a set of 80 composers whose working lives ranged across five centuries, in terms of syntactic and non-syntactic expressivity. These ratings revealed traditional and stereotyped attitudes and beliefs about composers' styles. Syntactic styles were engaged in at their highest point around the year 1700, and the non-syntactic styles moved progressively upwards in mirror image fashion. The results suggested to Smith that these two independent and, in many ways, opposing paths suggest that syntactical listening might de-sensitize the ear, as syntax, in his view, is a non-acoustic world.

The complaint that is sometimes expressed by certain undergraduate music students is that some methods of musical analysis actually destroy well-loved music for them. Adopting a Gestaltist stance that 'the whole is greater than a sum of its parts', they feel that the essential ingredient of a piece tends to become overlooked in the minutiae of its dissection. Quoting Cage (1961), Smith asks 'must we let syntax go in order to "let the sounds be themselves" '(p. 389). He also suggested that some listeners might actively seek out particularly syntactic or non-syntactic genres, for example, chamber music versus opera. This might well be borne out by further research on preference patterns should researchers choose to make use of this additional typology. With this in mind, we might interpret the results of Cattell and Payne quite differently using, as they did, largely novices and experts, respectively, in their research. It is probably wrong, however, to view these two dimensions as too clinically distinct. As Smith observes, it is possible that non-syntactic listeners may need some form of 'minimum syntactic glue' (p. 389), enjoying lushly emotional syntax in preference to lush emotional chaos.

The kind of distinction that we have discussed here certainly tends to be borne out by hemisphere studies in which different kinds of cognitive operations are said to be more localized on one side of the brain than the other. Although it may be an oversimplification, it is frequently maintained, that, although speech and linguistic functions tend to be located in the left hemisphere, spatial tasks, music, and singing appear to concentrated in the right hemisphere. As Sloboda (1985) has remarked, the picture is far from being a complete one and perhaps the 'best bet' at an explanation might be that 'analytic' strategies in a music task tend to be located in the left hemisphere, whereas more 'holistic' or 'global' perceptual strategies occur in the right hemisphere (pp. 264–5). Although we should not read too much into this notion at this point in time, it certainly relates well to our discussions here. Research into people's listening strategies suggests that they tend to adopt one or other stance, and this would certainly help to account for preferences, say, for Beethoven's Quartet in C sharp minor (Opus 131) as opposed to Respighi's *The Pines of Rome*. This is not to suggest, however, that these pieces cannot be listened to using the alternative strategy, or for that matter, a combination of the two, merely that, as Smith's musicologists attested, composers are frequently classified in this kind of way.

Zalanowski's (1986) research investigated the responses of a group of non-music undergraduates to programmes of absolute and programmatic music where the undergraduates had received different kinds of instructional approaches. The absolute music comprised the first 3 minutes of Schubert's Symphony No. 8 in B minor *'Unfinished'*, second movement, Andante con moto. The work selected to represent programme music was Berlioz's *Symphony Fantastique*, fourth movement ('March to the scaffold'). What she found was that teaching approaches that emphasized imagery (encouraging the listeners to form their own mental images) significantly enhanced the enjoyment and understanding of both types of music. However, while emphasis upon the story behind the music led to the best understanding of the programme music, the students' understanding of the absolute music was not facilitated by the more analytical approaches. What is of particular interest to us is that, when Zalanowski took account of hemisphere differences, those students who were right-hemisphere dominant benefited most from imagery approaches, whereas the left-hemisphere types profited more from analytical instruction. It will be seen that there are some important lessons inferred here for the music educator. Whilst it may well have been true that the right-hemisphere students responded more positively to the Berlioz, and the left-hemisphere students to the Schubert, nevertheless their respective preferences for different listening approaches is particularly important.

Whether or not preferences for analytic and holistic listening strategies can be invariably applied to expert as opposed to novice listeners in the way suggested by Smith (1987) has been challenged in some quarters. Sloboda (1985) cites research that suggests that left-hemisphere advantage is certainly not confined to musicians, and that some non-musicians will adopt an analytic stance in a music perception task (p. 264). We must be careful, though, to make a distinction between the strategies that a person might naturally choose to adopt in a specific and formal test situation as opposed to a more general and relaxed session. In other words, what may be emerging in some of this research is a listener typology based on people's attitudes about what the function of music is in their lives. Education and training will certainly influence this, as will a person's natural inclination to process information analytically or holistically. Nevertheless, many others will adopt different strategies for different activities. Those with stressful, analytical jobs may choose to use music for total relaxation, yet, if they decided to undertake formal music tuition, a perceptible shift to left-hemisphere processing might well take place.

The more recent work of Robertson (1993) suggests a much more explicit one-to-one relationship between musical style and hemisphere dominance. He maintains that brain scans reveal conclusively that atonal and discordant music stimulates the left hemisphere, and that the more concordant style of a Rossini string sonata activates the right hemisphere. Songs by Richard Strauss were found to involve activity of both hemispheres on the basis that both verbal skills and emotional insights were necessary. Developing the frequently voiced notion of the linguistic versus spatial/emotional divide, Robertson suggests that the music of different composers will reflect their originators' cerebral dominance. By way of example he cites Schoenberg as a composer driven by intellect and dissonance, whose music 'cannot neurologically offer emotional rewards to an averagely wired brain' (p. 24). In contrast he offers Taverner as a composer whose right-hemisphere dominance is demonstrated by his frequent use of sonority to elicit a predominantly emotional response. We shall certainly wish to return to this notion in Chapter 11 when we shall explore the personality characteristics of composers. What should interest us here is the suggestion that listeners' preferences can, amongst other things, be typed in terms of their hemisphere dominance in direct correspondence with that of composers. As we have seen, much of what has been discussed here aligns itself with this kind of view.

Perceptual style and listening attitudes

From our earlier discussions of Witkin's theory of 'psychological differentiation' in Chapter 3 we learnt that individuals tend to have a preference for perceiving objects in one of two alternative ways. The field-dependent person's perception is dominated by the overall organization of a piece of music, its parts being fused together and perceived as a whole. On the other hand, the field-independent person takes a more analytic stance, and is able to penetrate a piece in such a way that he or she can take delight in its various parts and appreciate how they contribute to the overall effect. The reader will immediately see how that psychological differentiation relates well to some of the research cited above that suggests that people tend to display one of two types of listening response to music. Whether these are labelled cognitive–associative, analytic–affective, syntactic–nonsyntactic, analytic–holistic, or indeed, left–right hemisphere dominance, may in the long run, not be of too much consequence. They may all address the same kind of view, namely, that listeners may be predisposed to attend to musical pieces in two fundamentally different ways.

As we noted in Chapter 3, several pieces of research into psychological differentiation and musical tasks suggest that many of the demands that music educators make on aspiring musicians are linked to field-independence. Aural and sight reading skills, as well as the ability to compose, appear to be acquired more comfortably by field-independent individuals. Furthermore, the ability to perceive underlying formal structures and to make judgements about musical textures have also been claimed to be facilitated by a more articulated perceptual style. For example, Ellis (1995) showed that field-independent types were significantly more able than field-dependent individuals to discriminate between homophonic and polyphonic musical styles. Research has also shown that field-independent people are more able to perceive certain musical transformations sometimes considered to be similar in kind to Piaget's conservation tasks (Matson, cited by Ellis and McCoy 1990). An example of a musical conservation task is the ability to identify themes that have undergone some form of musical transformation, say in a development section or in a set of variations.

Ellis and McCoy (1990) played examples of music in various forms to a group of students on a college introductory music course. They found that, invariably, those identified as field-independent were more able to identify structures such as rondo, theme and variations, ground bass, ternary form, and minuet and trio, than field-dependent types. The only form that did not significantly separate the two groups was fugue—the Amen chorus from Handel's *Messiah* and Bach's Fugue in C from the *Well-tempered Clavier*, Book 1. Of all the forms perhaps, as Ellis and McCoy conceded, fugue makes fewer demands on the listener to dis-embed, the single line entry tending to make the answer obvious.

Not only does field-independence appear to facilitate the acquisition of all these skills, so frequently seen as the bread-and-butter of music teaching, the research also suggests that those types of music that are dependent upon kinds of perceptual tasks may, to some extent, have their access closed to field-dependent types. This is particularly true in those instances where educators may restrict their learners' listening strategies to the more analytic type of approach. Also, as Schmidt (1985) has maintained, it is conceivable that field-dependent types may have a better developed sensitivity to expressive and stylistic qualities in music, aspects sometimes less emphasized by music teachers. Such a proclivity would certainly result in individuals naturally choosing to listen to the more sensual and emotional works in the concert repertoire.

Preferences of the Jungian types

Hedden's (1973) work, already referred to above, showed that those students who were more predisposed to take an 'associative' stance towards their music listening were more likely to show a preference for feeling as measured by the Myers–Briggs. As we might have expected, those whom he identified as the more 'cognitive' listeners were characterized by the preference for thinking. Myers (1993) reminds us, however, that we must not equate the thinking dimension with greater intellectual powers; it is more a matter of the fact that they 'run on different tracks' (p. 67). Frequently, feeling types will approach an assignment using their motives of feeling, only to undertake a form of double-checking afterwards using thinking as a back-up. This kind of process may well occur in both thinkers and feelers in their approach to music: each using their more dominant mode to make their first assessments of a piece, only to follow this up afterwards by reinforcing or testing it with the use of their more subsidiary attitude. However, in view of our brief discussion above concerning hemisphere dominance, we cannot fail to harbour a lingering thought that, perhaps, the thinking–feeling preference is somehow interconnected.

Lewis and Schmidt (1991) used the same test instrument as Hedden, but did not adopt his fivefold listening typology, preferring to calculate a composite score. Their intention was that this would separate the individuals who used a wide range of styles of listening from those who habitually adopt a narrow range. As the reader will appreciate, this is in many ways a

different research question to that of Hedden. What emerged in their results
was that the Myers–Briggs dimension most operative in connection with a
more catholic set of attitudes to music listening was the preference for intuition, as opposed to sensing. As Lewis and Schmidt remark in discussing
their results, intuition has been generally shown in the research literature to
be linked to creative abilities, particularly originality, imagination, and aesthetic values. Sensing, alternatively, has more frequently been found to
relate to more conservative and conventional attitudes. Myers (1993)
claimed that sensing types crave enjoyment (p. 63), and it is possible that not
only their listening strategies but also their preferences will be limited
because of this. Whether or not this notion is linked to Litle and
Zuckerman's excitement seeker's narrower preferences remains unclear.

These two pieces of research appear to be offering us two very different
messages. Although we know that musicians are generally characterized by
a combination of intuition and feeling, we must keep in mind that the
research cited here was carried out with groups who were not specializing
in music. Hedden's research may be suggesting that many so-called non-
musicians resort to analytical strategies that they more commonly adopt in
their other studies. Others, whom he showed to be more introverted, may
have been more comfortable using a more aesthetic, feelingful stance
towards their listening. The fact that the analytical group emerged with
higher musicality scores might, on the surface, appear to disprove this, but
it is not clear of what this musicality score was comprised.

Lewis and Schmidt (1991) appear to suggest that those Jungian types
most frequently represented in groups of musicians (intuitive feelers) display a distinct tendency to engage in a wider gamut of listening strategies.
Not only would this tend to suggest that they approach their listening with
the capacity to engage in more than one type of response at any one time,
but it also suggests that they would have the ability to mobilize their listening strategy more easily from one piece to another. Because of this they
would also display music tastes that would tend to be more catholic.

Preferences for popular music, rock, and heavy metal

Some readers might wish to question the amount of 'real' listening that
generally takes place in pop concerts. It might be for this reason that
researchers have traditionally kept clear of popular music, perhaps har-
bouring the view that it would introduce certain ill-defined and extramusical complexities. Although Cattell used light music in his inventory, a criticism that can be levelled against several researchers in this field is their
tendency to restrict their test items to what they saw as serious art music. For
example, Hargreaves and Coleman (1981) criticized Payne's work in this
connection and also criticized Wing's (1968) test for dismissing jazz as 'bad'

music. By way of example, Hargreaves and Coleman introduced traditional, modern, and avant-garde jazz in their research as well as blues pieces and 'muzak'.

Although there are signs that researchers are beginning to take more serious notice of popular music, the topic has traditionally been badly neglected, reflecting the belief that it is an inferior culture, overrun by drugs, promiscuity, and anti-social and violent behaviour amongst a small section of the adolescent population. Unfortunately, some of the research that has been undertaken with devotees of pop and rock music has approached the topic very much from this point of view. For this reason it does not sit altogether happily with the other research cited here, but, on the other hand, what little there is helps to attain a balance between what are often perceived as two totally different and distinct musical worlds.

Hansen and Hansen (1991) offer three alternative theoretical models that they consider might help account for any links identified between rock and punk music and observable personality factors, particularly as far as causal direction is concerned. Firstly, people's preferences may be largely determined by their personality characteristics—a tendency to gravitate to particular styles according to their currently held beliefs about themselves and their perceptions of social reality. This view is consistent with the commonly expressed opinion that the output from the music industry reflects the particular desires of its consumers. Secondly, theories of social cognition suggest the opposite causal direction: the notion that frequent exposure to certain powerful forms of music might actually help shape a person's attitudes and personality. Hansen and Hansen's third explanation is that any identifiable links of this kind both reflect *and* shape social reality. 'Young people may gravitate toward heavy metal music because they possess attributes that attract them to some aspect of the content, and these attributes are strengthened through frequent exposure to heavy metal' (p. 338).

In a series of experiments, Rawlings *et al.* (1995) set out to test the hypothesis that tough-minded individuals (those high on psychoticism) will show a preference for more aggressive types of music such as hard rock and heavy metal and, generally, for the harsh types of sound normally associated with such music. Alternatively, tender-minded people (those low on psychoticism) would prefer less aggressive and consonant music. The responses from a group of 9- and 10-year-olds and psychology undergraduates to recorded excerpts as well as two of Eysenck's personality tests were submitted to factor analysis. The results clearly showed that a liking for hard rock— excerpts from 'Wings of the storm' (White Snake), 'Patience' (Guns N Roses), 'Pinball wizard' (The Who), and 'Harvester of sorrow' (Metallicus)—was positively linked to psychoticism as well as extraversion, impulsiveness, and venturesomeness. However, a second factor showed that preferences for dance music, easy listening, and classical music were negatively related to psychoticism. These types of music were represented by pieces such as

'Simply irresistible' (Robert Palmer), 'On Saturday afternoon in 1963' (Ricky Lee Jones), and 'Serenata notturna' (Mozart), respectively.

Rawlings *et al.* also investigated whether the harsh, dissonant, and unpleasant chords associated with the more aggressive musical styles, as opposed to the more concordant and pleasant chords, when played in isolation from any musical context, would reveal the same patterns of results. This time the experimental groups were psychology and music undergraduates, and their patterns of preferences indicated that a tolerance, if not a liking, for dissonant chords—augmented, diminished triads, and three-note atonal clusters—was positively related to psychoticism (tough-mindedness). Those, on the other hand, who preferred consonant chords—major and minor triads—appeared to be characterized by low psychoticism and a certain degree of empathy. Neuroticism also appeared to be negatively linked to a liking for atonal chords.

In a final experiment, which generally confirmed the same patterns of results, Rawlings *et al.* used a smaller number of students, and this might have been responsible for the emergence of a few inconsistencies. However, what appeared clear from this research was that people's preferences for 'harder' and 'harsher' styles of music are significantly linked to Eysenck's psychoticism factor. As Rawlings and his co-authors concede, further research needs to clarify exactly what other compositional devices, besides harmonic features, most powerfully link with psychoticism. As they suggest, this might possibly be more associated with unresolved chords rather than dissonant ones, and we do not know the extent to which other aspects of harmony, melody, or timbre might also be involved.

Another important finding in their work was the suggestion that psychoticism appears to split into two separate factors: one negatively related to empathy, and the second associated with extraversion, impulsiveness, and venturesomeness. The first of these was found to be negatively related to 'softer' forms of music, whereas the second was linked to hard rock. As we have discussed in previous chapters, the negative end of psychoticism can be viewed as similar in character to Cattell's sensitivity factor. It would be reasonable, therefore, to speculate that the more sensitive person would be attracted to music that provides levels of quiet subtlety and introspection. Perhaps more importantly, the second factor, related to extraversion, might well be reflecting the high degrees of volume normally associated with hard rock. As we noted earlier, the higher thresholds of the extravert in terms of arousal would certainly account for this kind of result, the more introverted types actively wishing to avoid excessively high levels of stimulation. Although Rawlings *et al.* attempted to control the volume levels by setting the dance and easy listening pieces at a relatively soft level and the classical and hard rock at loud, it must be conceded that the levels of liking for particular styles might still have been influenced by prior experience of pleasant-unpleasant sensations.

One notoriously problematic variable that can complicate research in preferences for popular musical styles, particularly hard rock and heavy metal, relates to the social meanings that such music reflects. As Rawlings and his co-workers suggest, the social connotations of such music particularly link it to aggressive, radical, and rule-breaking attitudes to life: people's expressed preferences may, or may not, involve genuine aesthetic or appreciative responses. Certainly, Wheeler (1985) showed that a liking for rock music was not generally linked to preferences for any other kind of music. She also found that it appeared to be linked negatively to several aspects of personality such as obedience, ambition, preference for precision, order, and intellectual understanding.

The notion that popular music preferences, personality, and social judgements reveal a triangular relationship was examined by Hansen and Hansen (1991), particularly in relation to heavy metal and punk rock. Their expectation was that they would find connections between these music preference patterns and factors such as machiavellianism, attitudes to authority, sex, drugs, anti-social behaviour, and need for cognition. Their results suggested that heavy metal fans were characterized by less interest in cognitive endeavours, higher male hypersexuality, and machiavellianism (manipulative, cynical, or amoral forms of behaviour). Such an unflattering profile is surprising coming as it did from a group of, presumably, reasonably socially responsible university students, and one wonders what kinds of results would emerge from less establishment-orientated types. The results with the punk rock fans, in fact, showed that they were less accepting of authority and more prone to crime than heavy metal fans. For example, they showed tendencies towards shoplifting, driving fines, and possession of offensive weapons but, on the other hand, a lack of drug involvement. Whether or not these results relate well to Gold's (1987) finding that punk rockers reported more misunderstandings with their parents than non-punk fans is not clear. Both groups in Gold's research were delinquent anyway, which distances them somewhat from the university undergraduates studied by Hansen and Hansen. The suggestion remains, however, that their attraction to punk rock, and its associated life-style, may have caused particular relationship problems with their parents or, alternatively, that it was the expression of alienation and home difficulties, and the need for affiliation of a different kind.

As is so often the case in such studies, the causal direction has not been established, but Hansen and Hansen suggest that their particular results might best be explained by interactive socialization and social cognition theories, and particularly the latter. Citing their earlier work, they maintain that there is sufficient evidence to suggest that, quite apart from their preferences for such music, the content of heavy metal and punk rock actually influences and alters young people's attitudes and social judgements (p. 346). Whether or not this is a phenomenon that also occurs in other types and styles of music is debatable.

Summary

Although early attempts to measure personality itself through patterns of musical preferences were somewhat unsuccessful, considerable evidence has been generated subsequently to suggest that differing personality types are attracted to music of varying genres. This work suggests that neurotics tend to be more attracted to romantic and emotional styles, allowing the listener to identify closely with the elements of mystery and conflict. Alternatively, stable types appear more inclined towards classical styles in which form may be distinctly more apparent than its emotional content. In popular genres, there is some evidence that suggests that neurotic listeners prefer pop songs on to which they can project their personal problems.

Research also indicates that the more 'intellectual' and restrained a piece of music is, the more likely it is that it will attract the introvert who is generally prepared to do more work in terms of understanding it at deeper levels. Extraverts, on the other hand, appear to prefer music that is predictable, meets more immediate needs, and makes fewer demands on the listener. On the other hand, heavy metal and punk rock music tends to attract the more psychotic type of listener who prefers it for its more harsh and aggressive sounds. Rock music generally attracts those who are characterized by their excitement seeking; and jazz by extraversion.

A growing body of evidence suggests that listeners may be divided into two broad but distinct types on the basis of perceptual style. Researchers have adopted different terminology for this, referring to the distinction as analytic-holistic, objective-associative, or syntactic-nonsyntactic. Whilst there may be slight shifts of meaning between these, evidence suggests that listeners do, in fact, tend to be attracted to particular musical styles according to their more predominating perceptual style. Field independence–dependence also appears to bears some relationship with this kind of distinction.

Whether the analytic-holistic distinction is reflected in specific personality dimensions such as introversion–extraversion remains unclear. Although not overwhelmingly conclusive, some research with the Myers–Briggs suggests that the thinking–feeling preference is related to the phenomenon. At the same time we should note that sensing is related to conventional and conservative tastes, the more intuitive types displaying a far more catholic range of preferences. Some researchers have suggested that cerebral dominance may also be interconnected with analytic-holistic listening styles; others maintain that the distinction separates expert listeners from novices. On the other hand, some have speculated that composers themselves may also have a proclivity to one stance or the other, and that this will manifest itself in their compositional style.

EIGHT

Orchestral performers

Introduction

By the time that musicians take up their first appointments in orchestras we can view them as a highly specialized occupational group. The preceding chapters of this book have offered the reader a number of insights into the kinds of persons likely to have successfully manoeuvred their way through the preparatory stages of becoming a musician. Those who have received instrumental lessons from an early age, who have frequently been perceived as special by parents and somewhat different by peers at school, who have endured long hours spent in solitary practice, and who have applied themselves to hard work at college are likely to emerge with a fairly unique combination of personality traits. As we have observed, they are likely to be essentially introverted, reflecting the demands, not only of an internalized saturation with music, but also the effects that the acquisition of instrumental skills have over an extended period of years on a developing personality. We perceive their individualism as being essentially rooted in a fair degree of independence, which, combined with their introversion, renders them sufficiently confident to give expression to their feelingful internal life in public performances. To this picture we are required to add the musicians' highly developed sensitivity and imagination, which adds fuel and richness to their internal symbolic life, generating insight and levels of perception necessary in all artistic pursuits.

Lastly, we should not overlook the musicians' levels of anxiety, well embedded into their personality structure from studenthood onwards. As we noted in Chapter 5, its exact aetiology may, for the present, be unclear to us, and there may be a wide range of causes. These may range from the musicians' investment of so much of themselves in what may prove to be a precarious future; their deep feelings of being special and different from others; their continual striving for perfection in performance; their anxieties relating to vulnerability in the performing situation; and the uncertainties, competitiveness, and irregular hours involved in orchestral life.

It is against this kind of backdrop that a closer look at the different types of musician can take place, taking the view that there are several features of the kind described above that unite orchestral players but that, within this general description, there may be some fundamental variations. One aspect of these relates to the well-discussed antipathy between string and brass players, traditionally a part of orchestral folklore before receiving some fairly conclusive empirical support. However, before taking a closer look at these kinds of differences there are one or two general issues that require addressing. These might relate to needs that may well be operative at deeper psychological levels at the point when a person feels drawn to a particular instrument, sometimes without any ability to articulate why.

Take, by way of example, my own case, which occurred when I was about 11 years old. One day on my way home from school I took my usual route across some fields, but instead of walking straight through a churchyard I entered the little village church. Once inside, I was drawn over to the little one-manual organ, with its highly decorated display of pipes across the front. Having opened it up and located the handle I manually pumped some air into the bellows. Having drawn a stop at random, and already able to play the piano, I played a few chord progressions and immediately was presented with the rich sounds of the big diapason pipes directly in front of my face until, of course, the air ran out. The sensation of the speaking pipes coming to life and breathing their resonance over my face made such a lasting impression upon me that I *knew* from that moment on that I wanted to, and would, become an organist. Nothing mattered to me more, and all my efforts then on, and for several years after, felt as if they were focused on the achievement of this goal. As a result, the many hours spent practising in dark, cold, and deserted churches no doubt exerted upon my developing personality an undeniable impact. In fact it was not until many years later that an interpretation of the deep significance of this powerful experience began to dawn on me. The response of these rich, baritone pipes possibly presented me with the nearest thing that I had ever experienced to possessing the father from whom I had been separated from the age of 2.

Other musicians offer similar accounts, although not necessarily identifying any extramusical explanation. Sometimes the experience, frequently recognized as symbolic of something occurring at very deep levels, is similar to the incident just described, and appears to relate directly to the tone quality of the instrument. At other times it is a particular piece of music that the hearer feels the need to perform. In her biography of Jacqueline du Pré, Easton (1989) tells the story of how du Pré encountered the sound of the cello.

But the crucial musical event in her childhood, which she later recalled with perfect clarity, occurred just before her fifth birthday. 'I remember being in the kitchen at home, looking up at the old-fashioned wireless. I climbed onto the ironing board, switched it on, and heard an introduction to the instruments of the orchestra. It must have been a BBC *Children's Hour*. It didn't make much of an impression on me until they got to the cello, and then . . . I fell in love with it straightaway. Something within the instrument spoke to me, and it's been my friend ever since'. She told her mother, 'I want to make that sound'. (p. 26)

So much did it become her friend that, as Easton describes, du Pré now aged 11 and on holiday with her family in Dartmoor, 'suddenly burst into tears, explaining between sobs that she missed her cello' (p. 42). These are the kinds of experiences that are by no means uncommon in the childhoods of musicians, and that are highly charged emotionally and motivationally significant. Walters and Gardner (1992) refer to this kind of occurrence as a 'crystallizing experience' and attempt to explain it within Gardner's theory of multiple intelligencies. They describe the phenomenon as an 'overt reaction of an individual to some quality or feature of a domain: the reaction yields an immediate but long-term change in that individual's concept of the domain, his performance in it, and his view of himself' (p. 137). For du Pré, there is also a sense in which her chosen instrument filled a void and, somehow, became entangled in her relationship with William Pleeth, her teacher, who became 'her "cello daddy", dearer to her than her own father and the most enduring love of her life' (Easton, p. 34).

Howe and Sloboda (1991) also cite a number of instances where this kind of encounter occurred in the early lives of the talented musicians they studied. The outcome often takes the form of an obsessional relationship with an instrument from which the child finds it difficult to be separated. The instrument becomes endowed with a personality of its own; significant characteristics are projected on to it, and these may or may not be associated with a particular piece of music, or a specific musical style. Research that has pursued the reasons that children give for selecting instruments suggests that the sound quality is often a powerful determinant (Delzell and Leppla 1992; Fortney *et al.* 1993; Gordon 1991).

There are, however, some particularly negative influences operating also, which may serve in determining the kinds of people who persist in the playing of certain instruments in spite of such pressures. As Boulton and O'Neill (1994) have suggested, the playing of certain instruments at school can lead to peer group rejection and being ignored, if not bullied. Children appear to have very clearly delineated attitudes about what are socially acceptable and unacceptable musical instruments, and can be merciless in their treatment of those who choose to play inappropriate ones. As we shall see presently, the kind of gender-role stereotyping that was discussed in Chapter 6 does not only relate to those who play musical instruments; instruments themselves become endowed with a gender identity by children at an early age. Any suggestions of cross-gender matching can lead to peer group rejection with all the attendant unhappiness and reduction in self-esteem that can result.

Gender stereotyping of instruments

A fair degree of evidence suggests that children and adults have clear attitudes about which instruments are appropriate for boys to play and which
can be viewed as being more suitable for girls. For instance, Ables and Porter
(1978) found very consistent attitude patterns amongst adults revealing that,
whereas the clarinet, flute, and violin were perceived as appropriate instruments for girls to play, boys were considered to be more suited to playing
drums, the trombone, or the trumpet. These kinds of attitude appeared to be
fairly consistently held by boys from kindergarten onwards, whereas in girls
they tended to stabilize rather later around the age of eight and nine. Even
then, though, their range of choices was considerably wider than that of the
boys which was somewhat restricted.

Griswold and Chroback (1981) followed up Ables and Porter's work and,
using groups of music and non-music undergraduates together with a wider
selection of instruments, showed how the harp, flute, piccolo, glockenspiel,
cello, violin, clarinet, piano, and French horn were predominantly viewed as
feminine (listed here in decreasing order of perceived femininity). In contrast, the tuba, string bass, trumpet, bass drum, saxophone, cymbal, and guitar were seen as more appropriate for men to play (likewise, in decreasing
order of masculinity).

Reading between the lines of these two pieces of research, a number of
interpretations appear to suggest themselves. Certainly there seems to be a
tone quality, loudness, and perhaps pitch connotations to the selections
reported here. Instruments that are soft, subtle, and high-pitched appear to
be classed as suitable for girls to play; those that are large, powerful, and
lower-pitched have masculine connections. These two pieces of American
research might, of course, be influenced by the associations that wind band
instruments have with all the hype and macho image of American football.

In a piece of research with children in British infant schools Bruce and
Kemp (1993) organized a series of concerts during which string, woodwind,
and brass instruments were demonstrated by men and women on different
occasions. At the end of each concert the children were encouraged to move
forward to take a closer look at one instrument. The patterns of the children's choices showed that the girls were particularly attracted to the flute,
whereas the boys preferred the trombone. Closer examination of these patterns clearly showed the boys' and girls' choices were, in every case, influenced by the gender of the demonstrator. A particular example of this phenomenon involved 23 per cent of the girls actually choosing the trombone
when it was played by a woman; however, this dropped to 2 per cent when
the performer was a man. A similar pattern emerged in the boys' patterns of
preferences for the flute. It must be borne in mind, though, that the children
involved in this research were particularly young. Although the results
demonstrated that the gender associations of instruments appeared to be

well in place at this age, it is unclear whether the influence of the demonstrators' gender would have been quite so strong in older children.

Working with older children aged between nine and eleven, O'Neill and Boulton (1996) showed that the piano, flute, and violin were ranked more highly by the girls, and the guitar, drums, and trumpet by the boys. When asked about which instruments should or should *not* be played by girls and boys, very pronounced views also emerged. These showed no gender differences of opinion: both girls and boys strongly believed that the flute, piano, and violin should definitely not be played by boys, and that the trumpet, guitar, and drums were quite unsuitable for girls. When asked for their reasons why certain instruments should not be played by boys, the boys' and girls' answers clustered around statements such as 'never seen a boy play it', 'it's an instrument for girls', and 'boys don't like the sound'. Similar reasons were offered when the pupils were asked about the instruments that girls should not play, although both boys and girls also gave 'physical reason' in addition.

Another important finding of O'Neill and Boulton was the discovery that the beliefs and attitudes of those children who were currently learning to play musical instruments did not substantially differ from those who did not. It appears therefore that these children by and large were playing gender-related instruments and fitted comfortably into the attitudinal norms of the others. In other schools where a musical climate exists, and particularly where pupils have attained high levels of skill, players may find themselves belonging to a separate musical culture, a haven in which different norms can operate. For example, one wonders whether the results would be substantially different from members of a youth orchestra, or at a school for the musically gifted. Griswold and Chroback's (1981) research tends to suggest that this would not be the case. Their undergraduate musicians actually showed that they were *more* prone to gender stereotyping instruments than the non-musicians.

O'Neill and Boulton interpret their findings in terms of 'gender boundary violation' theories, offering an explanation for children as young as 5 revealing very rigid views about what they consider to be gender-appropriate behaviour. Clearly this is very much a similar notion to Bem's (1981) gender schema theory (see Chapter 6): individuals develop a personal and complex construct of gender-related associations into which they assimilate new information from close observation of the adult world. The individual's self-concept formation is also an inherent part of this schema which controls most aspects of behaviour and beliefs. This appears to be particularly delimited in boys who, as a result, need to be particularly vigilant and self-conscious about the ways in which they make manifest their masculinity. In terms of these research results it is reasonable to assume that an individual's attitudes towards music, its instruments, and performers all become an inherent part of a schema of this kind.

Their findings in the context of children's rigid gender role schema and attitudes towards musical instruments led Boulton and O'Neill (1994) to pursue questions relating to the social outcomes of playing certain gender-related instruments. As indicated above, they discovered not only that both boys and girls view many instruments in gender-stereotyped ways, but also that those who violate these norms by taking up playing cross gender-linked instruments can be seriously sanctioned through regimes of bullying or being ignored. As Boulton and O'Neill comment, children do not perceive this treatment as trivial; being bullied and suffering low popularity are distressing and particularly damaging psychologically for the recipients of the treatment. They can exert a powerful influence upon a child's initial choice of an instrument to play as well as his or her inclination to continue playing a 'wrong' instrument. Howe and Sloboda (1992) describe a number of cases of pupils who, on gaining places in schools for the musically gifted, show immense relief on being removed from such maltreatment. That certain children in ordinary schools *do* persevere in the face of such manifestations of disapproval might well be reflected in their personality typing, for example, in their significant levels of individualism, aloofness, and independence, identified in the earlier chapters of this book.

Intersectional perceptions in symphony orchestras

We might wonder whether the kinds of antipathy identified above might also manifest themselves in adult performing circles, and particularly in professional orchestras. Davies (1976, 1978) was one of the first to stumble upon similar phenomena during some unconnected research that he was carrying out with a Scottish symphony orchestra. Having interviewed about one-third of the orchestra and listened to the players' impressions of one another, he identified some very stereotyped patterns of interpersonal perceptions between the string and brass players. In some ways the woodwind players found themselves situated in the middle of the crossfire. The kinds of statements made about the brass players by the strings related to their lack of refinement, heavy drinking, lower intelligence, loud playing, and noisy behaviour generally. In the opposite direction, the string players were described as precious, oversensitive and touchy, delicate, serious, and high-minded. Although the interviewees could think of many exceptions to these stereotypes, nevertheless, all insisted that they seriously existed.

A similar piece of work was carried out by Lipton (1987) who not only investigated the patterns of perceptions between string and brass players, but also included woodwind and percussion sections. Another interesting aspect of Lipton's work was that he chose to study the self-perceptions of each section as well. What emerged regarding the views of string and brass players was very similar to Davies' findings, although they were not couched in quite so colourful language or as outspoken. The string players described the brass as loud, extraverted, macho, and masculine. Interestingly, brass players described themselves in very similar terms, claiming to be gregarious, loud, confident, and jovial. In contrast, the brass saw the string players as particularly confident, frustrated, quiet, and feminine. Similarly, the string players' self-perceptions focused upon their sensitivity, competitiveness, neuroticism, and insecurity. In many ways the percussion players were characterized in a similar fashion to the brass players as fun-loving, loud, and insensitive. The woodwinds were generally described as being quiet, sensitive, intelligent, and meticulous.

What arises from this kind of research is the notion that people tend to endow individual instruments with a personality of their own. Davies cites the double bass as an instrument that certainly cannot be taken very seriously, its mammoth proportions in relation to its relatively small sound is only one example of an absurdity that confronts us every time we attend an orchestral concert. But a close look at most instruments in the orchestra reveals that each can be perceived as possessing a 'personality' of its own, with traits that may not always escape becoming the focus of humour or even ridicule. Hoffnung's (1954) cartoons captured many aspects of these, whether it be the floor-wetting habits of the brass, the anxiety of woodwind players concerning the state and unpredictable behaviour of their reeds, the amorous relationship that ensues between string players and their instruments, and, of course, their yellow dusters! Many a Thomas Beecham story revolves around these kinds of instrumental characteristics, and the ways that the instruments of the orchestra are often presented in school classrooms may also result in the perpetuation of certain stereotyped attitudes. In the same way that owners are said to grow and look like their dogs, so do possibly the kind of perceptions about orchestral performers relate not only to the shape and characteristics of their instruments, but also the way that they are played, their sound qualities, and the repertoire with which they become associated. As Chapter 2 suggested, we should also not overlook the complexity level of playing particular instruments as well as the context in which those skills are acquired. What we need to explore here is whether these kinds of differences are reflected in hard personality data. Presently we shall take a look at the various types of instruments, their demands, repertoire, performing context, and, in doing so, review what literature there is concerning the personality types who play them.

In their attempt to assist parents in selecting the appropriate instrument for their children (as opposed to an automatic choice of the piano), Ben-Tovim and Boyd (1990) have provided a handbook. This encourages parents to consider a wider range of the child's attributes, such as physique, intellect, and personality, and attempts to relate these to the demands of particular instruments. Although they do not cite any research for their assertions, one wonders whether they drew upon certain personality studies. Their book has not been without its critics, principally due to what are seen as sweeping generalizations, the danger of which may be that they are too rigidly adhered to by parents concerned to do their best for their children. Herein lies the dilemma referred to in the 'Preface' of this book and in other sections. There are two main stances that we can take towards research of the kind cited here. Firstly, the one generally taken here is that personality studies of the musician can help inform us about the impress of musical involvement on the developing individual. The second view, requiring extreme caution, involves the adoption of these group tendencies as predictors of future success. Certainly, at some point in the future this might be possible, but it should be undertaken only after considerably more research, requiring the professional administration of tests that are not generally available to the public. Nevertheless, aspects of Ben-Tovim and Boyd's work are cited here when their observations, which are the outcomes of direct and extensive orchestral experience, appear to be particularly insightful.

String players

On the face of it we might expect the personalities of string players to reflect the temperamental impress of the particularly severe demands that characterize the playing of these instruments. It is often maintained that learners should start early and, having started, should engage in practice routines that need to be taken seriously. It would appear to be sheer determination and motivation that enables a child to maintain these practice schedules throughout the early stages of acquiring sufficient technique for the emergence of what can be considered to be a pleasing tone. On the face of it, string-playing skills appear to be far more complex than for some other instruments, interrelating finger, wrist, and arm movements and overall body posture. Inherently bound up with the development of these physical skills are the necessary aural skills, degrees of sensitivity to pitch and tonal nuance that will stand the player in good stead throughout the whole arduous learning process. It is easy to appreciate why Ben-Tovim and Boyd (1990) emphasize the need for aspiring violinists to be intelligent, sensitive, and conscientious. In particular, they claim that it is the well-behaved and not particularly gregarious child who is likely to make useful headway on the violin. They point out that, even in professional orchestras, string players do not generally mix widely, preferring to form close friendships with one or two people only. In connection with sensitivity, this would appear to be an important feature for string players but, in their case, involving much more than mere questions of managing intonation. String playing can be seen as a deeply sensuous mode of communication, a relationship between player and instrument in which the technical movements of bow against string are, themselves, a symbolic ritual of a sensuous partnership expressing deep inner realities.

It came as something of a disappointment in my own research to find that, paradoxically, the string players did not emerge with as strongly characteristic a personality profile as that of many other instrumentalists (Kemp 1979, 1981c). The most salient feature of string players appeared to be their aloofness (A–), confirming Ben-Tovim and Boyd's claim, and appearing to be in line with earlier findings about string players' introversion (Kemp 1971; Martin 1976). Table 8.1 shows a summary of all the research cited here that has adopted Cattell's inventories. Whilst admittedly working with very small numbers of school pupils and conservatoire students, Bell and Cresswell (1984), in common with Martin, also found the student string players to be introverted in comparison with brass players in terms of their aloofness (A–), desurgency (F–), and self-sufficiency (Q2+). These findings also endorse the general notion that, to make good progress, string players need to take a serious view of their commitments and to be comfortable in their detachment from the company of others. This picture is further supported by the string players' conscientiousness (G+) linked with high levels of self-sentiment (Q3+) which emerged in the comparison with the woodwind players. This combination helps complete the picture of string players' will power, their precise attitudes to their work, and, importantly, a certain compulsive disposition.

In her biography of du Pré, cited earlier, Easton (1989) highlights du Pré's introversion which comes over powerfully in several passages. In talking with a reporter about her childhood du Pré recalled that

. . . other children didn't like me. I was very introverted and desperately shy. Children are so quick to spot this. They knew of the existence of the cello and taunted me with it. That's when I went and talked to it, saying 'never mind; they have no idea how to play it'. I loved the fact that one could be so private with the cello and communicate one's innermost thoughts to it. It became a person, you could even say a love. (p. 47)

This passage also embodies so many insights about the outcome of the kind of encounter described on pages 140–1, that can lead to forms of identification with an instrument that are so strong as to amount to obsession. It encapsulates the sense of alienation that many musical children feel in relation to their contemporaries. The sense of the introvert's hidden depths and strengths comes across also in a remark of William Pleeth, du Pré's teacher, who was heard to say of her

There was this volcano in her, waiting to erupt. Once it started, it was an endless, tremendous force. There are so many aspects of such a talent: her musical memory, the speed of her development, the dynamic of her personality, the sort of burning lyricism, the drama. (Easton 1989, p. 44)

Table 8.1 Summary of research with string players

Researcher(s)	Type of group	HSPQ and 16 PF primary factors ¶											
		A	B	C	E	F	G	H	I	N	Q1	Q2	Q3
	String players												
Kemp (1979)	Secondary school	A−											
Bell and Cresswell (1984)	Secondary school								§I+				
Bell and Cresswell (1984)	Higher education	*A−	§B+	C−	*E−	*F−	§G+			§N+	Q1−	*Q2+	§Q3+
Martin (1976)	Higher education	‡A−				†F−		†H−				‡Q2+	
Kemp (1981)	Higher education	A−										†Q2+	
	Violinists												
Kemp (1979)	Secondary school			C−									
	Viola players												
Kemp (1979)	Secondary school					F−							
Kemp (1981)	Higher education			C+									
	Cellists												
Kemp (1981)	Higher education	A−								N+		Q2+	

* Significant difference between string and brass players only.
† Difference between string and both brass and woodwind players (not necessarily significant).
‡ Difference between string and brass players only (not necessarily significant).
§ Significant difference between string and woodwind players only.
¶ A−, aloofness; B+, high intelligence; C+, high ego strength; C−, low ego strength; E−, submissiveness; F−, desurgency; G+, conscientiousness; H−, shyness; I+, sensitivity; N+, shrewdness; Q1−, conservatism; Q2+, self-sufficiency; Q3+, high self-sentiment.

What has not emerged convincingly is any significant confirmation of Davies' (1976) finding that his professional string players were neurotic. Not only had he found them to be more highly neurotic than brass and wood-wind players as measured on Eysenck's test, but also they emerged as more anxious on a Cattellian inventory that he also used. The only manifestation of anxiety amongst groups of string players in other research was found in Bell and Cresswell's (1984) students who showed lower ego strength (C−) than the woodwind and brass players. This particular trait indicates a certain emotional instability and a tendency to be at the mercy of one's feelings.

The other disappointment, highlighted by Table 8.1, relates to the non-appearance of sensitivity, save that found in Bell and Cresswell's pupils in comparison, surprisingly, not with the brass, but woodwind players. We should not move on to a discussion of specific string instruments without noting the conservatism (Q1−) of Bell and Cresswell's student string players. Whilst bearing in mind the very restricted size of their groups, the string players were found to be significantly more conservative than either the woodwind or the brass. The nature of such a difference may not be immediately interpretable, although one can speculate that a degree of respect for traditional ideas and values might correlate with aspects of the work ethic of the instrument and of orchestral life.

Because my own work involved sufficiently large numbers of participants I was able to break down the groups further into players of certain individual instruments (Kemp 1979, 1981c). We must be cautious, though, about making too many categorical claims on the basis of one set of results. However, some of these features are not without interest. For example, the secondary school violinists were characterized by lower ego strength (C−), a tendency to be easily upset and emotional. As a contributory trait of anxiety, its emergence is certainly interesting, and interpretable very much in terms of Boulton and O'Neill's (1994) thoughts about the victimization of pupils who play certain instruments that are unpopular. After all, half of this group of violinists were boys.

Traditionally, one often suspects that viola players have moved 'downwards' from the violin. The viola is not usually a young person's first instrument, requiring a greater degree of strength and, more importantly, greater arm length and larger hands. In orchestras the viola player is frequently perceived as the 'failed' violinist, someone whose progress on the violin has been rather chequered and who, although wishing to continue orchestral playing, needs to find parts that are generally a little easier. The secondary school viola players did not reveal traits that one would associate with this situation, for instance, perhaps lower levels of intelligence, introversion, and conscientiousness. Instead, what merely emerged was a suggestion of desurgency (F−) very much, of course, associated with higher introversion. On the other hand, the student viola players were found to be particularly emotionally stable (C+), leading one to speculate that the 'safer' performing situation effects a reduction of the higher levels of anxiety claimed by researchers such as Davies to characterize most string players.

Ben-Tovim and Boyd (1990) maintain that the cello requires a quiet and reflective intelligence and work that is equally conscientious and sustained as that required by the violin. They also suggest that cellists are often of a shy temperament. The 34 cellists in my research very much confirmed these suggestions, displaying significant levels of introversion over and above that shown by all the string players. In fact, they emerged as even more aloof (A–) than the rest of the string players who, as we have seen were already characterized by aloofness. Their other trait, also associated with introversion, was self-sufficiency (Q2+) which emerged along with a definite level of astuteness (N+). This is an interesting combination: the cellist's introversion combines with a social awareness, two qualities that, at face value, do not relate well together. Perhaps Ben-Tovim and Boyd have an important insight in this respect when they suggest that cellists are characterized by a 'quiet and unstressed sociability' (p. 97).

Surprisingly, in view of the very different characteristics of the double bass, my 32 student players did not emerge with any particular personality differences from those of other string instruments. Viewed as a totality, Table 8.1 can be perceived as suggesting that the temperament of string players reveals a serious and hard-working ethic. The strong evidence of introversion supports this, as does their conscientiousness and will power. When we come to a discussion of brass players it may become rather obvious as to the basis on which certain animosities might ensue in orchestral circles.

Woodwind players

In many ways, woodwind instruments present a less cohesive picture in terms of their characteristics than do strings. Quite apart from their obvious similarity, in that they are all blown, there is quite an appreciable divergence, which might possibly be reflected in the personalities of their respective players. As we have seen, the higher pitched woodwind instruments are often perceived as being women's instruments, perhaps due to their treble pitch and lack of the kind of power frequently exercised by the brass. The treble pitch may be particularly significant; it allows the young player to 'sing through' their instrument, thus encouraging a close identification with it. Alternatively, the strength necessary for playing the oboe and the bassoon might result in them being seen as more suitable for boys who are older. Whilst certainly not wishing to perpetuate these kinds of stereotypes, recognizing their existence in discussions of woodwind players' temperaments may help us to account for certain differences that emerge in the research. Another less contentious aspect relates to the notion that results are far more quickly forthcoming on the flute, clarinet, and saxophone than on the dou-ble-reeded oboe and bassoon. Within their first few lessons learners are able to produce simple but reasonably pleasing melodies on the former, much to their own delight and that of their parents. The availability of immediate results versus long-term application to master techniques, as with the strings, may prove to have a direct bearing upon the personality character-istics of those players who have demonstrated levels of success.

Before moving on we should, perhaps, mention Freud's concept of the 'oral character' for it is sometimes thought that it might have a bearing on a person's choice of wind instrument. Without pursuing this at any depth, let it suffice to say that Freud (1905) maintained that all children move through a number of phases of sexual development during which attention is focused on the various erotogenic parts of the body . The first of these is the oral stage and involves the child's unconscious attempts to re-experience the pleasure of feeding at his or her mother's breast. As so frequently observed by parents of small children at this stage of development, the child's auto-matic reaction is to experience all new objects via the mouth. Anyone who, for a particular reason, becomes fixated at this pre-genital stage can be said to be an oral character, and this may manifest itself in over-eating, excessive drinking, smoking, and so on.

Kline and Storey (1977) set out to investigate Freud's theory using two specially devised tests, one testing oral optimism (characterizing those who received indulgent breast feeding), and the other testing oral pessimism (those who experienced frustration at the breast). Their results emerged with clear evidence of both syndromes, showing the former to be linked to stable extraverts, and the latter to neurotic extraverts.

The purpose of this psychoanalytic diversion is prompted by the thought that wind players might be differentiated from other instrumentalists as being fixated at the oral stage. It is an attractive notion. After all, oral opti-mists have been shown to have a preference for sucking; pessimists, being more sadistic, prefer biting. Pen-chewers, for example, have been shown by Kline and Storey (1980) to be oral pessimists. It occurred to them that the woodwind members of a university orchestra would be significantly more orally fixated than the non-woodwind. Unfortunately, no relationship was found and, in discussing their results, they considered that this may have been due to the amateur status of the orchestra members. They also specu-lated about the fact that many were equally good at playing other instru-ments, a factor that may have influenced their results. Nevertheless, it remains an interesting notion and, as Kline and Storey indicate, might be worth following up with groups of professional players specially selected on the basis of their single-instrument orientation. The thought persists that pursuing differences, not only between the orchestral sections, but also with-in them, might highlight differences that can be interpreted in these terms.

Another rather psychoanalytic notion worth mentioning at this point relates to the playing stance of certain wind instruments. Those instruments that tend to be thrust forward in what is sometimes seen as an aggressive, sexual fashion, as opposed to being cuddled and caressed, might become entangled with people's gender schema at the more unconscious levels. If the phallic stance of the trumpet, trombone, and saxophone connect in this kind of fashion with what is perceived as male sexuality, then these instruments would naturally have strong gender associations and be seen as inappropriate for women. Later, when we discuss the attributes of the trumpet and trombone and their ability to penetrate the complete fabric of the orchestra, the common attitude that the brass section is a natural male preserve becomes even more understandable.

In the light of all the possible differences between woodwind instruments mentioned above, some of which are more subtle than others, we might expect to find a corresponding variation between their players' personality characteristics. If this is found to be the case, then attempting to find a personality description for woodwind players generally might cause us problems. Any differences in the composition of these groups, involving the balance of instrumentalists, would certainly cause this. A glance at the summary of research in Table 8.2 suggests that this is the case, and certainly Bell and Cresswell (1984) support this view. For example, Davies (1976) found his professional players to be the most introverted and adjusted in comparison with the other two sections. Martin's (1976) research, while supporting the introversion in his conservatoire students, also found them to be less controlled, revealed by their lower conscientiousness (G–) and a tendency to be undisciplined (Q3–). On the other hand, Kaplan (1961) found woodwind players to be highly controlled, at the same time showing that their high levels of sensitivity and self-confidence were linked to high achievement. Bell and Cresswell's (1984) school pupils also showed a combination of desurgency (F–) and conscientiousness (G+) indicating the effects of a mode of upbringing that is supportive and encouraging. Bell and Cresswell's results with conservatoire students revealed a mixture of traits that fails to suggest a cohesive pattern of higher-order factors, namely, lower intelligence (B–), emotional stability (C+), artlessness (N–), radicalism (Q1+), and self-sufficiency (Q2+). As Table 8.2 shows, some of these traits only emerged with one other orchestral group. Nevertheless, these marginally support the pattern of introversion and adjustment found by Davies.

My own results (Kemp 1979, 1981c) showed that secondary school woodwind players were somewhat phlegmatic (D–) but at the same time, adventurous (H+). The first of these suggests the presence of anxiety; the second indicates extraversion and, possibly, independence. In undergraduates, some signs of introversion were found, taking the form of shyness (H–) and self-sufficiency (Q2+), and confirming the findings of Martin and Davies. Additionally, they were discovered to be more radical (Q1+), supporting

Table 8.2 Summary of research with woodwind players

Researcher(s)	Type of group	A	B	C	D	E	F	G	H	I	L	M	N	O	Q1	Q2	Q3	Q4
Woodwind players																		
Kemp (1979)	Secondary school				D−													
Bell and Cresswell (1984)	Secondary school						F−	*G+	H+							*Q2		
Bell and Cresswell (1984)	Higher education		§B−	§C+						I−			N−					
Martin (1976)	Higher education	†A−					‡F−	†G−	‡H−						Q1+	†Q2+	†Q3−	
Kemp (1981)	Higher education								H−						Q1+	Q2+		
Kemp (1979)	Professional (men)	A−		C+		E−					L−	M+						
Kemp (1979)	Professional (women)			C+		E−					L−	M−						
Flautists																		
Kemp (1981)	Higher education											M+						
Oboe players																		
Kemp (1979)	Secondary school			C−	D+													Q4+
Kemp (1981)	Higher education													O+		Q2+		Q4−
Bassoonists																		
Kemp (1981)	Higher education		B−											O+		Q2+		

The factor columns (A–Q4) are given under the heading *HSPQ and 16 PF primary factors* ¶.

* Significant difference between woodwind and brass players only.
† Difference between woodwind and both strings and brass players (not necessarily significant).
‡ Difference between woodwind and brass players only (not necessarily significant).
§ Significant difference between woodwind and string players only.
¶ A−, aloofness; B−, low intelligence; C+, high ego strength; C−, low ego strength; D+, excitability; D−, phlegmatic; E−, submissiveness; F−, desurgency; G+, conscientiousness; G−, expediency; H+, adventurousness; H−, shyness; I−, tough-mindedness; L−, trusting; M+, imagination; M−, practical; N−, naïveté; O+, guilt proneness; Q1+, radicalism; Q2+, self-sufficiency; Q3−, low self-sentiment; Q4+, high ergic tension; Q4−, low ergic tension.

Bell and Cresswell's results, a characteristic that only rarely appears to be associated with any aspect of instrumental performance. The third group, the professional woodwind players, demonstrated certain elements of adjustment, taking the form of emotional stability (C+) and a trusting nature (L–), which again, support Davies' findings with professional players. Another feature of this group was their lack of independence, manifest not only by the trustingness (L–) already mentioned, but also by their submissiveness (E–), and the women's lack of imagination (M–).

Apart from certain manifestations of introversion and adjustment (lack of anxiety) that appear in a fragmentary way across groups of woodwind players, there appears to be even less agreement over the remaining characteristics. Whether these reflect differences at the various developmental levels or, as suggested above, different balances of instrumentalists within groups is unclear. Clearly, very little in the way of personality outcomes of either form of oral fixation appears to be in evidence here.

What kind of person is attracted to the flute? Ben-Tovim and Boyd (1990) suggest that it is the shy, lonely child who enjoys his or her own company that progresses well, leaving the aggressive and dominant child looking for an instrument that requires more energy and produces more sound. Add to this the distinct 'pastoral' connotations of the instrument, and it is fairly easy to understand why the flute tends to be a 'no go' instrument for many highly gender-stereotyped boys. My 42 student flautists emerged with only one characteristic, a significant level of imagination (M+), in comparison with all other woodwind players. This trait is interpretable in three very plausible ways: firstly imagination links with pathemia, a certain feelingful and sensitive disposition, as discussed in Chapter 4; secondly, it links with the kind of independence suggested by Ben-Tovim and Boyd; and, finally, it suggests 'subjectivity' one of Cattell's second-order factors not commonly apparent in performing musicians, although hinted at by Ben-Tovim and Boyd who saw flautists as being 'dreamy and forgetful' (p. 47).

Clarinettists are looked upon as rather more sociable than flautists, and tend to be bright and alert. According to Ben-Tovim and Boyd the clarinet particularly suits boys who are good at practical activities such as model-making; and they maintain that it is more likely to attract them because of the bigger sound and its slightly lower register. Disappointingly, no significant characteristics emerged for them in my analyses.

The oboe stands out from the flute and clarinet in several ways. Besides being far more expensive, it requires a good deal of strength in terms of wind control and pressure, and considerable hard work and application. Ben-Tovim and Boyd suggest that the oboe is one of those very special cases of the kind already described where an individual feels deeply compelled to play it for reasons that may not be at all clear. They maintain that prospective players must possess high levels of willpower, 'the oboe is not for extroverts; determined, tight-lipped, stubborn children do best' (p. 53). Such a specific set of requirements tends to suggest that oboe players' personality profiles would be equally as specific. One respondent in Davies' (1978) interviews referred to oboe players as neurotic, adding that the instrument itself is neurotic. On questioning her more closely about this, she said that '. . . minor defects, leaks, sticking pads, and other faults are forever developing . . . this, coupled with an obsession about 'reed' problems, serves to keep the hapless oboe player in a perpetual state of fear' (p. 204).

What emerged in connection with my group of 33 secondary school oboe players was, indeed, a convincing picture of anxiety, demonstrated by their low emotional stability (C–), excitability (D+), insecurity (O+), and high ergic tension (Q4+). No other features emerged, and one is led to assume that anxious individuals may possess the physical attributes of tension necessary for oboe playing. Alternatively, it may be that repeated exposure to the high levels of pressure in the head and upper chest, as well as the muscular tension of the lips, face, diaphragm, added to the technical problems mentioned above, generate particularly high levels of anxiety, which are more lasting. That both trait and state primary factors appear to be involved suggests, perhaps, that the effect is in both directions.

In the light of the above, the student oboe players' 'profile' is even more mystifying. In demonstrating a total absence of anxiety, in fact, distinct tranquillity (Q4–), the results suggest, on the face of it, that something fairly dramatic might occur after secondary school and during selection for conservatoire or university. It must be borne in mind, though, that composite groups of undergraduate students are generally found to be anxious, whereas the whole secondary school group were certainly not. This disparity between the overall baselines for the children and undergraduates might account for the emergence of what appears to be a straight reversal. An alternative explanation, which may be more convincing to the reader, is that the more anxious school oboe players, particularly those whose anxiety is trait-orientated, drop out of oboe playing and do not proceed to study performance in higher education. Ben-Tovim and Boyd suggested that children should actively resist any pressure by a school to take up the oboe simply because a spare instrument is available, or because a player is required in the orchestra. This view tends to be supported by these results.

Finally, we come to the bassoon, which, interestingly, Ben-Tovim and Boyd maintain is attractive to slow learners because of its warmth and 'human' sound (p. 55): also, its music is comparatively easy to read. They suggest that bassoon players are 'pleasantly gregarious', tending to be the practical jokers in the orchestra. Some aspects of this description is borne out by the research: in comparison with other woodwind players the 30 undergraduate bassoonists in my study were found to be rather less intelligent (B–), although the notion of their gregarious nature is not borne out by their self-sufficiency (Q2+). They were also more apprehensive (O+) which is rather more difficult to account for, unless, of course, their lower ability levels were somehow the cause of anxiety to them in connection with their other studies. Alternatively, this manifestation of anxiety may have tentative links with that found in the young players of the other double-reed instrument, the oboe.

What may come as something of a surprise to the reader is the tendency towards introversion of woodwind players in this research. Woodwind players are far more exposed in orchestral playing than, say, the string players who group themselves together in such a way that any slight mishap by one player may well go unnoticed by the listener. Not so with the woodwind: not only do they play as individuals, but many composers' orchestrations frequently highlight them as a 'choir' for the purpose of contrast in which they may still feel particularly exposed. The aspect of personality that may reflect this much more is the distinct adjustment identified by several researchers. As we discussed back in Chapter 2, we should not fall into the trap of considering introversion as indicative of timidity; far more it can

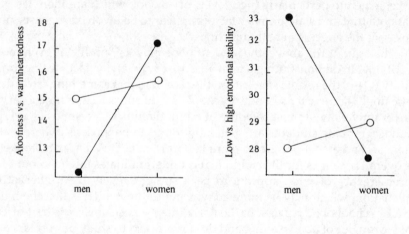

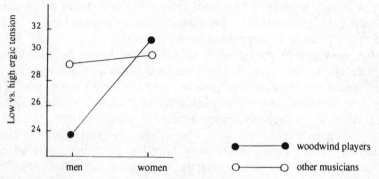

Figure 8.1 Gender differences on aloofness, emotional instability, and ergic tension between professional woodwind players and other musicians.

be interpreted as an inner strength and resourcefulness that allows the individual to deal with exacting demands with hidden levels of resilience.

We should not pass on without considering a further and interesting feature of the professional woodwind players' personality pattern. In Chapter 6 we discussed the notion that musicians are generally found to be somewhat androgynous, that is, displaying certain personality traits that are more associated with the opposite sex in general populations. What emerged in my results was that, on some of these traits, a definite trend emerged for the woodwind players to preserve these gender-linked differences. Thus, as shown in Figure 8.1, whereas gender differences of other professional musicians on aloofness (A–), emotional instability (C–), and ergic tension (Q4+) were minimal, those in woodwind players were more gender biased. This suggests that it appears to be important for woodwind players to preserve certain aspects of 'la différence', and, as Figure 8.1 suggests, this is rather more a male phenomenon than a female one. It may well prove to be the case that these patterns are interpretable as the effects of male woodwind players tending to overcompensate, feeling the need to appear masculine despite their playing the more female gendered instruments.

Brass players

After what has been said and written about brass players by writers such as Davies and Lipton we might expect highly characteristic personality profiles to emerge for them. Although we must bear in mind at all times that we are dealing in generalities, we might expect to find significant levels of extraversion, suggestions of lower sensitivity, as well as the retention of certain gender-related traits of the kind already located in woodwind players.

If we consider the actual tasks of learning and playing brass instruments there are several important points to note. Firstly, they are often perceived as being reasonably easy to master, and often allow the early lessons to take place in groups. In fact, of course, in parts of the brass band movement beginners may be assimilated into the back rows to pick up the techniques on the job. I vividly recall engaging in this kind of process myself as a member of an RAF station band during national service, working my way upwards through the lower cornet parts as my technique and range developed. (Never, though, did I ever master the technique of changing my band cards on the march, periodically scattering them on the ground, and leaving them to be picked up by the bandmaster at the rear!) Back in the bandroom, whilst doing very little damage to the overall performance, I was able to engage in a highly effective, and multi-faceted learning process. More importantly, in terms of our discussions here, I was able to undertake this learning in a setup that allowed the opportunity to socialize, developing the requisite skills in the company of others who were similarly minded. Much the same process can happen in schools; a whole brass ensemble can be taught together from the very first stages, and a considerable amount of learning engaged in jointly. The resultant camaraderie amongst brass players is clearly of a different order to what we have seen in the members of other sections. The long hours of solitary practice of the string and woodwind players are traditionally not seen as nearly as important for most brass instruments. This, of course, is not to suggest that individual practice is not necessary, or that it does not take place.

Another important feature of the brass section is their sheer power: that half a dozen players can totally obliterate the sound of the rest of the orchestra without difficulty is a common fact. Only particular personalities will seek out this kind of prominence, for it involves a degree of exposure that would be uncomfortable, for example, for many string players. As a trumpet player himself, Davies (1978) is very aware that brass players have nowhere to hide once an error has been made; the perpetrator is left to shrug it off as a one-off occurrence. Certainly a bad or missed entry cannot be allowed to diminish the possibilities of the next one being absolutely perfect. A resilience and strong self-concept would appear to be imperative for personal survival in these circumstances. Since brass players do not have the visual cues offered by keys, being wholly dependent upon their lips, ears, and three valves with which to determine their whole range of pitches, these personal qualities would appear to be of paramount importance. As Davies observes, all other instruments offer a fair degree of visual and tactile cues about where to 'place' the initial note of a new entry: brass players are merely left to imagine the note aurally, adjust the tension of their lips accordingly, and hope for the best—rather like leaping into the dark. All this appears to be highly stressful, and one might expect to find elements of anxiety in brass players who are repeatedly called upon to perform in this fashion. Davies suggests that, possibly, this stress tends to be dealt with by the brass players' reported heavy alcohol intake, traditionally always being the first in the bar during any interval. Alternatively, any high levels of adjustment and extraversion they possess might allow them to cope without serious symptoms of stress.

Another important aspect, not to be overlooked, is the association that brass playing has with the northern areas of England. Despite the demise of the coal mines, prestigious bands such as the Black Dyke and Grimethorpe enjoy a worldwide reputation. Davies suggests that the working class image of the brass player as a beer-swilling, cloth-capped, and somewhat uncultured individual may account for the kind of stereotype to which we have already referred. It may also help account for the masculine image of brass playing, particularly as, as Davies observes, there certainly exists no parallel in the world of string playing. The various bands of the armed forces and their associated repertoire also assist in perpetuating the male stereotype. It would be very wrong, however, to consider that this is the only way to perceive brass players. Many excellent players have come from the Salvation Army movement which, in some ways, conjures up a very different kind of image.

Let us then take a look at what the research has to say about measurable personality traits of brass players to see whether the stereotype, so deeply embedded in orchestral folklore, can be empirically maintained. Certainly, Davies (1978) discovered that they were the most extraverted section of the orchestra as well as being the least neurotic. In his very early research, Kaplan (1961) also found them to be uninhibited, referring to them as 'turbulent' as well as insensitive; in fact he showed that sensitivity was actually counterproductive to brass playing success. The lack of inhibition is well supported by Martin (1976) who found all the primary factors of extraversion (A+, F+, H+, and Q2−) in his brass-playing undergraduates as compared with the string and woodwind players. Whilst Bell and Cresswell (1984) supported the extraversion of brass-playing undergraduates (F+, Q2−) they also discovered them to be lacking in control (G− and Q3−). A summary of this research is shown in Table 8.3.

It may be worth adding at this point that Bell and Cresswell are the only researchers to suggest that brass players are independent, revealed by their dominance (E+) and surgency (F+) in comparison to string players. This is not without interest since Schmidt (1985) claimed that brass players were relatively field-independent types. Viewed in this way, the notion that brass players possess a more articulated perceptual style may add another perspective to their more autonomous behaviour. However, this is very much a side issue and, as mentioned above, their independence is not universally established.

My own work (Kemp 1979, 1981c) showed conclusively that lower sensitivity (I−) and lower intelligence (B−) are linked to brass playing. We can be reasonably confident about this claim simply because these same traits emerged consistently in the profiles of the secondary school, higher education, and professional brass players. To save myself from being lynched by the brass player-participants at an international research seminar when I first presented these findings, perhaps in cowardice, I presented the following kind of gloss.

It has to be recalled that the complete group of musicians in this research was considerably more intelligent and sensitive than the non-musicians. In this context it might then be more accurate to refer to the brass players as not sharing the high levels on these traits as the other two groups.

The reader may view this as something of a cop-out, but it has to be said that, in all research of this kind, we must keep the nature of the baseline (or norms) in mind at all times. Viewed from an educational standpoint, these results may well indicate how brass playing can be viewed as an opening for pupils who might be misfitted on other instruments. However, as

Table 8.3 Summary of research with brass players

Researcher(s)	Type of group	A	B	E	F	G	H	I	M	O	Q2	Q3	Q4
	Brass players												
Kemp (1979)	Secondary school		B–					I–					
Bell and Cresswell (1984)	Secondary school				§F+	§G–							
Bell and Cresswell (1984)	Higher education			*E+	*F+	G–					Q2–	Q3–	
Martin (1976)	Higher education	+A+			+F+		+H+				†Q2–		
Kemp (1981)	Higher education (men)		B–		F+	G–		I–		O–	Q2–		
Kemp (1981)	Higher education (women)		B–		F+	G–		I–		O+	Q2–	Q3–	Q4+
Kemp (1979)	Professional		B–					I–	M–				
	Trumpeters												
Kemp (1979)	Secondary school				F+						Q2–		
Kemp (1981)	Higher education											Q3–	
	Horn players												
Kemp (1979)	Secondary school				F–						Q2+		

* Significant difference between brass and string players only.

† Difference between brass and both string and woodwind players (not necessarily significant).

§ Significant difference between brass and woodwind players only.

¶ A+, outgoingness; B–, low intelligence; E+, dominance; F+, surgency; F–, desurgency; G–, expediency; H+, adventurousness; I–, tough-mindedness; M–, practical; O+, guilt proneness; O–, self-assured; Q2+, self-sufficiency; Q2–, group-dependent; Q3–, low self-sentiment; Q4+, high ergic tension; Q4–, low ergic tension.

mentioned earlier, all research that relates to group differences should be interpreted with special caution particularly by people tempted to use it for predictive purposes with individual children.

In common with those of Davies and Martin, the brass players from higher education institutions in my research also demonstrated moderate signs of extraversion, although not as unequivocally as in the pattern found by Martin. Here they showed very consistent manifestations of surgency (F+) and group dependency (Q2–), supporting the notion of their social demeanour and happy-go-lucky attitude to things generally. The brass player's extraversion may well be interpretable in terms of my earlier suggestion concerning the higher thresholds of arousal in extraverts discussed in Chapters 2 and 7. Not only will extraverts be able to perform more efficiently under stressful conditions, they will also be more comfortable producing the sheer amount of volume of which they are capable.

Finally, in the groups of professional brass players we find a rather more complicated picture with regard to anxiety. Whereas the men displayed certain elements of adjustment, specifically a self-assured and secure disposition (O–) coupled with a relaxed and tranquil attitude (Q4–), the women were apprehensive (O+), possessing a low self-sentiment (Q3–), and exhibiting a tense and overwrought state (Q4+): a persuasive picture of anxiety.

The different patterns of the men and women in respect to these traits is an important phenomenon and they are shown diagrammatically in Figure 8.2. Unlike most other groups in this research the trumpet and trombone players were not numerically matched gender-wise; the male–female ratio being 20:9 and 24:5 respectively. This may have exercised a distorting effect, particularly as the group of horn players was composed of equal numbers. Viewed another way, there were nearly twice as many female horn players as there were female trumpet and trombone players together, whereas in the men the three groups were equal. The outcome of this may well have been for the men and women to emerge with different patterns on the anxiety-adjustment dimension accountable by differences between trumpet and trombone players versus horn players. We shall return to this a little later.

The only other finding of note was the professional players' lower imagination (M–), which, in combination with the lower sensitivity mentioned earlier, suggests the presence of cortertia—its only manifestation in any of my findings. It will be recalled that, in Chapter 4, we found that most musicians were characterized by pathemia, tending to live at the level of feeling and affect. Cortertia, on the other hand, indicates quick activation times, and an alert and energetic disposition. Whether or not this relates to what was observed in connection with the field-independence of brass players is unclear. Both findings do, though, tentatively suggest that fundamental differences in cognitive style exist between brass players and other musicians. These might be of a kind which, together with other differences already

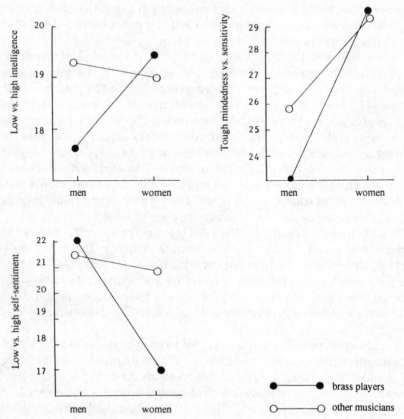

Figure 8.2 Gender differences on intelligence, sensitivity, and self-sentiment between brass players and other musicians in higher education.

described, suggests at the very least 'chalk and cheese' sets of interpersonal attitudes and the emergence of persistent prejudices.

Due to the lack of gender balance in the groups of trumpet and trombone players (caused by the dearth of women players at that time) it did not come as much of a surprise to me when the results of the further analyses were somewhat inconclusive. Those for trumpeters and horn players are shown in Table 8.3. The school trumpet players in direct comparison with the horn players emerged as being significantly more extraverted, being surgent (F+) and group-dependent (Q2–). By the same token, of course, we can therefore say that the horn players were more introverted, or at least less extraverted. The undergraduate trumpet players merely demonstrated a lack of discipline and carelessness about rules (Q3–). Perhaps it is worth adding at this point that Wills and Cooper's (1988) work had highlighted trumpet players as one of the most extraverted and the least neurotic of all their groups of popular musicians. Incidentally, they also identified them as the most high scoring group on Eysenck's lie scale.

Another glance at Figure 8.2 offers some further insights about the student brass players. Because of the disparity between the numbers of men and women it is reasonable to assume that the differences between the female brass players and non-brass players will be more attributable to the horn players than for the men. If we follow this line of reasoning, we might be tempted to consider that the greater differences among the men on intelligence and sensitivity than among the women is due to characteristics more attributable to trumpet and trombone playing than to horn playing. By the same token, we might be forgiven for assuming that the greater disparity on low self-sentiment (Q3–) between the female brass players and non-brass players, than in the case of the men, is a reflection of horn player's slight susceptibility to anxiety. Certainly, what is often said about brass players does not always appear to relate directly to horn players. They are frequently seen as being temperamentally quite different. This may be due to the particular technical difficulties of horn playing, involving many more hours of solitary practice than on other brass instruments. In some ways the horn can be said to enter into the spirit of symphonic music more than the other brass who are often perceived as merely tolerating it, particularly the music of the classical period in which they see themselves as very much underemployed.

Percussion players

In common with woodwind players, percussionists may also be characterized by a diversity that might cause some problems to the researcher. Although there is little research into their temperament, there appear to be some strong gender associations that are worth mentioning. As we observed earlier, Griswold and Chroback (1981) showed that the bass drum was perceived by undergraduates as having distinct masculine connotations. Ables and Porter's (1978) groups claimed the drums to be the most masculine of instruments, the trumpet and trombone, in fact, being viewed as less so. In the context of this particular research, 'the drums' were probably associated with pop groups in which, of course, most of the role-models would have been male. The same conclusion was arrived at in Delzell and Leppla's (1992) study in which, again, the drums were perceived as even more masculine than the trumpet and trombone. The research of Fortney et al. (1993) refers specifically to 'percussion' and here also the male preference emerges nearly as strongly. Although the research of Wills and Cooper (1988) focused entirely on musicians working in the popular fields, jazz, rock, and pop, it is probably worth mentioning that such drummers emerged as the most extraverted of all their instrumental groups. We shall return to Wills and Cooper's work in more detail in Chapter 10.

In the absence of research into specific orchestral percussion and timpani players we are left to speculate that the exhibitionistic aspect of some orchestral percussion playing, for example, the playing of cymbals and xylophone, might be perceived as having particular male connotations. Thus, there may emerge certain associations with extraversion and possibly independence. Builione and Lipton's (1983) research showed that percussion players were perceived as being extraverted by all other sections of a high school orchestra; at the same time the brass and woodwind players also viewed them as masculine. As with most of these pieces of research it is not clear whether timpanists were included. The picture, for them, has to remain obscure, although, from personal experience, I know the overwhelming feelings of power that can overtake a timpanist, particularly when, during a loud and sustained dominant pedal, one has this overwhelming feeling that the whole orchestra is somehow under one's direct influence and control.

Summary

The study of the personality characteristics of different types of orchestral players occurs within the context of a rich backdrop of folklore that is frequently apparent in musical circles. It relates to certain beliefs and attitudes about the kinds of people who choose to play particular instruments, and thus tends to divide orchestras into very different camps. Empirical research offers confirmation of some aspects of these attitude patterns, even of one or two of those not considered to be altogether complimentary.

Possibly connected with these stereotyped attitudes are those more prevalent in schools, which concern certain gender-related qualities with which pupils tend to endow musical instruments. Broadly speaking, children often perceive string and woodwind instruments as being effeminate, particularly those in the upper registers; alternatively, brass instruments and the drums are often considered macho. These gender-related stereotypes appear to be formed in children's minds from a very early age, and pupils who play mismatched instruments may, as a result, be bullied and ostracized by their contemporaries. Some evidence has emerged that suggests that these attitudes are also shared by those who play musical instruments themselves, although possibly not by the more gifted.

The most striking aspect of string players appears to be their introversion, particularly in terms of those factors that have been shown to relate more closely to musicianship, namely, aloofness and self-sufficiency. These qualities can be interpreted as reflecting the slow progress that is generally forthcoming on string instruments compared with some others. String players' serious approach to their work and their strong work ethic, which their levels of introversion reflect, may well be interpretable by the more extraverted as giving themselves airs of superiority.

Woodwind players, often caught in the crossfire between the other sections, are also revealed by research as being introverted despite the fact that, in the early stages, most of their instruments tend to provide more immediate results than in the case of the strings. However, woodwind players' introversion appears to be coupled with a degree of imagination and radicalism that eludes the string players. There is also some evidence to suggest that male woodwind and brass players are not as androgynous as male string players, thus helping to establish the belief that the latter are effeminate.

Research with brass players supports several of the views expressed about them by members of the other orchestral sections, particularly in terms of those observations that relate to their considerable extraverted qualities. Brass-playing skills may be developed in more social environments, and it is generally recognized that progress can be reasonably rapid, thus eliminating the need for a more introverted temperament. Other differences identified in brass players relating to their lower levels of personal discipline and intelligence may also help confirm some of the more scurrilous views expressed by the very different string players. Furthermore, percussion players, and particularly drummers, appear to share certain extraverted qualities of brass players.

NINE

Keyboard players, singers, and conductors

Introduction

In the last chapter, which focused upon the orchestral musician, we became
more fully aware that, within a general personality description of the musician, there are several different patterns of variations that occur according to
the specific characteristics of instruments and their repertoire. It was conve-
nient to organize the chapter in this fashion so that, amongst other things,
the research concerning intersectional attitudes in orchestras and certain
gender identities of instruments might also be considered. An additional
consideration, of course, is that orchestral musicians have one particular
thing in common: they are all subject to the control and musical directions of
a conductor. In this context we can begin to see orchestral players as having
relinquished some aspects of their artistry and individuality. This chapter
might also reflect few cohesive features; after all, the modes of performance
of pianists, organists, singers, and conductors take on very different aspects,
yet, being 'non-orchestral', they might be expected to reveal higher levels of
individuality, less conservatism, and more imagination. This chapter has,
unfortunately, another particular feature: there is a dearth of research relating to these groups.

Pianists

The piano is often viewed as the instrument with the highest failure rate. If
this is true it may be due to the high numbers of children who commence
piano lessons on the basis of parents considering that 'it would be good for
her to play a musical instrument' with little consideration given to other
alternative instruments. When interest begins to flag and little progress
appears to being made, parents can sometimes assume, quite wrongly, that
this is due to a lack of 'musicality' rather than a child being misfitted to the
particular demands of the piano. Unfortunately, and all too often, that is the
end of the story for many children. Others who *do* struggle on and make
headway through sheer application and hard work sometimes find that, on

taking up a second instrument, progress is so rapid that they discover that the piano was not their natural instrument for all the previous years. It is clear that the piano makes considerable demands upon young children, particularly if lessons are started at a very early age. After all, it requires equal dexterity of all 10 fingers, considerable co-ordination, high levels of mental agility involved in the simultaneous reading of two lines of music in different clefs, and all the rapid eye movements that this demands. Bearing all this in mind, we might be led to suspect that pianists would tend to be introverted, on the basis that it is the *extent* of the numbers of hours spent in practice that might determine levels of introversion. This is certainly the notion that was proposed during the course of the last chapter.

In developing the above kind of thinking, we might expect pianists to be above average in intelligence, taking a conscientious attitude towards their school work, and tending to spend long periods quite happily on their own. As Ben-Tovim and Boyd (1990) remark, the piano may well be an ideal instrument for an individual of this type who may be an only child or one with siblings who are much older. It is these kinds of children, they maintain, that tend to develop a strong, prolonged, and mature relationship with their teachers. An important component of this kind of syndrome of individuality would feature our expectation that pianists would be autonomous types, very much more radical and musically imaginative, in other words, traits reflecting an ability to create their own interpretations.

In emphasizing the solitary nature of the piano, Ben-Tovim and Boyd liken it to the guitar and the harp both in terms of their difficulty levels and the self-containment of their players. Their line of thinking is that single-line instruments are all designed for group music-making and, in that sense, offer less of an opportunity for the child to remain solitary. On the other hand, because the piano, harp, and guitar are harmonic as well as melodic instruments, Ben-Tovim and Boyd maintain that they do not immediately require co-operation with other players. They are, then, *musically* self-contained and therefore more likely, in their view, to appeal to the child who is less extraverted. Some may wish to challenge the notion that an instrument's *musical* self-containment is linked to the player's level of introversion by citing the introverted string player as merely tolerating the social aspects of the orchestral situation in order to benefit from it musically. Also, of course, pianos are very often situated within the living area of homes and also, apart from practice rooms, are found in fairly public places in institutions. In this sense pianos are rather public objects, and those who choose to play them do so possibly in the certain knowledge that a good proportion of their practice will take place within earshot, if not the view, of other people. Unlike most other instruments the piano does not allow the learner to choose a quiet, solitary environment in which to practise.

In my early work (Kemp 1971), which will be discussed in more detail in Chapter 11, I compared the profiles of a group of composers in higher education with a matched group of performers. In a subsidiary analysis, I carried out a comparison between string players and pianists that suggested that the latter were inclined to be more sensitive (I+), imaginative (M+), and radical (Q1+). However, although both groups contained composers and non-composers, the balance was not uniform, there being a higher preponderance of composers amongst the pianists than among the string players. That the composers had been found to be particularly imaginative and radical might have accounted for these results, unduly influencing the results on these two factors. Of course, there is another notion, which should not be overlooked here. These characteristics may be *shared* by pianists and composers. After all, any inclination towards imagination and radicalism can be interpreted as not only a sign of the composer's creativity but also of the pianist's autonomous interpretative ability. Neither should we overlook the tendency for many composers to be pianists, often interpreted as a reflection of the comprehensive musical aspects of piano playing assisting in the process of composition. Also, of course, many composers actually undertake their compositional work at the keyboard. In other words, these results could suggest that the two groups are temperamentally quite similar. The sensitivity, however, can still be interpreted as a hallmark of the pianist; the composers and non-composers exhibiting an identical level.

Later, I was able to return to the question of the pianist's personality by adopting much larger groups of both pianists and composers. What emerged clearly suggests that any link between composers and pianists that appeared in the earlier research was, indeed, spurious. At the secondary school level the results with the pianists showed them to be significantly more shy (H–) than the non-pianists. Although the results of this part of the research were disappointingly thin, this one factor supports the view taken by Ben-Tovim and Boyd that pianists are natural loners who like privacy and show a disinclination to join in or to participate in group activity (Kemp 1979). In discussing the shyness (H–) factor in Chapter 2 in the context of introversion, the point was made that the factor is not normally operative in the personalities of musicians at either pole. The fact that it is emerging here in the personalities of young pianists might be telling us something quite profound.

Cattell's shyness factor involves the social withdrawal and timidity aspects of introversion that we have maintained throughout all the chapters of this book form no part of the musician's introversion. The musician's introversion is of a very different kind. The H– person is, according to Cattell *et al.* (1970), intensely shy and tormented by unreasonable thoughts of inferiority. In terms of upbringing, shyness is associated with strict discipline in the home and particularly anxious and apprehensive mothering. It may therefore occur to the reader that the emergence of this factor may be telling us something about the forms of upbringing of young pianists. Is it just possible that this group of 79 pianists (41 boys and 38 girls) was revealing just one aspect of the impress of the kind of close, if not intrusive, parenting that young pianists so very often receive? Many will come from musical homes—the presence of a piano will frequently indicate this; and this may reflect the level of parental involvement and the kind of vigilance that ensures that regular practice takes place, that teachers' instructions are being carried out, that practice is focused on particular weaknesses of pieces and exercises, and so on. Cattell (1973) actually suggests that the factor reveals the outcome of 'maternal solicitousness, which invites dependence' (p. 167). This makes the point perfectly, and also raises another connotation of the shyness factor—its involvement in the second-order factor of dependence. Neither should we overlook the fact that shyness is a constituent primary trait of anxiety. Seen from the perspective of the three higher-order factors, the shyness factor suggests that this group of young pianists may not be particularly healthy from a psychological point of view.

In view of the rather meagre result with the secondary school pianists it came as a surprise to find the pianists in higher education emerging with an extensive profile of traits that suggest quite a different picture (Kemp 1981c). Far from being introverted, the students displayed significant inclinations to be both outgoing (A+) and group-dependent (Q2−), suggesting that, if shy children do well on the piano initially, either they may not be suited temperamentally to pursue their studies into higher education, or that some significant development takes place in the meantime. The former interpretation would appear to be the more probable; those children who are possibly being driven to practice and are dependent upon parental supervision merely drop out at the earliest opportunity.

Besides their relative extraversion these pianists appeared also to be very well adjusted, showing evidence of strong self-sentiment (Q3+) and a relaxed attitude (Q4−). As we noted in Chapter 2, research tends to suggest that achievement in school is associated with extraversion and that, later on, it becomes more facilitated by introversion. The total reversal of this pattern in pianists is curious and not immediately explicable. Whatever role anxiety plays in other musicians it clearly does not occur here. These 104 pianists (25 men and 79 women) were characterized by high levels of self-sentiment, a strong self-image, and a persistent nature, yet by taking a relaxed attitude to life generally.

Another important feature of the pianists' personality was the combination of traits of submissiveness (E−), conscientiousness (G+), and the high self-sentiment (Q3+) referred to above. Taken together, these three features suggest that the more mature pianists were brought up in particularly supportive and encouraging home environments by loving and respected parents who took a close interest in their musical development (Kemp 1995). This group was also inclined to be conservative (Q1−) and a long way from possessing the radicalism of the composer suggested by the earlier research. Any hypothesized temperamental connection between the two groups is certainly not upheld by these results, an observation that will become even clearer in Chapter 11.

The relative extraversion of these pianists is an interesting phenomenon, and encourages us to consider seriously whether life in a university music department or conservatoire keeps the pianist in the forefront of musical activity. Whereas most orchestral types will satisfy many of their perform-ing needs by playing in various ensembles of different types, pianists may experience more exposure by being forced to perform either on their own or as accompanists. If this is true, it suggests that extraversion is, after all, linked to some forms of performance, particularly when the performance is very exposed as in a piano recital. Certainly, this does not necessarily run counter to our earlier discussions concerning the overall introversion of the musician. But what it *does* highlight is that, whereas many orchestral types function reasonably well in spite of their introversion (on the basis that they possess considerable internal strengths), those who are more likely to per-form solo in recitals, or possibly as accompanists, may require a somewhat different type of temperament.

What is particularly striking about these results with both groups of chil-dren and adults is that their differences appear to occur in direct contrast to other musicians at both levels. In other words, child pianists show signs of being introverted and anxious when their fellow musicians of a similar age are not; student pianists, on the other hand, are extraverted and stable when the student non-pianists are introverted and anxious. If nothing else, these results suggest that pianists appear to be quite separate from other musi-cians, displaying a temperament that may reflect their different life-style and musical involvement. Also notice that both the children and students appear to show the effects of the impress of parental support, although their respec-tive patterns are quite different. However, in the case of the children this appears to be non-productive and possibly harmful; in the students it may be interpreted as being effective, both in terms of the students' achievement levels as well as in their stable personalities. Their submissiveness, consci-entiousness, and conservatism, reflecting the styles of their upbringing (Kemp 1995), will not enable them to set the world on fire. As we shall see in Chapter 11, they generally appear not to be at all suited to creative enter-prise. However, their particular combination of traits would allow them to be very effective leaders.

Organists

All of what was said initially about the demands of piano playing would seem to apply even more so to the organ, particularly the church organ. One only has to consider such key aspects as the simultaneous reading of *three* lines of music, the physical co-ordination of hands and feet, the manipulation of two or more manuals, stops, tabs, and pistons, and so on to realize there is much here to suggest even higher levels of the personality traits associated with skill development. Add to this the notion that the organ is probably the self-contained instrument *par excellence*—and the reader might also consider how much time, until the arrival of the home organ, the organist spent practising in the solitude of, very frequently, deserted churches. From my own experience, I vividly recall Saturday evenings invariably spent in dark, empty churches throughout my adolescence, spending what little pocket money I received on electric blowing, still at that time a rare acquisition for most of the East Kent village churches. The motivation was, of course, playing for services the following day with a sense of pride and confidence, as well as all the sensations of achievement that followed. What was, of course, being blocked out, possibly without realizing it, was any thoughts of engaging in the alternative social activities pursued by most of my school contemporaries.

Seen in this way, we might wish to speculate that organists would also emerge as introverted, yet very much possessing the inner strength of purpose that allows them to perform regularly in the church setting, albeit frequently hidden behind discreet curtains. Another important feature, of course, is the size and power of many pipe organs—an aspect that might appeal to the introvert who, nonetheless, needs certain opportunities to feel powerful and omnipotent. No wonder the organist is perceived by most other musicians as 'a race apart'. We should not overlook, either, the fact that many organists are expected to be choir trainers, necessitating levels of leadership involved in taking rehearsals and conducting. That some church organists actively avoid the choir training role may suggest that the two temperaments are not necessarily unitary. Consider also the extent to which the church organist's and recitalist's principal diet is often their beloved Bach. Burt (1939) would probably suggest that this might ease the organist in the direction of introverted stability. Nevertheless, let it be reiterated that here we have been discussing the traditional church organist, shiny trousers and all. The relatively new arrival of the home organ, particularly with full keyboards and pedalboard, may bring about a new breed of organist hitherto unknown save perhaps as the rarer one of the theatre organist.

My research (Kemp 1979) drew together 42 student organists (25 men and 17 women), and these were compared with the somewhat larger group of pianists. What emerged, rather surprisingly, was that the organists largely shared the same levels of extraversion: outgoingness (A+) and group dependency (Q2−); adjustment: strong self-sentiment (Q3+) and low ergic tension (Q4−); and control: submissiveness (E−) and conscientiousness (G+) demonstrated by the undergraduate pianists. The fact that organists emerged as sharing the same levels of extraversion as pianists may well lead us to continue to speculate about its involvement with solo performance. Most of their playing, apart from the occasional orchestral piece requiring an organ part, is carried out by organists either in solo or as prominent (sometimes far too prominent!) accompanists.

The only trait that showed the organists to be significantly different to the pianists was shrewdness (N+), a trait that was also found to be linked to cello-playing students. Having not featured in our discussions up to this point, perhaps some explanation of this factor is necessary. Cattell *et al.* (1970) describe the factor as one, not only relating to social awareness, but particularly associated with the acquisition of technical skills and with occupations which require mental alertness and precision. According to Cattell, the N+ person is also astute, emotionally detached and disciplined, and 'esthetically fastidious' (p. 99). Clearly, there are several important aspects of the organist that appear to be captured within this factor, not the least being the technical efficiency required to handle the complexities of organ playing. In spite of these multifarious mechanical demands, organists are required to remain in touch with the more musical aspects of performance. That some organists never achieve success at this tight-rope act often leads to them being accused by other musicians of lacking sensitivity. Cattell's remark about aesthetic fastidiousness relates well to the frequent charge that organists have narrow musical interests outside their immediate repertoire.

FACTOR N		
Low score NAÏVETÉ N–	versus	High score SHREWDNESS N+
Forthright	vs.	Astute
Unpretentious	vs.	Worldly
Genuine, but socially clumsy	vs.	Polished, socially aware
Has vague and injudicious mind	vs.	Has exact, calculating mind
Gregarious, emotionally involved	vs.	Emotionally detached and disciplined
Spontaneous, natural	vs.	Artful
Has simple tastes	vs.	Aesthetically fastidious
Lacks insight	vs.	Insightful regarding self
Has blind trust in human nature	vs.	Smart, cuts corners

Box 9.1

There is one interesting twist to this profile: it was said of pianists that they fail to display any signs of creativity, and thus would not make effective composers. Whilst this group of organists would share this profile, nevertheless organists are traditionally expected to be expert improvisers. Many church-going readers might wish to challenge this, particularly those who have to endure the meaningless meanderings of some organists called upon to fill in during a hiatus in worship, and may wish to cite the research results here as evidence that they should not be allowed to do it! Nevertheless, the tradition persists and one only has to think of the great improviser–organists, Marcel Dupré and Pierre Cochereau, for example, whose improvisations were extraordinary feats of organ performance and creativity to realize that, at the height of organ-playing achievement, the two skills certainly appear to be related, at least for some.

Singers

The singer is, in many ways, quite unique within our discussions here. Singers have no visual or tangible instrument on which to focus their attentions, or towards which to direct the attention of an audience. They cannot 'hide' behind an instrument that offers a personality for them to project; there is no musical partnership that allows a sense of stability or companionship in performance. The singer's instrument is personal, invisible, and very complex, and in a performance it is the vocalist's personality that is presented, together with any vocal defects that are perceived as belonging directly to him or her. Singers cannot project their problems on to troublesome reeds, sticking pads, and other technological difficulties; there are different boundaries in operation. Whereas other instrumentalists have to be very aware of 'what is me' and 'what is not me', the singer has to take ownership of everything that occurs, including the defects of the 'instrument'.

Peter Piers, in talking about Kathleen Ferrier, the contralto, referred to this very aspect of singing, explaining that 'a violin is played by a person; a piano is played by a person; but a voice *is* a person' (Piers 1978). In view of this observation we might be forgiven for persisting with our notion about a link between extraversion and solo performance, not of course that the singer always performs solo, but that those in higher education and professional life are clearly expected to do so fairly frequently. Given the levels of self-assurance that appear to be necessary to undertake vocal performance either in lieder, oratorio, or opera, we might wish to speculate that singers would project a highly specific pattern of personality traits comprising, not only extraversion, but also adjustment, independence, and, possibly, sensitivity.

However, we should not overlook the potential sources of anxiety and stress in singing. Howard (1982) describes the wilderness of instructions and advice for singers—a bewildering and depressing picture of conflicting theories

... for instance, that voices are born and not made; that though born, they can at least be made over; that one should sing as little children scream, or as an adult whispers, or as a dog yawns; that a refined 'technique' is the singer's salvation; that one should dispense with all technique and sing 'naturally'; that speech and singing are the same and should be developed coordinately or one 'from' the other; that the two are entirely different and must be developed separately; that the singer must 'drive' the voice by a great effort of muscle and breath; that singing should be totally effortless and free of all tension. (p. 33)

That the processes of learning to sing are so subjective seems to encourage a plethora of contradictory theories, which may leave singers, at best bemused, and at worst, highly anxious and constantly unsure about whether they are performing correctly or doing themselves untold damage. Singing students may well find themselves moving from teacher to teacher in constant search for a 'guru' who, by use of a particular form of metaphor, somehow manages to 'speak their language'. This whole process may be very anxiety-provoking.

According to Howard, here is yet another cluster of conditions peculiar to the singer that we may interpret as a potential source of, if not tension, a high level of 'body sensitivity'. These issues are: firstly, that singers cannot hear themselves as others hear them; secondly, each sound they produce will be accompanied by a particular sensation; and, thirdly, singers have to learn to detect particular body sensations that connect with their more desirable sounds as, of course, identified by their teachers. At least, in Howard's view, all the vocal theorists, various schools of thought, and voice therapists are united on this. In this way we can begin to understand the nature of singers' dependence upon their teachers. Despite what was suggested above regarding extraversion, we might now suspect that singers need to give a particularly introverted attention to themselves. They may also require a special kind of sensitivity that allows them to perceive the interrelationships between their body sensations and the desirable qualities of their vocal tone.

In the light of the little research that has been published, certain aspects of these notions and speculations become clarified. Martin (1976) found his secondary school singers to be particularly extraverted on all four primary factors, although the level was higher in brass players. In my research I chose not to pursue a group of secondary school singers, the reason being that serious individual singing tuition, apart from that in choir schools, does not tend to start until later. There were, however, 58 student singers in the higher education group (36 per cent men and 64 per cent women), and a small number of professional singers (Kemp 1979, 1981c). The student singers upheld our initial idea that they would be extraverted and, like Martin's younger singers, demonstrated high levels on all the primary factors of extraversion: outgoingness (A+); surgency (F+); adventurousness (H+); and group dependency (Q2–). Unlike those of Martin, the extraversion of these student singers was *higher* than found in the brass playing group. As expected, independence also emerged highly significantly, the group showing distinct dominance (E+) and suspiciousness (L+) in addition, of course, to the F+ and H+ factors mentioned above. Finally, levels of pathemia were manifest in their high levels of sensitivity (I+) linked with factor A+ already identified.

As Figure 9.1 shows, in combination, these second-order factors present a very convincing picture of a well-integrated person, and, whilst the results with the professionals were not so extensive, they did confirm the students' level of extraversion (A+, F+, and H+). Viewed in its totality, the pattern of extraversion, independence, and pathemia suggests that the musician without an instrument appears to attract a very different type of person. Certainly, we have found that brass and keyboard players also tend to be extraverted (but at lower levels and on fewer factors). However, apart from extraversion, the singer exhibits significant independence, which these other types of musician do not demonstrate, and their high levels of sensitivity also serve to separate them from all other groups of musicians.

Perhaps then, we now have sufficient evidence on hand to be reasonably confident that extraversion is linked in some way to the capacity to perform solo. We should not, though, totally discount the interpretation of introversion in instrumentalists as being a reflection of the level of difficulty of their instruments. It is reasonable to adhere to the notion that the more extensive are the hours of confined practice, and the greater the level of technical difficulty of instruments, the more introverted will be the performer. Whether singers *do* practise for such long hours as, say string or woodwind players is debatable. Certainly, singers tend to be very concerned about protecting their voices from overuse and strain and, as a result, may not spend excessive hours in practice routines. However, these two explanations, one relating to long periods of secluded practice, the second to the demands of solo

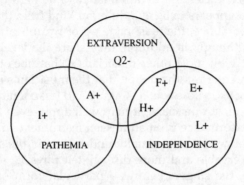

Figure 9.1 A model of the student singer's personality.

performance, may not operate in conflict; it may merely be that the two influences operate in opposite directions until an optimum and comfortable point on introversion–extraversion is attained.

All the research on singers cited here has dealt with singers as a composite group. In this connection, Wilson's (1984) research that set out to investigate whether personality differences would emerge in connection with high- and low-pitched voices is particularly apposite. As Wilson observed, tenors are often considered to be short, stocky, and broad-chested individuals in comparison with baritones and basses. Likewise, although less obviously, mezzo-sopranos and contraltos are generally thought to be taller than sopranos. These differences, Wilson considered, would also interrelate with other traits such as emotionality and sex-drive.

Having assembled the self-assessments from six groups of singers and two control groups, he found that all the singers were more extraverted than the controls; the sopranos and tenors emerging as the most extraverted. Furthermore, Wilson's work demonstrated a clear and consistent relationship between high- and low-pitched voices within each of the male and female clusters. For example, on emotionality, the sopranos emerged with the highest level, followed by the mezzos, and then the contraltos. A similar pattern revealed itself for the tenors, followed by progressively lower levels in the case of the baritones and basses. Other dimensions on which the same pattern occurred were aggression, unreliability, conceit, being difficult (as opposed to amenable), femininity, and libido. In comparison with the non-singing controls, the singers were, in addition to being less extraverted, more intelligent and modest. On most of the other characteristics, the controls were to be found within the middle of the range within their respective groups. As Wilson observes, there may well be hormonal factors operative in these results, not only in body typing, but also in temperament. Whilst some caution is necessary in interpreting results from self-assessment profiles, nevertheless there are certain interesting similarities with the other results cited here.

Finally, let us return to a topic discussed in Chapter 4, namely, that musicians tend to be characterized by a tendency to be high on pathemia. The singers' pathemia appears to be of a different kind from that discussed earlier. As mentioned above, theirs is made up of warmheartedness (A+) and sensitivity (I+), although, in addition, they share the levels of imagination (M+) in common with most other musicians. What does this suggest? We may well wish to entertain the notion that the musician's pathemia reflects a certain tendency to operate at a 'feelingful' and less cognitively sharp level. If this is true for most musicians, it may well apply even more strongly to singers whose performance is on an unseen instrument, an instrument that is felt and that cannot be conceptually understood in the same way as one that involves observable and more directly felt physical skills. In the way suggested above, the singer requires a particular form of sensitivity that allows him or her to develop an 'outgoing sensitivity', a sensitivity that, as we have seen, has to be shared totally with the teacher during the learning process. It is this form of sensitivity on which the singer appears to be dependent for ultimate success.

In connection with singers' sensitivity, we should not overlook the feeling–thinking dichotomy suggested by Jungian theories. This accords well with singers' more body-orientated modes of performance, involving a head to torso stance and, as a result, their functioning is more orientated towards the limbic system and less cerebral. It is often assumed by general musicianship teachers in higher education that singers often display lower levels of music reading skill in comparison with other musicians, and this, if true, may well be accountable in these terms. Another observation that can be made at this point relates to some research by Dunbar-Wells (in press) with singing teachers. In questioning them about their singing teaching methods she discovered a surprising inability to explain their teaching techniques and rationales in any clear fashion.

The singer's more feelingful approach to vocal production is exemplified by Licia Albanese's explanation

When you sing about being in love you must have love on your face. When you are angry you must have an angry face . . . You see, I think in terms of qualities. I feel I can see the tone. You have to treat one note with velvet cloth, another taffeta, another chiffon. I think very much in terms of texture. (Hines 1994, p. 21)

The main thrust of these findings are not without importance in education. Singers do appear to be amongst the most 'integrated' of all musicians in terms of personality development, as suggested by Figure 9.1. It would be reasonable, therefore, to claim a central place for singing in the school curriculum, leaving the more demanding of instruments for those children who are particularly temperamentally suited to pursue them.

Conductors

In a different sense, the conductor is also a musician without an instrument. Most, if not all, will have been instrumentalists who, by these means, will have first developed the ability to interpret the music of others. In conducting, though, he or she plays vicariously through the skills and musicianship of others, making demands in terms of an internalized vision of the piece— demands that are required to be communicated, sometimes verbally, frequently gesturally. In orchestral conducting, the internalized vision will be dependent upon extensive knowledge and experience gained through one's own playing, but also with working contact with other instrumentalists.

Having a well-internalized internal vision was presented in Chapter 2 as very much the hallmark of the introvert. It is the capacity to sustain a symbolic and imaginative internal existence in which art objects are cherished and kept alive through a process in which they are allowed to enter the unconscious where they continue to be 'worked upon'. As discussed in the earlier chapter, this appears to be a feature of most musicians. However, in the conductor, particularly if he or she is going to produce performances that reveal new insights, this internal process has to involve radical and particularly imaginative processes leading to insightful interpretations. In other words, there has to be something of the composer in the mind of the conductor, although, in the case of the latter, the creative processes have to operate within well-defined boundaries. This may result in the frequently observed levels of identification that occur between certain conductors and composers. For example, it is generally recognized that Klemperer was an outstanding conductor of Beethoven's and Mahler's works; and one might go a long way before bettering Colin Davis's recordings of the Sibelius symphonies; likewise Barenboim's interpretative skills in Mozart; and Simon Rattle's performances of twentieth century works of, say, Boulez and Tippett. In these and many other instances, it is as if the conductor so closely identifies with the thought processes of the composer that the work springs to life in new ways, with new revelations and depths of meaning as if, in some mystical way, the conductor acts as a kind of medium. Certainly there is no research that supports this kind of speculation, but the idea that music preferences reveal the personality of the perceiver may well be strongest in these very special relationships between conductors and composers.

The conductor's internal processes by which composers' works are rediscovered and reworked are, of course, only the first part of their work. Clearly, the matter of bringing a performance into being is dependent upon a responsive and skilled orchestra. But these things apart, the next aspect of the process is dependent upon the conductor's personality in projecting and articulating, in one manner or another, his or her internalized 'vision' of the piece. What conductors often find is that there is a limit to what can be described purely verbally during a rehearsal. There comes a point where interpretations need to be communicated non-verbally, taking the form of gesture and, sometimes, facial expression in which highly subtle feelings are articulated through expressive movements. The involvement of body movement in this form of music-making is significant. As we have observed earlier, the concept of pathemia appears to capture the notion of 'body-thinking', of the kind that has been considered of importance to both instrumentalists and singers. That sensitivity and imagination are linked to body feelingfulness appears to have even more significance in the case of the conductor. Every time a conductor mounts the rostrum we are able to witness in operation a process whereby his or her deeply internalized conception of a piece, perhaps even unconscious responses, are communicated to players in a gestural form of a kind not dissimilar to that adopted by dancers and actors. But the musician's introversion may well mean that this 'performance' is a well-controlled one, and there are many examples of the great conductors whose repertoire of gestures are kept well in check: Klemperer, Boult, Groves, and Boulez amongst them.

The process is a complex one: after all, there is no point in a conductor developing profound and deeply internalized interpretations and expressing these kinaesthetically, if the gestures are not understood by orchestras and choirs. In making a case for the structured teaching of conducting, Durrant (1994) cites Dickson's (1992) three-stage method of coaching conductors in the use of expressive gesture. Firstly, the body's responses to music are explored; secondly, these responses are conceptualized; and, thirdly, kinaesthetic skills are then applied to the processes of music making. In this way Dickson believes that the conductor's conceptualization of the music is enhanced, gestural techniques are improved, and better communication with performers is achieved.

Then, of course, there is the whole area of rehearsal management. Not only is it important to possess all the attributes alluded to here, but there are also all the organizational aspects of rehearsal taking, which make further demands upon the conductor. Orchestras are noted for the difficulties with which they can present conductors and, besides these more social considerations, there are all the pressures imposed upon conductors due to the expense and shortage of rehearsal time. Imposing one's own interpretation upon a group of individualistic types, many of whom will have played particular pieces under other conductors requesting alternative interpretations, and doing so within the shortest possible time make excessive demands upon the conductor of a very different kind. In this sense the conductor is more like a school teacher keeping a class of what may potentially be unruly types in some semblance of order. Certainly, it may not be an easy matter dealing with a group of musicians as diverse as those discussed in the last chapter. Treading a critical tight-rope, poised between the string players with low thresholds of arousal, and the very different temperaments of the brass players perhaps needing more flamboyant approaches, requires extreme levels of diplomacy and sensitivity. Much of what will be discussed in Chapter 12 in terms of class management and control might, therefore, be related to the conductor. Certainly, some who have written about the work of conductors have frequently stressed the importance of leadership qualities. Conductors such as Boult (1963) and Groves (1960) have emphasized the need for self-confidence, self-discipline, and control. Alternatively, Hindemith (1952) considered that a conductor's dominance was of paramount importance.

Whilst admitting that leadership qualities in different walks of life require different trait combinations, Cattell *et al.* (1970) suggested that extraversion, adjustment, and modest levels of cortertia characterize leaders generally (p. 244). In the absence of any published research on the conductor, we are left dependent here upon my own unpublished results (Kemp 1979). Those music students in higher education who regularly undertook conducting activities were indeed much more extraverted right across the board of traits: outgoing (A+); surgent (F+); adventurous (H+); and group-dependent (Q2–). They were also significantly adjusted, emerging as more emotionally stable (C+), self-assured (O–), and relaxed (Q4–) than those who did not undertake conducting engagements. A clear manifestation of independence was also apparent, the conductors demonstrating dominance (E+) alongside the F+ and H+ factors that overlap with extraversion. One interesting similarity that conductors appear to have with pianists in this study is their tendency to display leadership qualities. Whether this indicates a natural inclination for pianists to be temperamentally suited to conducting remains unclear. As we would have expected, the cortertia claimed by Cattell to characterize the natural leader failed to appear in either the conductors or pianists.

As we have noted in earlier discussions, it is important to bear in mind the baseline used for comparison purposes. Indeed, it is correct to maintain that conductors appear to be more extraverted, adventurous, and adjusted in comparison with non-conducting musicians. However, we need to bear in mind that conductors are still musicians and that their personalities still reveal aspects of the musician's personality. In discussing this point, Pollack (1991) points out that the more extraverted conductor will engage and interact more readily with an orchestra, even to the extent of being open to suggestions. On the other hand, the more introverted, who keep their evaluating and critical processing internal, run the risk of not giving sufficient feedback to the players. In terms of the general population norms, conductors could be described as *ambivert*, displaying introverted aloofness (A–), only marginal surgency (F+) and adventurousness (H+), and extraverted group dependency (Q2+). On the other hand, they can still be viewed as anxious in comparison with the general population. Their independence, of course, does not conflict with the musician's profile for, as we have observed at various points and will do again in Chapter 11, independence appears to be related to manifestations of 'higher' musical abilities.

This discussion would not be complete without acknowledging that conductors may be divisible into those more comfortable with orchestras and those more comfortable with choruses. Several, of course, such as Colin Davis, Solti, and Barenboim, appear equally at home with both. Whilst having no evidence for this, we might wish to speculate that those more attracted to working with the more introverted orchestral types might themselves be more predominantly introverted. Conversely, those who prefer working with the more extraverted members of choral societies might tend to reveal more evidence of extraversion. After all, with these groups tending to operate at different thresholds of arousal, those sharing the same levels might be expected to communicate more efficiently without either inducing too much anxiety or, on the other hand, understimulating those they conduct.

Summary

Unfortunately, rather less information is available concerning the personalities of non-orchestral musicians, and we are largely left to speculate about the fragments of evidence that are available. It might be thought, for example, that they would be more radical and imaginative given their greater freedom from the conductor's baton, apart, that is, from any choral work that they engage in.

It is often thought that keyboard players would be solitary types in that their chosen instruments are more musically self-contained. However, what is suggested by the available research is quite the opposite: pianists and organists appear distinctly *extraverted*, and this is indicated by those very traits displayed by most musicians in the opposite direction. In other words it appears that pianists' and organists' warmheartedness and group-dependency temperamentally separate them from other types of musician. Even brass players, who are also group-dependent, do not display any suggestion of warmheartedness. What also distinguishes keyboard players from all other adult musicians are their higher levels of conscientiousness and self-sentiment coupled with their distinct conservatism and lack of anxiety.

The only characteristic that emerges as distinguishing organists from pianists is their shrewdness, which Cattell more fully describes as embracing a capacity to acquire precise technical skills and high levels of mental alertness. These qualities may be seen as invaluable for the development of the complex techniques of organ playing. Whilst the reader needs to be cautious about claiming too much from one set of results, what is particularly surprising is that these keyboard players do not appear to be temperamentally suited to creative or imaginative activity. This is surprising in view of the common belief that composers frequently come from a keyboard playing background.

Because singers are musicians without objective and tangible instruments, their performing orientation is predominantly body focused. This appears to reveal itself in their higher levels of extraversion and their sensitivity and independence in comparison with all other musicians . Singers can therefore be perceived as particularly integrated types, possessing the necessary composure and 'togetherness' for their processes of solo performance. At the same time they tend to display a distinct perceptual style indicated by their high levels of pathemia. This more feelingful than cerebral style may well have important implications for the ways in which singers are taught, and may account for subtle differences in their responses to more academic forms of education.

As one might expect conductors also emerge as extraverted and this features as a part of their well-adjusted and independent outlook. This kind of temperament is in line with previous research on leadership qualities in various fields. However, traits that perhaps might be considered to be significant for the conductor's work, such as radicalism, imagination, and sensitivity, do not emerge in the research.

TEN

Musicians in popular fields

Introduction

In the absence of a large body of personality research on musicians working at the popular end of the music profession, an important aspect of this chapter will be a return to those notions, entertained in Chapter 7, that relate to the personality characteristics of listeners' different music preferences. At that point we were able to consider ways in which the main dimensions of personality, extraversion, neuroticism, and psychoticism appear to be linked with listeners' attraction to various popular music styles. Bearing those observations in mind, it would be reasonable to frame hypotheses that allow us to explore the notion that those who spend their lives playing these different types of music through choice would also exhibit these features. After all, it would appear reasonable to speculate that those who play certain styles of music do so as a direct result of the impact that the music made upon them initially as listeners.

We must, however, bear in mind that musicians will often need to take work that is on offer or becomes available to them, and this may well serve to blur the boundaries between the two kinds of musician in personality terms. In those cases where classical performers are prepared to move over into the more popular arena, purely for the purpose of making a living rather than choice, it is conceivable that such enforced transitions might result in generating certain levels of anxiety and stress. However, working in the worlds of jazz and rock may be less accessible on technical grounds for some classically trained instrumentalists, and conceivably less acceptable to others.

It has, therefore, to be borne in mind that many musicians working in popular music will have received a formal music training and, because of this, may well still exhibit those temperamental characteristics that can be interpreted as reflecting the impress of that type of training. Others, performing in heavy metal groups, for instance, are less likely to have come through this route, and may exhibit very different combinations of traits. This might appear to be particularly true when one bears in mind the more anti-social and delinquent connotations of heavy metal and punk rock of the kind discussed in Chapter 7. However, in the absence of any sizeable body of research with performers of popular music, we are left to speculate about all the possible influences on their personality development of a kind that we have already considered in the context of other kinds of musician. Quite apart from the impress of receiving a formal professional training, other aspects of instrumental choice, musical preferences, life-style, and the nature of the working environment are all likely to impact upon the popular musician in the same kind of way. Let us take a look at the three main dimensions of personality that have received a small amount of investigation in the context of those musicians working in the popular field. In doing this, we might expect to develop insights into very different types of musician.

Extraversion

Perhaps the most prevailing notion about musicians working in the popular field is that they are all extraverted types, the common view being that they carry out their work in clubs and other environments that offer considerable opportunities for social interaction. However, we should bear in mind the not insignificant amounts of studio recording work that are also often undertaken by these kinds of musician. But perhaps one of the most obvious links with extraversion, particularly in the context of what was discussed in Chapter 7, relates to music preferences. Evidence was cited that suggested fairly conclusively that extraverts tend to be drawn to those types of music that tend to appeal instantly, that meet immediate needs and offer fairly short-term rewards. In contrast, it is the introverted listener who selects less accessible styles, and who is prepared to make all the necessary effort in the process of understanding it. Extraverts actively seek out styles of music in which they can become totally engaged, but the engagement is more likely to be orientated to a global perception of pieces of music, rather than particular aspects identified as a result of any process of intellectual analysis. However, this is not to suggest for one moment that, merely because certain styles may be classified as 'easy listening', they necessarily require lower levels of technical proficiency in the players.

It has been suggested that the music listening habits of extraverts reflect their active seeking out of high levels of arousal. Because of this, it is reasonable to suspect that extraverts will prefer the high levels of volume, and vigorous, rhythmic, if not aggressive styles frequently found in pop and rock music. In this context Dollinger's (1993) findings are of considerable importance to us because he is one of the few researchers who particularly studied the interrelationships between personality and preferences for a wide selection of musical styles, including hard rock, pop, and jazz. During this work he showed that jazz lovers are, indeed, characterized by their general extraverted temperament. In contrast, those who prefer hard rock are more characterized by a very particular aspect of extraversion (as measured on the 'big five'), excitement-seeking.

Wills and Cooper's (1988) research set out specifically to study the effects of work pressure on a group of 70 musicians working in popular fields, including jazz, rock, pop, and dance music. The work of this group would have included a wide variety of live engagements and recording sessions in all manner of environments from theatre orchestras, ballrooms, and jazz clubs, to studio work accompanying singing groups on television and radio. Disappointingly, this group as a whole, emerged with fairly unremarkable scores on extraversion, leaving us to conclude that this was a fairly homogeneous group in terms of this dimension and its links with the playing of various instruments. However, we might be led to consider whether, within this group, the jazz performers' extraversion was being offset by the introversion of some of the other players who reflected a more conventional musical training. In contrast, Dyce and O'Connor (1994), who adopted an inventory measuring the 'big five', found their group comprised mostly of rock players to be significantly high on extraversion as well as arrogant and dominant in comparison with student norms. In addition, they were characterized by their openness to experience (a big five factor independent of extraversion), which, as we have already noted, Dollinger (1993) discovered to be linked to preferences for jazz as well as soul/rhythm and blues, and classical styles.

Neuroticism and stress

The 70 musicians studied by Wills and Cooper were found, in comparison to non-musicians, to be distinctly neurotic, and this they interpreted as an outcome of the precarious life-styles that the popular musician tends to lead. As they point out, a considerable amount of this performing work is carried out in the evenings, thus depriving these musicians of engaging in leisure activities alongside those in nine-to-five employment. In addition, the enforced and inevitable separation from partners and families, sometimes for extended periods, would also tend to generate stress and anxiety. Neither, as a rule, do those working in the popular music fields enjoy job security, pensions, and other benefits. Also, it is frequently the case that their work arrangements can be terminated or cancelled with little prior notice, very much adding to their sense of stress and feelings of being undervalued. However, it should be kept in mind that neuroticism, or anxiety, as we saw in Chapter 5, is a feature that tends to manifest itself in the profiles of most musicians.

The important question here is whether stress can be seen as any more prevalent in popular musicians than in others and, if so, whether there are specific sources of stress that are peculiar to them in terms of their work demands and life-style. Unfortunately, due to the absence of any

specifically comparative research, there are no data which can shed light on
this question. It is clear from Wills and Cooper's (1988) research that these
musicians are also subject to some of the same kinds of stress that other
musicians experience. For example, they appear to impose upon themselves
high standards of performance in a similar way to other musicians; an observation that was made in Chapter 5. Making this very point, Wills and
Cooper cite statements from popular musicians such as:

If you've got high standards, you're trying to keep up to them all the time.

You have your own standard to keep up to, and you know that all eyes are on you.
I get upset if I think I've made a mess of something.

I made a positive decision to do gigs that I would find creative and musically reward-
ing. It's hard facing up to shortcomings in your playing. I'm very ambitious on a creative level. I don't want financial reward. I'm always setting goals for myself.

I don't want fame and fortune, but I want a good reputation in the music business.
There's a constant pressure to keep up your standard. I won't play music that's really
bad. It ruins your reputation. (p. 45)

In this sense popular musicians appear very similar to their orchestral counterparts in the way that they seem to drive and pressurize themselves
towards high standards of performance. As we saw in Chapter 5, this search
for perfection can be very intertwined with their perceptions of their own
self-worth and, if taken to excess, can amount to a very damaging form of
self-punishment.

   This may interact with another distinct source of stress that may well
prove to be particularly prevalent in popular musicians. This relates to what
they consider to be other people's low estimation and devaluing of them.
Wills and Cooper cite musicians who offer insights into the different forms
that this may take.

Most people regard musicians as one step up the 'social ladder' from rapists and
muggers, and it's this 'alienation' from the non-musician that I believe creates all the
problems.

There's a fair amount of hatred of musicians by club owners, because they have to
pay Musicians' Union rates.

The talents and abilities that jazz musicians have are used in musical situations that
are far beneath their capabilities, and this causes tremendous resentment and frustration.

The state of the management/agency situation is scandalous . . . It's a total fiasco in
which the musician *again* bears the brunt, and which alienates him even further. In
addition, robbery within these areas, and the record industry, is actually *legal*. How
else can a musician feel but downtrodden. (pp. 46, 50–1)

   The musicians' commitment to music as an inherent part of their self-
concept formation, Pruett (1991) has suggested, frequently appears to result

in feelings of grandiosity and omnipotence. The musician becomes increasingly 'hooked' on peoples' adulation and admiration and will strive all the more to earn it. However, when this does not occur and in those circumstances where the musician feels something of a social outcast through being devalued or exploited, this may well result in feelings of alienation, resentment, and stress. The popular musician may feel very acutely that in the eyes of other musicians, as well as the public at large, the status of their gig and commercial work is rock-bottom despite all the efforts they may make to maintain their high personal musical standards. In Cattell's terms, we may suspect that they suffer particularly low levels of ego strength.

However, in apparent contrast, certain manifestations of arrogance were found by Dyce and O'Connor in their rock and country groups, although this arrogance was found to be linked to distinct levels of neuroticism. Their explanation of the neuroticism focuses on these groups' ever-changing working environments as well as the unstable nature of their employment. Clearly, the precarious nature of the musicians' work in the popular fields is a key issue. Ironically, this can frequently result in problems of work overload. As one of Wills and Cooper's musicians commented 'It's a stress when, if you've been working hard, you have to decide whether to turn gigs down to get a rest. You're worried that if you do turn gigs down, people won't ring again' (p. 48). Because engagements and gigs do not necessarily occur regularly, the fear of too little work and the thought that the telephone might cease ringing may result in players tending to overwork themselves by accepting additional engagements during already busy periods. Thus many of these people, probably in common with freelance musicians generally, can suffer from entrapment in a dilemma in which they find themselves fluctuating between these two sources of stress. However, in common with our discussions in Chapter 5, Dyce and O'Connor also maintained that a certain degree of neuroticism can make a positive contribution to a performance. The mental tension possessed by the neurotic may enable him or her to perform with a greater sense of passion (p. 172). However, our alternative explanations outlined above should not be overlooked.

With this kind of thought in mind we might care to note that the group of popular musicians studied by Dyce and O'Connor was made up of 48 guitarists, 44 bass players, and 46 drummers. It would have been interesting to know whether the high neuroticism that they reported for the total group was equally shared by each of the instrumental subgroups. Wills and Cooper's (1988) results suggested that neuroticism was particularly high in their guitarists, with pianists and trombone players not far behind. Whilst there is little in our earlier discussions that supports the appearance of neuroticism in these particular instrumentalists, nevertheless we might be led to speculate whether these musicians are revealing temperamental characteristics that might result in a penchant for more aggressive musical styles and that overtly express elements of conflict. As Chapter 7 indicated, particularly in connection with Payne's work, neurotics tend to prefer more emotionally charged music in which 'abnormal' and anxiety-provoking connections can be made by listeners and, presumably, performers. In other words, we might wish to speculate that the effective performance of those styles and types of music that we have observed as being attractive to the neurotic listener is dependent upon this aspect of the performer's temperament.

Psychoticism

Another feature of the musicians that emerged in Wills and Cooper's (1988) research related to their high levels of psychoticism. This is of particular interest to us because the trait has not so far featured in the personalities of any other musicians cited in this book, although, of course, in Chapter 8 some lower sensitivity was generally found in brass players. It may therefore be reasonable to consider the possibility that those who are drawn, or at least prepared, to play the various styles of popular music for a living are not only characterized by a reduction in the high levels of sensitivity we find in most groups of musicians, but that sensitivity tends to be replaced by a distinct level of tough-mindedness. In other words, the broader factor of pathemia that was noted in Chapter 6 as being as feature of most musicians is not revealed in those working in the popular field. However, we should be cautious about forming any conclusions about this as none of the research cited in this chapter made use of Cattell's inventories. Eysenck (1992b) has described his concept of psychoticism as a dimension that takes us progressively through aspects of criminality, impulsiveness, hostility, aggression, and so on through to schizophrenia. At the opposite pole of high empathy, he suggests that people are conventional, socialized, and altruistic. Although the attentive reader will have noted Eysenck's placement of conventionality versus creativity as a direct reversal of what we might have expected from a more Cattellian view, space does not allow us the opportunity to pursue this here.

On further investigation, Wills and Cooper discovered that the particularly high levels of psychoticism were, in fact, related to guitarists, drummers, bass players, and trumpeters, and the lowest levels belonged to the trombonists. Whilst caution is also called for due to the small numbers involved in these groups, we might wish to speculate about these patterns, particularly in terms of these instrumentalists' counterparts in the world of orchestral playing. For example, although in Chapter 8 we certainly witnessed lower levels of sensitivity in brass players generally, no evidence of lower sensitivity in bass players emerged. We are therefore left to conclude that either Wills and Cooper's musicians were somewhat unrepresentative of their instrumental types, or that these musicians' involvement in more popular musical styles was exercising a powerful impact upon their personality typing.

At this point, then, we may choose to return to our earlier discussions about preferences for musical styles. Certainly, guitarists and drummers in pop and rock groups appear to assume a 'hard' exterior. As we noted in Chapter 7, Rawlings *et al.* (1995) had found those listeners who claimed to prefer hard rock to be higher on psychoticism compared with those who preferred dance music and easy listening. In generalizing from their results, they concluded that all musical styles that can be perceived as being 'hard' or 'harsh' as well as dissonant are likely to attract psychotic types. This would appear to be particularly true of punk rock with its anti-social and aggressive connotations which we might well expect to attract more psychotic types, particularly in view of Eysenck's notion of 'criminality' within the psychoticism factor. Support for the notion that guitarists and drummers spend a considerable proportion of their time playing for pop gigs is offered by Wills and Cooper. However, it should be pointed out that these findings relate to a much wider sample than those used in that phase of their research that had pursued personality differences. In the light of the trombone players' low psychoticism, further tentative support for the notion that psychoticism is negatively linked to easier listening interestingly is also offered by Wills and Cooper by showing that trombonists working in this field are more likely to make their living playing for commercial sessions. Clearly, there are far fewer openings for them in pop or rock.

Types of work

An interesting outcome of Wills and Cooper's (1988) extensive work in this field, which would, otherwise, be virtually unresearched, is their description of those musicians who undertake various forms of work in the popular music field. On the basis that it is the work environment that strongly influences the person's ability to adjust and feel secure and fulfilled, these will be briefly reviewed here. However, it will be noted that general personality differences within these groups were not investigated.

Firstly, Wills and Cooper found that those who perform in the jazz idiom most closely exhibited the kind of temperament found in the 'sensitive, dedicated artist', in other words, possibly those working in the field of orchestral playing. Performers of jazz appear to identify more strongly with their work and receive enjoyment and fulfilment from it. Perhaps because of its importance to them, the work is especially stressful for them, and they appear to suffer from anxiety more than the other musicians in the popular field do. In particular, Wills and Cooper reported a tendency for them to become stressed by anything that frustrated their work, very much disliking the artificial atmosphere of the recording studio and over-amplified music.

They found this group to perform at the lowest levels on the Type A1 score (the most extreme form of Type A coronary-prone behaviour), interpreting this as reflecting the group's greater 'inner-orientation' and lack of interest in achieving material success. This is what we might expect in a musician who needs to develop the kind of creative improvisatory skills necessary in jazz playing. In common with the composer, we might expect those skilled in the sophisticated forms of improvisation found in some forms of jazz to exhibit high levels of independence and pathemia. In the absence of research we can only speculate about this.

On the other hand, the pop/gig musicians were characterized more than any other type of musician by their need to be successful in the commercial world of pop music. Wills and Cooper found that the highest stressors for this group related to the general atmosphere of hostile competitiveness. They tend to clash with those with whom they work, experiencing potential conflict particularly with those types of recording managers and agency executives who have little understanding of their high musical ideals. Career management was important to them, and confrontations with music management were also identified by them as stressful as, indeed, were any conflicts and clashes that occurred within their working relationships. The group also experienced problems in handling the kinds of pressures involved in gaining recognition and fame. This was experienced by particular members of famous bands who felt under extreme pressure to maintain their performing standards in order not to 'let the side down'. Wills and Cooper found this group to be the most prone to health problems, suffering feelings of inertia and depression and, as a result, likely to resort to drug-taking.

Commercial gig musicians, Wills and Cooper found, were the poor relations of the popular music world, earning the lowest wages and picking up odd bits of work wherever it could be found. They identified them as the most highly stressed of popular musicians, experiencing problems with instruments that they could not afford to maintain properly, and suffering anxiety due to the demands of those instrumental parts that they found more difficult to read and play. They tended to suffer from psychosomatic ill health and appeared to achieve little real enjoyment in their work.

Wills and Cooper claimed that pop/session players shared some of the aspects of the pop and commercial/gig musicians, standing midway between them on several characteristics. They were the second highest paid, and their most common stressor was the maintenance of their performing standards. As Wills and Cooper suggest, the world of the recording studio is a highly competitive one, time is short and expensive, and there is enormous pressure to 'get it right' within the shortest possible time scale. As a result, they found this group most frequently resorting to drug taking—cannabis, amphetamines, and cocaine.

The commercial/session musician was found to be the most secure and least stressed of all the groups. Wills and Cooper observed that they were rather older than the others, and tended to live a more secure kind of life— frequently married with responsibilities for children. The greatest stressor for them was the sheer amount of sound amplification in the music they were required to play and, although they did not resort as a rule to drug-taking, they were heavy consumers of alcohol and tranquillizers. The competitive nature of their work was, perhaps, reflected in the high incidence of Type A personalities in this group. However, Wills and Cooper also observed that, in a sense, these types tended to compete against themselves as much as others, imposing upon themselves high personal goals.

Finally, Wills and Cooper suggest that the commercial/residency musicians can be perceived as being one rung up the ladder from the commercial gig musician on the basis that their longer-term residencies offer them a fair degree of stability of employment. Nevertheless, musicians in this group tend to receive little in the way of job satisfaction, and yet, curiously, their greatest stressor is the maintenance of the high musical standards that they set themselves. They appear to resort to smoking and, as Wills and Cooper remark, this may possibly be due to the higher boredom factor.

In summary, perhaps it is important for us to highlight, once again, the notion that there may well be two broad types of musician embedded within research of this kind. Firstly, there will be the classically trained musician who, for one reason or another, has taken the decision to work in the popular field, making all the necessary adjustments that this would have involved. These adjustments of life-style, working environment, working colleagues, and musical styles might well be reflected in certain necessary adjustments to these musicians' personality. For example, although they may well relate to a description not too far removed from that of the musician as described in our earlier chapters, one might expect them to reveal adjustments of the kind discussed here that would allow them to operate in a hard, commercial, and highly competitive world.

The second type of musician may not have come through the formal training route, and may, as a result, have more experience of the world outside music. They may be more extraverted, not only because they have been less dependent upon others, making their own way into the profession by sheer effort, but also because they may not have spent such long hours in secluded practice routines as have other musicians. In fact, of course, many of their skills may have been developed in group enterprise. In some ways they may be more musically spontaneous, less rigid in the musical procedures that they are prepared to adopt. On the other hand, they may lack the sensitivity of the average musician and, as a result, may be prepared to perform more exaggerated, aggressive, and highly amplified musical styles. The reader will be aware of the wealth of research hypotheses for further research lingering here.

Summary

There are several complex issues relating to the study of the musician working in popular music fields, and several of these we are left to speculate about due to the dearth of research in this area. Certainly, research into music listener preferences might offer suggestions for research hypotheses: for example, do the players of heavy metal and rock share the same kinds of trait combinations as their audiences? There may be several reasons why this may not be so. Musicians are not always able to choose the kind of work they accept and, besides, they may have worked their way through music college, developing the same high levels of performing skill as their orchestral colleagues. As a result, they may well be expected to share the same kind of basic temperament.

With these thoughts in mind we might expect to discover evidence of poor adjustment in some of the groups of popular musicians. Unfortunately, there is little comparative research that directly pursues questions relating to temperamental differences between musicians working in these two very contrasting worlds. The small amount of published work available focuses upon the different types of musician working within the world of popular music performance.

Despite the fact that listeners to popular musical styles, particularly jazz and rock, appear to be extraverted, surprisingly little hard evidence for higher levels of extraversion is forthcoming for these types of musician. Whilst some research suggests that these jazz and rock players are extraverted in comparison with student norms, this may tell us very little in the light of students' well-known levels of introversion. Other research indicates that drummers and guitarists, those perhaps most likely to play pop and rock, are the most extraverted in this field.

Neuroticism and stress appear to characterize the popular musician as much as their classical counterparts, and this is interpreted as an outcome of their precarious life-style: job insecurity, separation from home and family, and so on. What they also appear to have in common is their tendency to impose upon themselves the same high performing standards, perhaps in order to develop their feelings of self-esteem. On the other hand, some members of this group of musicians may be sensitive to the kinds of exploitation that they may suffer, revealing low self-esteem as a result, and perceiving their work as being of low status. As might have been expected, psychoticism appears high in drummers, guitarists, and trumpeters, and this manifestation may relate to the hard and harsh musical styles engaged in by these instrumentalists.

It appears that those musicians working in the field of popular music, whether it be playing jazz, pop, or commercial styles, and either as gig or session players, or in residence, reveal contrasting levels of anxiety and stress. These levels may be directly caused by differences in job security,

pay, pressure, status, working relationships, all making an impact on players' sense of well-being, job satisfaction, and dedication, and physical and
psychological health.

ELEVEN

Composers

Introduction

Throughout the chapters of this book the musician has been described as a special kind of creative person: one who possesses the temperament conducive to the performing function of bringing compositions to new life through the processes of interpretation. But, of course, this act of creativity, hopefully developed in all performing musicians throughout their education and training, can be viewed as being totally dependent upon the higher-order creativity of the composer. It is the composer's creative endeavours that stimulate the creativity in performers, mobilizing their sensitivity and imagination through the impact of the composer's creative energy embodied within a work. Through the act of interpretation a process of re-creation occurs in which a performer may leave his or her personal imprint upon the music, within the structures delimited by the composer. Similarly, listeners may also engage in a somewhat similar, but sometimes less disciplined process in which they make personal interpretations through their own perceptual processes and by projecting upon the music certain symbolic responses. Unlike those of the performer, the listener's interpretations may remain personal and totally private, and may not be subject to any public scrutiny or social sharing.

The composer then is often viewed as the musician *par excellence*, and, certainly within the literature of music, the preponderance of biographical study of composers' lives and work vouches for the attention we are prepared to give them, and the pedestal on which we are prepared to place them. These kinds of attitudes towards composers are more predominant in Western culture and may also relate to the rather romanticized view of the creative artist of earlier times. In other cultures where less emphasis is perhaps placed upon the new and the innovative, the notion of the composer as a specialist who drives the 'world of music' does not occur. Traditionally, the study of Western music has largely consisted of the study of the significant and outstanding compositions of a relatively small number of people who have come to be considered exceptionally talented and whose music has stood the test of time. Composers are revered, their significant works continue to inspire new generations; and their profound compositions touch people, even to the extent of 'calling' them as in vocation, to a life-long dedication to music.

The research discussed in the following sections develops a view of the composer as a special kind of musician who possesses particular abilities that are reflected in exceptional levels of certain traits of personality. In many cases these traits are also found in other musicians but at more modest levels. This is a very different stance from the one taken by writers such as George Bernard Shaw (1962) who, holding the orchestral musician in low esteem, was critical of 'muddled headed people who imagine that every man who can play a string of notes written down by Mozart or Bach must have the heart and mind of Mozart or Bach'. Performers, he maintained, need not be able to make any distinction between Beethoven and Brahms any more than a compositor makes between Shakespeare and Tennyson (pp. 111–12). Such a jaundiced view of the orchestral player may possibly reveal just as much about G.B.S. as about the state of London's orchestras at the turn of the century.

Disposition towards creativity

The enormous proliferation of research into personality and creativity that mushroomed throughout the 1960s and 70s, particularly in America, was founded upon the belief that the study of personality would unlock the door to our understanding of the nature of creative talent perhaps just as effectively as the study of abilities. Whilst space does not allow any detailed review of this body of literature, the names of Barron and MacKinnon require mentioning as researchers whose work exercised an important impact upon this field for many years. Several of these studies involving various creative groups support the view that they are particularly endowed with the aspects of personality described in the earlier chapters of this book. For example, in her summary of research with creative scientists, Roe (1961), another key researcher in the field, described them as

. . . independent and self-sufficient with regard to perception, cognition and behavior . . . they have high dominance; they have high autonomy; they are bohemian or radical; they are not subject to group standards and control; they are highly ego-centric . . . They have strong egos . . . less compulsive superegos than others . . . They have no feelings of guilt about the independence of thought and action mentioned above. They have strong control of their impulses. Their interpersonal relations are generally of low intensity. They are reported to be ungregarious, not talkative . . . There is an apparent tendency to femininity in highly original men, and to masculinity in highly original women, but this may be a cultural interpretation of the generally increased sensitivity of the men and the intellectual capacity and interests of the women . . . They show much stronger preoccupation with things and ideas than with people. (p. 458)

My own review of a large body of research that had used Cattell's 16PF with a wide variety of creative groups generally showed them to be introverted, independent, sensitive, imaginative, radical, and expedient (Kemp 1979). The picture with regard to anxiety is a little more contentious and, as we shall observe later, appears to be more associated with creativity in the arts than in the sciences. This raises the question as to whether anxiety is an inherent component of artistic existence, as discussed in Chapter 5, or whether it is more related to manifestations of high levels of creativity.

Composers' characteristics viewed through Cattell's factors

Some time ago I undertook a small pilot study that attempted to identify the temperamental requirements of performance and composing. I adopted groups of student composers and performers as well as a third group of students who claimed that they were neither interested in music nor creative (Kemp 1971). Intergroup comparisons revealed that the ability to compose music appeared to be significantly linked to self-sufficiency (Q2+), and expediency (G–), and what Cattell called 'subjectivity'—a combination of imagination (M+) and radicalism (Q1+). The comparison between the performers and the group of non-musicians, on the other hand, suggested that sensitivity (I+), imagination (M+), self-sufficiency (Q2+), and ergic tension (Q4+) were more linked to performing aspects of musicianship. When these results are seen diagrammatically (Figure 11.1), the extent to which the composers differ from the performers can be seen as being roughly of the same order as that by which the performers differ from the non-musicians. This would seem to suggest to us that those factors that separate the performers and composers (a composers' profile) are the same factors that separate the performers and non-musicians (a musicianship profile). As Figure 11.1 suggests, the only factors that depart from this pattern are expediency (G–), which characterizes the composers, and relative conscientiousness (G+), which is demonstrated by the performers. Similarly, ergic tension (Q4+), the most important element of anxiety, appears to be connected with performance, the composers emerging with somewhat lower levels. The outcome of this small study therefore suggested that it might not, after all, be possible to distinguish a specific set of creativity correlates that are separate from those of performance. In other words, those that appear to be connected with musical creativity also seem to be associated with the performing temperament or, more specifically, with the imaginative processes involved with interpretation. However, as pointed out earlier, the differences between the composers and the performers, being of the same order as those between the performers and the non-musicians, indicate that the temperamental requirements of composition make serious and additional demands upon the individual over and above those of performance.

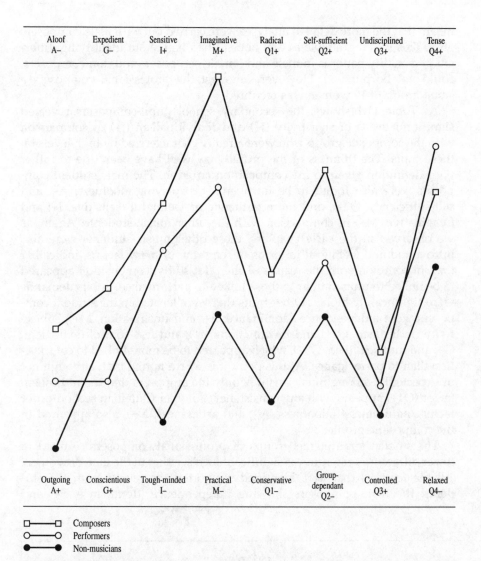

| Aloof
A– | Expedient
G– | Sensitive
I+ | Imaginative
M+ | Radical
Q1+ | Self-sufficient
Q2+ | Undisciplined
Q3+ | Tense
Q4+ |

| Outgoing
A+ | Conscientious
G+ | Tough-minded
I– | Practical
M– | Conservative
Q1– | Group-
dependant
Q2– | Controlled
Q3+ | Relaxed
Q4– |

☐———☐ Composers
○———○ Performers
●———● Non-musicians

Figure 11.1 Personality differences between student composers, performers, and non-musicians. (Data from Kemp 1979, 1981b.)

Later, I was able to return to the same kind of question, not only in connection with students in higher education but also with professional composers (Kemp 1981b). As in the earlier study, inclusion in the group of student-composers was dependent upon them pursuing composition seriously as a first study. The professionals were all members of the Composers' Guild of Great Britain. Amongst the schoolchildren, those who claimed to compose seriously were selected for inclusion in the criterion group. As in the pilot study, the dearth of female composers in higher education at that time meant that the more detailed analyses were carried out with male composers only. This was regrettable as any hopes I had had about identifying different personality patterns in male and female composers and non-composers, could not be pursued. However, amongst the professional composers a small group of 10 women was recruited.

As Table 11.1 shows, the secondary school pupil-composers revealed significant levels of sensitivity (I+) and individualism (J+) in comparison with the composite group who were already characterized by high levels on these traits. The thinness of the profile may well have been due to rather poor definition given to the composition criterion. The male student-composers were also found to be introverted (displaying aloofness, A–; and self-sufficiency, Q2+), and more pathemic or feelingful (sensitive, I+; and imaginative, M+) in comparison with the other music students. Again, as we observed in the early chapters, these other music students were also introverted and feelingful in terms of the same primary factors, indicating that, in common with the results of the pilot study, composition appeared to be linked to traits similar to those linked to performance, but its demands were significantly higher. Other traits that were located in the student composers were independence (dominance, E+; and imagination, M+), subjectivity (radicalism, Q1+; and imagination, M+), and less control (expedient, G–; and undisciplined, Q3–), which appeared to be more linked to composition than to performance. At this point it is worth noting that, although not unexpectedly, among musicians it is only in composers that the radicalism factor (Q1+) appears with any consistency. Another Cattellian second-order factor, 'naturalness' (aloofness, A–; and artlessness, N–), also appeared in the composers' profile.

The smaller sizes of the groups of professional composers resulted in fewer differences emerging at significant levels, either in the men or women. All the features that *were* identified supported the results with the students: the male composers showing independence (dominance, E+; and

FACTOR Q1		
Low score CONSERVATISM Q1–	versus	High score RADICALISM Q1+
Respecting established ideas	vs.	Experimenting
Tolerant of traditional difficulties	vs.	Liberal
Inclined to moralize	vs.	Free-thinking

Box 11.1

Table 11.1 Summary of research on composers

Researcher	Type of group	16 PF primary factors *										
		A	B	E	G	I	J	M	N	Q1	Q2	Q3
Kemp (1979)	Secondary school composers					I+	J+					
Kemp (1971)	Higher education male student composers				G-			M+		Q1+	Q2+	
Kemp (1981b)	Higher education male student composers	A-		E+	G-	I+		M+	N-	Q1+	Q2+	Q3-
Kemp (1981b)	Male professional composers		B+	E+	G-			M+				
Kemp (1981b)	Female professional composers			E+							Q2+	

* A-, aloofness; B+, high intelligence; E+, dominance; G-, expediency; I+, sensitivity; J+, individualism; M+, imagination; N-, naïveté; Q1+, radicalism; Q2+, self-sufficiency; Q3-, low self-sentiment.

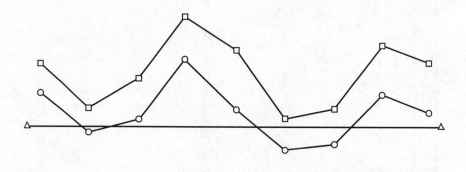

Aloof A–	Dominant E+	Expedient G–	Sensitive I+	Imaginative M+	Naïve N–	Radical Q1+	Self-sufficient Q2+	Undisciplined Q3–

Outgoing A+	Submissive E–	Conscientious G+	Tough-minded I–	Practical M–	Astute N+	Conservative Q1–	Group-dependent Q2–	Controlled Q3+

□———□ Composers
○———○ Performers
△———△ Student norms

Figure 11.2 Personality differences between male frofessional composers, performers, and student norms. (Data from Kemp 1979, 1981b.)

imagination, M+) and lack of discipline (G–) along with the addition of higher intelligence (B+). The female composers supported the male independence (E+): they also shared the students' introversion (self-sufficiency, Q2+) which the men did not. Figures 11.2 and 11.3 show in graphic form how the profiles of composers, in comparison with those of performers, deviate far more significantly from general population norms on those traits found to separate the groups most significantly.

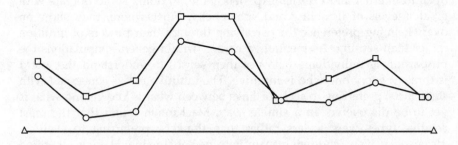

| Aloof | Dominant | Expedient | Sensitive | Imaginative | Naïve | Radical | Self-sufficient | Undisciplined |
| A– | E+ | G– | I+ | M+ | N– | Q1+ | Q2+ | Q3– |

| Outgoing | Submissive | Conscientious | Tough-minded | Practical | Astute | Conservative | Group-dependent | Controlled |
| A+ | E– | G+ | I– | M– | N+ | Q1– | Q2– | Q3+ |

□——□ Composers
○——○ Performers
△——△ General population norms

Figure 11.3 Personality differences between male frofessional composers, performers, and general population norms. (Data from Kemp 1979, 1981b.)

The point was made earlier in the 'Preface' that Cattell always maintained that the rarity of particular specialist occupational groups within society would be reflected in profiles that were exceptionally deviant from general population norms. In this way the demands of highly specialized skills (the examples that Cattell always offered in this connection were airline pilots and brain surgeons) would be reflected in the temperament of the practitioners. Composers appear to be no exception to this rule.

Composers' characteristics viewed through Jung's preferences

MacKinnon's work is significant, not only in his attempts to develop a theory of the creative personality, particularly in architects, but also in connection with establishing the use of the Myers–Briggs Type Indicator in America. In a key paper MacKinnon (1962) showed that creative writers, mathematicians, and architects were predominantly perceptive as opposed to judging types. As we have noted earlier, perceptives tend to evade any temptation to prejudge events and objects, preferring to remain open to internal and external experience and, in doing so, to operate with greater levels of flexibility and spontaneity. Furthermore, they show an overwhelming preference for perceiving through their powers of intuition rather than sensing. As mentioned earlier, within general populations the proportion of individuals who use their senses to understand the world is three to every one who is intuitive. The intuitive is less concerned with static facts, preferring to seek for links between what is known and what is yet to be discovered. In a similar way, MacKinnon found that the most creative types were feelers rather than thinkers: preferring to evaluate ideas subjectively, endowing them with personal value. Having identified high levels of introversion in the creative groups, especially amongst those orientated towards the arts, MacKinnon was able to claim that, of the 16 Jungian types, that which was most representative of his creative groups was INFP. In some similar work with fine artists, Simon (1979), cited in Myers and McCaulley (1985), showed that levels of creativity were related to these same four dimensions: 80 per cent were introverted (I); 95 per cent intuitive (N); 70 per cent feelers (F); and 75 per cent perceptive (P).

As mentioned in earlier discussions, although I adopted the Myers–Briggs Type Indicator in my earlier research, the results with the student and professional composers have remained unpublished. In returning to these data, it has emerged that composers follow something of the same pattern of preferences as the creative types in MacKinnon's work. I found the student-composers to be particularly introverted (79 per cent), intuitive (87 per cent), with feeling (72 per cent), and perception (72 per cent) (see Table 11.2). The table also shows the dispersion of the 39 composers amongst the 16 Jungian types, and indicates that there is a clear clustering in the INFP cell as in the findings of MacKinnon and Simon. Compared with the entire group of student musicians the composers were considerably more introverted, perceptive, and intuitive. However, there was a very slight reduction in feeling (76 per cent of the general group had shown a preference for feeling).

The professional composers' results on the Myers–Briggs are also shown in Table 11.2. The professionals also emerged with high levels of introversion (79 per cent), intuition (84 per cent), and feeling (87 per cent) compared with their performing colleagues, and a swing away from judgement (J) to

Table 11.2 Dispersion of composers amongst the Jungian types

Composer	Sensing types (%) with		Intuitive types (%) with	
	Thinking (T)	Feeling (F)	Thinking (T)	Feeling (F)

Introverts (I)

With a preference for judging (J)

	ISTJ	ISFJ	INTJ	INFJ
Students	0	3	15	10
Professionals	0	5	5	37

With a preference for perception (P)

	ISTP	ISFP	INTP	INFP
Students	0	5	8.5	38
Professionals	0	5	3	21

Extraverts (E)

With a preference for perception (P)

	ESTP	ESFP	ENTP	ENFP
Students	0	0	3	8.5
Professionals	0	3	0	10

With a preference for judging (J)

	ESTJ	ESFJ	ENTJ	ENFJ
Students	0	5	3	3
Professionals	0	0	3	5

Jungian type	Students (%)	Professionals (%)	Jungian type	Students (%)	Professionals (%)
E	21	21	TJ	18	11
I	79	79	TP	10	3
S	13	16	FP	51	39
N	87	84	FJ	21	47
T	28	13	IN	72	66
F	72	87	EN	15	18
J	28	58	IS	8	13
P	72	42	ES	5	3
IJ	29	50			
IP	51	29			
EP	10	13			
EJ	10	8			
ST	0	3			
SF	13	13			
NF	59	74			
NT	28	10			
SJ	8	8			
SP	5	8			
NP	56	34			
NJ	31	50			

perception (P) is also apparent. Despite the professional composer's preference for perception when viewed as a separate dimension, a tendency for
them to cluster around the INFJ type is noted. In the following sections we
shall attempt to pull together what the Jungian and Cattellian results are
telling us.

Further interpretation of the composer's temperament

Because of the above discovery that several of the important facets of the
composer's personality coincide with those of musicians generally, although
at significantly higher levels, it is incumbent upon us to revisit some of these
features in an attempt to interpret them in terms of the composer's craft and
life-style. It may not be sufficient to interpret them glibly as indicating that
composers are merely a brand of supermusician. Most, of course, will be, or
will have been, very able performing musicians. One has only to consider
outstanding examples of composer–performers such as Bach, Mozart, Liszt,
Brahms, and Boulez amongst others of our own time, to realize that the two
skills may be inextricably bound together.

Firstly, let us consider the composer's particularly high levels of introversion and independence, which were reflected in both sets of results reported
above: directly in the 16PF and inferred in the Myers–Briggs. The INFP type,
which represented a good proportion of the student composers, appear to be
driven by their inner core of values and are fascinated by opportunities to
explore complexities. They are capable of great concentration and bursts of
energy; they have the capacity to take an individualistic stance towards projects (Myers and McCaulley 1985, p. 25). They emerge as fairly self-contained
people, feeling their obligations to their work very strongly but revealing little desire to influence others. This appears to change at the professional level
and, although they continue to be stimulated by difficulties and by solving
them, they are more inclined to want to liaise with people, especially in starting new movements and trends. The INFJ type has a gift for intuitively
understanding complex problems, is particularly insightful, creative, and
visionary; conceptual, symbolic, and metaphorical; idealistic, complex, and
deep (Myers and McCaulley 1985, p. 29). Thus, the personality of the more
mature composer appears to reflect the ability to work with others and to
feel a sense of commitment to group and shared enterprises.

Clearly, these characteristics of independent individualism can be identified in so many composers both dead and living that their importance
hardly requires any discussion. One has only to consider the degree to
which so many composers have clung doggedly to their personal aspirations in the face of considerable hardship. Then there are those like Handel
and Schumann who pursued music in the face of parental opposition, or
Tippett whose sheer personal drive triumphed despite parental indifference.

The history of music is peppered with the stories of those who persisted with their composition whilst experiencing all kinds of opposition, ridicule, and poor reviews. Take Bruckner's obstinate determination to become a musician and composer against all odds, and Elgar's persistence over a period of 20 years to be taken seriously as a composer, while having to be satisfied with a modest job as bandmaster in an asylum. Janáček also experienced enormous obstacles set against him, having to wait until well into his sixties to experience success. Similarly, Schoenberg had to fight considerable resistance in the most difficult circumstances, his burning conviction of his own self-worth driving him on until he eventually experienced acceptance in middle age.

Having studied the correspondence of some of the great composers, Gall (1978) presents a convincing picture of the composer's persistence and drive in the face of all kinds of adversity.

It is hardly possible to read the records of great musicians' lives . . . without being struck by the preponderance of tragedy, of frustration, of self-sacrifice, revealed in such documents: . . . those who . . . had to live in obscurity such as Bach, Schubert, Wolf, or achieved right at the end of lives of untold toil and drudgery a haphazard recognition by a small minority, such as Berlioz or Bruckner. It looks as if the inevitable corollary of greatness were martyrdom . . . Again and again one marvels at the strength of resistance a creative will was able to give a frail, ailing body, and the meagre encouragement on which such a creative urge could be maintained. (p. 448)

The research cited in the present chapter supports this kind of picture of the self-motivated composer, obsessional about his or her work, even in circumstances in which most people would give up the struggle. The combination of introversion and independence certainly provides a description of the type of personality that may be characteristic of large numbers of successful composers. What remains unclear, however, is *why* this appears to be the case. What are the psychological benefits of these facets of personality? Several answers to these questions have been explored in the earlier chapters of this book in the context of performing musicians. In our present discussion of the composer, some of these notions will take on a particular significance.

In Chapter 2 our conclusions concerning introversion revolved around musicians turning their energies inwards, needing time for reflection, solitude, and separation; we also emphasized the importance of the musician's internal and symbolic life and of a particularly well-developed musical memory. The point was made that this turning inwards, involving the development of a rich internal world of musical creativity, could be perceived as being the locus of the composer's powers of imagination and innovation and sense of omnipotence. This pattern of the autonomous introvert's mind is further enriched by the presence of high levels of sensitivity, feelingfulness, imagination, and radicalism revealed in Tables 11.1 and 11.2. It is within this kind of personality structure that the composer finds his or her own identity and the sense of drive, ambition, and autonomy.

This already complex form of independence takes on new connotations if we reconsider some of the aspects of independence discussed in Chapter 3. For example, the ability to tolerate high levels of ambiguity and conflict, and the distinct preference for complex ideas are particular features of the creative person. Furthermore, the kinds of perceptual freedom of the field-independent, and the sense of liberation from the constraints of the more socially accepted norms of behaviour are also features that not only keep recurring in the literature but that can also frequently be identified in most of the composers we might wish to cite. One has only to take a brief look at the lives of Britten and Tippett, for example, to see the extent to which both refused to adhere to socially expected norms. In the case of Tippett this occurred from an early age, for example, in arguing his way out of organized religion and cadet corps whilst still at school, and, of course, the pacifism of both men was paramount, leading them to object to active service in the 1939–45 war.

At several points we have observed how frequently we find the musicians investing their whole complex identity in the process of becoming successful musicians. The serious downside of this is that the concept of self can so easily be fragmented and destroyed for these people if their personal ambitions are not realized. This appears to be true just as much, if not more, for the composer whose personality development appears to have been wholly invested for the precise purpose of living a life of composition. Copland (1952) put this very effectively when he asked

> ... why is it so important to my own psyche that I compose music? What makes it seem so absolutely necessary, so that every other daily activity, by comparison, is of lesser significance? And why is the creative impulse never satisfied; why must one always begin anew? To the first question—the need to create—the answer is always the same—self-expression; the basic need to make evident one's deepest feelings about life. But why is the job never done? Why must one always begin again? The reason for the compulsion to renewed creativity, it seems to me, is that each added work brings with it an element of self-discovery. I must create to know myself, and since self-knowledge is a never-ending search, each new work is only a part-answer to the question 'Who am I?' (pp. 40–1)

Is it this kind of quest for self-actualization that drives a composer like Tippett to pursue composition against all the odds, and to continue being productive into his nineties? This may well be so. Certainly we can observe his continuing desire to draw new ideas and problems into his works, and to struggle at new accommodations as if his compositions were somehow a symbolic playing out of real life issues. Tippett describes the process as a deeply internal one: 'I feel the need to give an image to an ineffable experience of my inner life. I feel the inner life as something that is essentially fluid in consistency.' (Bowen 1981, p. 156)

In a sense, of course, every time a composer engages in his or her art, a struggle takes place. This struggle relates to the classic conflict between the individual and society, between personal freedom and external control, between free-flowing creativity and accepted stylistic norms. All artists, composers amongst them, are called upon to handle these opposites within themselves, reconciling their need to exercise their personal autonomy as artists but at the same time knowing just how far their sense of freedom and personal identity may diverge from well-worn and generally accepted stylistic procedures. In this way we may well begin to see how composers' introversion and independence empower them to handle this internal conflict in such a way that an acceptable and comfortable rapprochement is arrived at.

Storr (1976) maintains that artists' quest for identity involves them in working out the tensions between these kinds of opposites in order to bring about new integrations within themselves. It is these processes that allow their egos to develop new levels of wholeness and strength. In Storr's view this is one reason why composers' works frequently fall into early, middle, and late periods. These reflect a gradual shift in ego identity as new problems are worked through and new integrations take place. It may well be this that drives the creative person onwards, ever exploring new opportunities and new problems and adopting new techniques, thereby causing disequilibrium in their internal state, and new crises to be solved. It is precisely this kind of process that particularly attracts the schizoid person, offering identification with the experience of making whole, and offering restoration to a fragile or damaged ego. It is a process in which the individual may experience a degree of omnipotence and sense of authority and superiority, bringing order out of internal chaos. Storr cites the case of Chopin, as described by Georges Sand as 'shutting himself up in his room for whole days, weeping, walking, breaking his pens, repeating and altering a bar a hundred times, spending six weeks on a single page' (p. 66). Beethoven, too, was prone to considerable amounts of struggling to work through compositional problems, reworking passages several times before emerging with a solution that was acceptable to him.

Musical creativity and psychopathology

It may be for the reasons discussed above that certain people with psychopathological problems are attracted to artistic pursuits. Many writers have commented upon the fact that composers as a group appear to be overendowed with people who appear to suffer from psychiatric symptoms. Cattell and Butcher (1968) maintained that it was their anxiety levels that differentiated scientific and artistic creative groups, observing that, whilst the latter tended to have higher anxiety levels, musicians were less anxious than writers. Beethoven, Ravel, Bartók, and Warlock were singled out for special mention as having unhappy and stormy lives.

In an extensive study, Post (1994) examined the biographies of 291 world-famous figures renowned for their creativity in an attempt to determine the incidence of psychic abnormalities, disorders, and illnesses amongst them. His results showed that 31 per cent of composers, compared with 38 per cent of painters, and 46 per cent of writers suffered from serious forms of mental ill-health. Only politicians (17 per cent), scientists (18 per cent), and thinkers (26 per cent) were found to be less prone to mental ill-health. Amongst the composers he identified as suffering severe psychopathology were Berg, Berlioz, Bruckner, Elgar, Falla, Gounod, Martinů, Moussorgsky, Puccini, Rachmaninov, Reger, Satie, Schumann, Scriabin, Tchaikowsky, and Wagner. Amongst those whose symptoms were less severe but still marked were Chopin, Grieg, Mahler, Mendelssohn, Rimsky-Korsakov, Rossini, Schoenberg, Sibelius, Stravinsky, and Wolf. Post also hypothesized that the very high rates of psychiatric problems commonly reported in creative people would *not* be found in the outstandingly creative. Presumably, this was formulated on the basis that greater success in creative endeavour would result in greater effectiveness of certain defence mechanisms, and thereby, a reduction in psychiatric symptoms. The hypothesis was rejected, however, supporting the view that there appears to be some kind of causal relationship between psychopathology and creativity. This is important in terms of our discussions here simply because the results reported earlier in this chapter appear to support this. After all, the achievements of the groups of composers whose results are shown in Table 11.1 would have been significantly more modest in comparison with those cited by Post.

Although the groups of performers discussed in Chapter 5, generally tend to show higher levels of anxiety (see Table 5.1 on page 92), the student and professional composers cited in this chapter do not display either any marked reduction of anxiety, or any increase. One is forced, therefore, to reconsider whether the musician's anxiety can be viewed purely as a manifestation of performance stress or whether there is a separate cause. This needs raising, since the composers would not have been subject to these particular kinds or degrees of stress.

Closer study of Post's findings with the outstandingly creative reveal that some types appear more prone to different forms of psychiatric disorders and illness. It is of particular significance that, of all the groups he studied, the composers appeared to be most prone to anxiety and related disorders. On the other hand, musicians were the least susceptible to depressive illness—writers appearing to be more than twice as vulnerable. As a result, we may be left to question whether the kinds of 'cathartic' processes that composers engage in *do* help keep neuroticism in check particularly in comparison to some of these other creative activities. Storr (1976) appears to take the view that, although creative persons tend to display psychopathological symptoms, confirming the popular belief that artists are 'mad', they do in fact possess greater ego-strength and a superior controlling apparatus with which to deal with the situation.

More recently Storr (1992) has returned to a discussion of mental illness in composers and concedes that there certainly appear to be thought processes in common between the mentally ill and the creative. The mentally ill, he maintains, are overwhelmed by the threat of confusion and disorder. On the other hand, creative persons, whilst being aware of this threat, see this as a challenge and are able to create new order in their works, and thus master it. Storr observes that

Robert Schumann and Hugo Wolf are examples of composers who suffered from manic-depressive illness. Although ultimately defeated by the severity of their mental disturbances, there is no doubt that their creativity was partly a product of their instability. Rachmaninov also experienced severe depression. This condition can be so extreme that it prevents production altogether, but *liability* to depression and the threat of its recurrence can act as a spur to creativity. Berlioz, when suffering tormenting depression and anxiety, told his father that without music he could not go on living. Tchaikowsky, who also endured severe bouts of depression, wrote 'Truly, there would be reason to go mad if it were not for *music*'. (p. 104)

An interesting insight into Beethoven's understanding of the compositional process is offered by Caldwell (1972) in a discussion of the String Quartet No. 6 in B flat, Opus 18. The final movement is assigned a title—La Malincolia—a fairly unusual thing for Beethoven to do. The movement consists of several sections that alternate between slow, melancholic, and tortuous sections, and highly elated, even playful ones. Caldwell describes the first

as representing an inhibited mood in which there is no expansion or elaboration, just a struggle to keep going despite the agony:

The fast theme, alternatively, bristles with energy and restlessness, with violent leaps in a carefree style:

After a while the depressive mood descends again without warning, and then the different mood swings appear to occur more frequently. Caldwell sees within these fluctuations Beethoven's attempt to depict manic-depressive illness, moving from painful, depressive mood states with their attendant psychomotor retardation, through to feelings of restless elation and psychomotor acceleration. No suggestion is being made here that Beethoven was manic-depressive, although his mood swings are well-documented in biographical literature. More importantly, Caldwell suggests that Beethoven had some degree of understanding of such mental problems and made use of them as a part of his mental imagery, thus shaping his creativity. In a sense, of course, one can see how Beethoven's attempt to interlink his knowledge of human mental illness with his inner creative processes was the natural outcome of the more emotional and *Sturm und Drang* (storm and stress) styles that marked a new turning point in attitudes to the nature of musical expression.

After Schumann's attempted suicide, his committal to an asylum, and eventual death from starvation, Liszt, who appears to have understood perceptively the kind of struggle endured by Schumann, commented:

No one can fail to recognize that instead of venturing, conquering, discovering, Schumann strove to reconcile his romantic personality, torn between joy and pain, and often driven by a dark urge towards the fantastic and the bizarre, with the modalities of classical form, whereas the clarity and symmetry of such forms lay beyond his characteristic spirit . . . this struggle against his true nature must have caused him great suffering . . . (Quoted in Jamison 1993, p. 207)

We are left with at least two important issues. The first relates to Post's identification of a link between certain psychopathological problems and musical creativity and the second to Storr's suggestion that there may be some form of commonality between creative processes and the modes of thinking of the mentally ill. Both of these issues certainly deserve further serious investigation. It would appear quite reasonable to speculate that those types of people whose minds tend to be preoccupied with holding their fragmented personalities together would be naturally drawn to the processes of working through problems and attempting reconciliations.

Before we leave this point, the reader is invited to consider an example of this process that comes immediately to mind. In the first movement of his Second symphony in D, Opus 43, Sibelius shares his sketchpad of musical fragments with the listener in a strikingly diffident and hesitant way. The symphony, often considered to depict the quiet, pastoral aspects of Finland, may, however, reflect at deeper levels Sibelius' way of dealing with his inner suffering and melancholy. The movement commences with a fragmentary idea played by the strings:

A few bars later, this offers an accompaniment to the seemingly jocular first theme played by the flutes and oboes:

While this idea is extended, additional fragmentary material is introduced, still maintaining a hesitant, enigmatic atmosphere. After a number of intro-spective afterthoughts played by the horns, a new theme appears played by the violins:

There follows a passage, improvisatory in character, during which snippets of ideas are shared around the orchestra. A more agitated pizzicato passage on the strings makes its appearance:

This heralds a new theme played by the upper woodwind while the strings resume the earlier strumming passage:

The development and recapitulation that follow represent a working through of these ideas which, whilst not becoming fully reconciled, are brought into a closer proximity, are more comfortable in each other's com-pany, and are presented with a greater depth of knowledge and awareness.

After an early performance of the symphony in Stockholm in 1903, Wilhelm Stenhammar, the Swedish musician, wrote to Sibelius saying

... you are in my thoughts daily since I heard your symphony ... it is indeed a large catch of marvels that you have brought up out of the depths of the unconscious and the inexpressible ... Give humanity hope, give us the drama! You do not need it; I, too, can dispense with it; but all the many who turn away from a riddle they cannot solve, they require it . . . You have stirred me so much that I cannot forget it. (In Ekman 1946, p. 173)

Quite what Stenhammar had experienced was clearly difficult for him to articulate, but the performance had exercised a profound impact upon him. Is it pushing the speculation too far to suggest that he had, as a composer himself, identified exactly with Sibelius' personal struggle to reconcile the opposites that haunted his mind?

Let us return now to the question which, although it cannot be answered here, is nonetheless important. This relates to the shared levels of anxiety demonstrated by the groups of more modest composers and the performers cited in this book. One possible way of accounting for this is that musicians who work in both areas are attracted to the process described above—the making whole, the reconciliation of conflicting elements, the renewal of broken or incomplete objects. The shared levels of anxiety of the composer and performer possibly suggest that they take part in two forms of a similar process. The composer engages in a God-like, omnipotent act of creating something of beauty out of disparate and primitive elements. The performer is invited to engage in the same process, albeit one step removed, identifying with the God-like being, striving for glimpses and insights into his or her processes of creation, and identifying with the very act of creation through the process of re-interpretation. Each new piece on which a composer or performer works invites each to engage in a struggle to deal with a depressive state of fragmentation, hopefully to emerge triumphantly, victorious over acutely felt destructive powers. Was it this kind of experience that prompted Holst to write 'Music, being identical with heaven, isn't a thing of momentary thrills, or even hourly ones. It's a condition of eternity' (Gall 1978, p. 425). This kind of response may, of course, also be experienced by the music listener: offering those who, because of their inner needs, are attracted to conflicting elements and their resolution an opportunity to bring order to their internal conflicts. Storr (1988) puts it this way:

. . . outer happenings and inner experiences interact with one another; which is why . . . hearing the integration of opposing themes in a piece of music gives the . . . listener the marvellous experience of a new unity as if it were within his own psyche. (p. 200)

Compositional style

In Chapter 7 we discussed the ways in which listeners' preferences for the music of particular composers might possibly reveal different personality types. The early work of Burt (1939) was cited in connection with this kind of suggestion, particularly with respect to the dimensions of neuroticism and extraversion (see Figure 7.1 on p. 123). Burt suggested, for example, that neurotics might be more attracted to the music of Wagner, Richard Strauss, Liszt, Berlioz, Debussy, Delius, and Chopin. Here, we might wish to speculate whether it might be possible to see this kind of interrelationship from the perspective of the composer's personality. Might the thought processes and states of mind of the composers reflected in their output be precisely what attracts certain types of listeners? Again, we might wish to speculate about Payne's (1967) classical/romantic dichotomy and suggest that a style of composition that emphasizes structure and form might be more likely to be composed by someone with a stable (non-neurotic) personality type. Alternatively, a more romantic style of music, emphasizing changing mood states and lack of stability, might be found to be generated by a more neurotic composer.

Chapter 7 also cited research that appeared to support the idea that a person's introversion might be related to the degree to which he or she is prepared to engage in an analytical style of listening. Conversely, it was suggested that the extraverted listener is more attracted to music that offers more immediate forms of satisfaction. Again, if it is possible to theorize that certain types of listener are attracted to various musical styles on the basis that their personalities reflect particular states of mind and a predilection to think in particular ways, may not these differences apply to the composers who created the music in the first place? Some readers will be uncomfortable with this kind of argument maintaining that what is in the mind of the composer may be quite different to what is perceived by the listener. But that is a somewhat different question. Here we are talking about far deeper psychological needs as expressed in music, as well as different cognitive styles that may provide reasonable degrees of access to it. Certainly we are not entertaining the notion of direct communication of 'meaning' between composer and listener with the performer operating as some kind of medium. Certainly, Post's research findings tend to support Burt's idea in that he identified Wagner, Richard Strauss, Liszt, Berlioz, Debussy, and Chopin as suffering some degree of psychopathology. One is left to speculate that Burt's groups of listeners were somehow sensitive to the mind states of these particular composers. However, the introversion–extraversion of the composers identified by Burt is perhaps less conclusive and more difficult to sustain, although we might wish to entertain the argument that Bach's music reveals a more analytical mind (introverted attitude) than that of Handel which may offer more immediate rewards.

This brings us to another important aspect of Chapter 7 that involves the syntactic-nonsyntactic and analytic-holistic listening styles, as well as hemisphere dominance. A body of research was discussed that suggested that all these appeared to relate to a dichotomous typing of listeners. If we are tempted to continue our speculations that this kind of research can be turned around to focus upon the personalities of composers according to their style of output, we can certainly draw encouragement from the work of Robertson (1993) in doing so. In a brief paper, which hopefully heralds more detailed research, Robertson suggests that the musical styles developed by certain composers directly reflect their hemisphere dominance. With his collaborator Peter Fenwick at the Maudsley and Bethlem Hospital, London, Robertson maintained that the relative dominance of composers' hemispheres might relate to the ways their styles develop. More specifically, Robertson and Fenwick considered that the more intuitive composers would produce emotional music, adopting the rhythmic and concordant 'language' of the right hemisphere. In this connection Robertson cites a number of examples of right-hemisphere composers: Janáček, in his use of bright and frenzied ostinati and increasing neglect of musical syntax; Wagner, Debussy, and Liszt's use of erotic arousal; Philip Glass's repetitive and minimalist structures, involving Eastern-style hypnotic effects; and John Taverner's extensive use of sonorities and contemplative atmosphere. On the other hand, composers with more dominant left hemispheres, he claimed, include Schoenberg, whose arrhythmic music is driven by intellect and dissonance, denying emotional rewards to most listeners. Boulez is also cited as another composer whose music rejects orthodoxy and strives for a 'new musical language based on rigorous theory' (p. 24), indicative of a more analytical left-hemisphere type of processing.

Clearly, this research is still at an early and speculative stage, but it certainly offers a line of investigation which deserves further exploration. Robertson and his colleagues have also given some consideration to the involvement of the limbic system, which has been referred to at various points in this book particularly in connection with the role of the hypothalamus. They suggest that the spiritual quality of Taverner's music may be accounted for by the activation of the right limbic system which, as we have noted earlier, may help explain levels of emotional arousal in listeners. In Taverner's music repetition is used to create a flat emotional climate in which the smallest novelties may have a disproportionate emotional effect. In this way they help support my earlier suggestion (Kemp 1992) that the interplay between repetition and change can charge music with the sensations of stability and stress.

Summary

In the Western world it is composers' creativity that exercises a driving force upon the health and vitality of musical life. The creative energy within their works stimulates and inspires performers to new heights of interpretative creativity and concert audiences to new levels of imaginative experience and insight. The composer can be seen as the musician *par excellence* who, whilst sharing much in common with the general musician, is often suspected as possessing additional, nearly superhuman qualities.

Generally speaking, the composer's creative disposition can be described in similar terms to that of creative types in other fields: a unique combination of introversion, independence, sensitivity, imagination, and radicalism. Certainly the small amounts of research with composers at the student and professional levels tend to support this kind of profile. These findings particularly emphasize high levels of introversion, independence, pathemia, and radicalism well above those that may be found in musicians generally. Viewed from a more Jungian perspective these same groups are found to demonstrate a perceptual style that is hinted at by the Cattellian results. The Myers–Briggs particularly highlights composers' introverted, intuitive, feelingful, and perceptive stance towards their work.

Studies of composers' lives indeed often reflect these kinds of qualities. They appear to be individualistic, they have a capacity for solitude, and they are attracted to complex and ambiguous symbolic enterprises. Throughout musical history there are many examples of composers displaying the capacity to cling doggedly to their aspirations despite serious obstacles, engaging in extraordinary bursts of drive and creative energy. It is suggested here that this intense creative impulse, engaged in with a sense of visionary zeal, may at its roots relate to a personal need to create internal order and wholeness. Musical works reveal how the composer's craft largely comprises the synthesis and analysis of fragmentary musical ideas. In adopting these contrasting and complementary processes composers bring creative order to chaos, ambiguities, and conflicts within them. In this way they may maintain an equilibrium in their levels of neuroticism and stress. It may be for this reason that composers do not reveal higher or lower levels of anxiety than other musicians, although their roots may be as different as the manner of its control.

This kind of stance supports the frequently articulated view that, to get to know a composer, one should start with his or her music. Composers' works frequently reveal considerable insights about their personalities and perceptual styles, and can open up windows on their internal worlds and psychological needs.

TWELVE

Music teachers

Introduction

Questions about what makes a good teacher are raised each time an interviewing committee meets to fill a vacancy in any school. Candidates are questioned about their interests, professional experience, teaching approaches, and accomplishments, but underlying these sometimes quite perfunctory enquiries is a concern to know how the candidate relates to people, how robust they will be in the rough and tumble of the classroom, whether they will be able to teach efficiently and imaginatively, and whether they will 'fit in' in the staffroom. As far as music teachers are concerned, there may well be other considerations about the candidates lurking in the interviewers' minds: is this person a good musician? does she possess the requisite skills to conduct the orchestra, the wind group, and the choral society? has he the enthusiasm and resourcefulness to interest the more recalcitrant pupils in worthwhile musical activities? has she sufficient musical flexibility and knowledge to engage in those musical genres that lie closer to the pupils' musical enthusiasms? will he achieve good advanced level examination results? and so on. Each of these kinds of question can be seen to relate to an aspect of the candidate's personality as far as it can be assessed within the confines of the interview.

The same procedures, of course, are carried out during the processes of selecting students for courses of teacher education and training, whether this be at undergraduate or postgraduate level. In the case of the latter, the candidates have graduated, or will be about to graduate in music. These applicants perceive themselves as reasonably developed musicians, often wishing to embark upon a profession in which they are able to continue practising music, while at the same time sharing their musical enthusiasms with children. Of course, the selection procedures will involve the identification of the requisite kinds of musical skills and knowledge necessary for teaching, but the other agendum concerns the ways that candidates' personalities relate to the kinds of question raised above. What may underlie the process, either consciously or unconsciously in the minds of the interviewers, is the belief that these two issues are distinct: what makes a good musician does not necessarily guarantee good potential as a teacher, and vice versa. The present chapter pursues this kind of dilemma. Now that we have attempted to develop some kind of understanding of the musician's personality in the preceding chapters, we may be able to assess the ways in which the typical musician is, or is not, naturally temperamentally suited to classroom teaching.

The rapid and extraordinary growth in teacher education that took place in Britain during the 1960s and 70s generated an upsurge in research that attempted to establish empirically whether classroom teaching success was, in fact, characterized by a specific and consistent profile of personality traits. The underlying hope, of course, was that researchers would be able to identify a profile of characteristics that selectors might adopt for predictive purposes. A review of a large body of British research with student teachers carried out during this period tended to suggest that they can be viewed as fairly introverted, independent, anxious, pathemic, as well as lacking in conscientiousness (Kemp 1979). Such a general description of groups of students, regardless of levels of success in the classroom, may be unhelpful to our discussions here, particularly as most of this research was undertaken at the very time when entry to the then colleges of education was probably at its easiest. What should invite our caution in particular is the observation that this profile of traits resembles very closely the profile that we would normally expect in higher education students generally. Also, it will not have escaped the reader's attention that this kind of personality profile is not dissimilar to that identified in undergraduate musicians, although it would be reasonable to suspect that these traits would be more significantly identifiable in their case.

Another similar literature review, but this time dealing with research that had adopted successful classroom teaching as a criterion, showed a very different picture (Kemp 1979). Although the pattern was far less conclusive, indications emerged that suggested that some of the characteristics of the general groups mentioned earlier were reversed when actual teaching effectiveness was considered. In fact, extraversion and conscientiousness were found to be linked to either teaching practice grades or some other form of evaluation of serving teachers' classroom performance. With this thought in mind that at least these two traits are linked to classroom teaching success in teachers generally, let us move on to discuss the personality characteristics of the music teacher. In doing so, we may wish to bear in mind that the variability and inconclusiveness of the above research in terms of other traits may have been due to the personality effects of the teachers' variety of disciplines.

Cattellian view of classroom music teachers

The earlier research with music teachers was undertaken with American groups (for example, Michael *et al.* 1961; Krueger 1974) and this tended to suggest that music teaching success was somehow linked to adjustment (C+, H+, L–, Q3+, and Q4–) and conscientiousness (G+ and Q3–). Whilst it is easy enough to interpret these two second-order factors as relating closely to classroom stability and management, we should note that they represent a direct reversal of the traits usually featuring in a musician's profile. Extraversion, however, appeared to have a more complex link with teaching success. The groups of music teachers here 'split' the dimension, displaying signs of adventurousness (H+), but counterbalancing this by a manifestation of the musician's introverted self-sufficiency (Q2+). Similarly, a certain ambivalence occurred on independence, in that dominance (E+) and adventurousness (H+) featured in the profile, but were offset by a lack of imagination (M–), and suggestions of trustingness (L–)—a trait that one would not readily associate with the classroom teacher! Clearly, differences between the British research on general teachers and the American work with music teachers are to be expected. Whilst both adopted the effectiveness criterion, the differences may have been due to British and American cultural differences, but, more importantly perhaps, to the fact that the American research was focused on *music* teachers. Thus, the present chapter pursues this kind of issue, raising questions about the ways in which musicians are required to adjust to the world of schools and various types of teaching.

It was the notion that the musician's pattern introversion, independence, anxiety, and lower conscientiousness, identified in earlier chapters, would somehow render him or her misfitted to classroom teaching that led me to incorporate groups of teachers into my main research project (Kemp 1979). What was being sought, of course, was evidence that those musicians who had taken the conscious decision to become classroom teachers and who had been selected for training would reveal a significant modification to the musician's profile. The expectation was that certain of the musicianship-linked traits would occur, either at their opposite poles or, at least, at reduced levels. The group of classroom student teachers comprised 49 secondary postgraduate certificate in education students and 60 college of education undergraduate students mostly at the primary level.

This group indeed showed, in a comparison with other full-time music students, a reduction of the musician's introversion at highly significant levels, emerging as outgoing (A+) and group-dependent (Q2–). This will not come as a surprise to readers, particularly those engaged in the supervision of music students on school experience. It is, perhaps above all, the internal restraint and aloofness of musicians that can so often entrap them in a pattern of communication difficulties, particularly with larger groups of pupils in the classroom setting. The introversion of the musician, as discussed in earlier chapters, has emphasized the 'living inwards' aspect of the dimension, rendering the individual somewhat detached and removed, particularly in settings where effective interaction is of paramount importance. Being so bound up with their own internal world and values may frequently prevent them perceiving how the more extraverted types think and operate or, indeed, approach aesthetic activities from different viewpoints. Disappointingly, no other distinctive characteristics emerged in the student teachers save that of conservatism (Q1−). This factor, however, is not without some degree of significance. It will be recalled that, whereas radicalism (Q1+) does not feature in the profile of musicians generally, it *does* occur in those types where higher levels of creative and interpretative skill are required. The reader will be aware that this was particularly true in the case of the more skilled performers and composers. The emergence of conservatism in teachers, like extraversion, does not come altogether as a surprise. It is, after all, a trait frequently found in leaders, and particularly elected leaders (Cattell *et al.* 1992), who may well feel that manifestations of unconventional and eccentric behaviour are not appropriate in their positions of authority. In a similar way student music teachers may also feel constrained to adopt a less 'artistic' persona in the classroom to the extent of making efforts to appear 'normal' and conventional.

On the basis of these results we may assume, as far as this group of student teachers are concerned, that those other aspects of the musician's personality, namely independence, anxiety, and lower conscientiousness, were not particularly debilitating in the context of the classroom. However, it must be borne in mind that these student teachers were not necessarily able to display high levels of teaching skill. As already indicated, they had merely applied and been selected for training. We are therefore left to speculate as to whether these traits reveal *actual* music teaching potential or merely the foibles of their interviewers' selection procedures and criteria.

A further finding, not without significance, relates to the varying patterns of gender differences amongst the student teachers and the other music students. These interactions on the three primary factors, (A, Q2, and Q1), are shown diagrammatically in Figure 12.1 to which the positions of the specialist performers have been added for comparison purposes. There are two main observations that can be made about these. Firstly, and as already indicated in passing, the general linear trend of both male and female student teachers, in comparison with the general music students, is maintained by the specialist performers. In terms of these three apparently creative music traits, it might tentatively be argued that those who are not temperamentally suited, or able, to pursue a career as performers or composers may find themselves more adjusted to work in classrooms.

Secondly, the difference in the patterns of men and women on these traits is not without significance. On outgoingness–aloofness both the performers and the general music students display a reversal of the gender differences

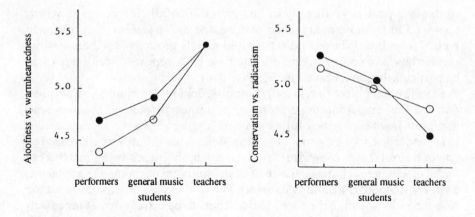

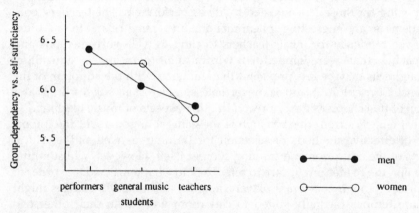

Fig. 12.1 Differences between student teachers, specialist performers, and general music students on outgoingness, conservatism, and self-sufficiency.

normally found in general populations. However, these converge in the teachers, possibly indicating that any signs of psychological androgyny may be out of place in classrooms. An alternative view might be that there exists an optimum level for both sexes on outgoingness for those likely to be successful in teaching. In a similar way, the results on the other extraversion–introversion factor, self-sufficiency–group-dependency, revealed the same kind of trend. Whereas men are normally more self-sufficient in general populations, the main group of music students showed a reversal of this pattern. Again, however, we find student teachers adopting those patterns of gender differences more usual and acceptable in the world outside music. Curiously, on the third factor, the opposite pattern occurs. Although the gender differences of the performers and general music students appear to be directly in line with the population norms in which men tend to be more radical than women, the music teachers deviate fairly widely from this. Whereas both male and female groups of teachers assume greater levels of conservatism, it is the men who appear to feel the need to be particularly conventional in the classroom.

During a later piece of research (Kemp 1982c) I returned to the same question but this time adopting a group of postgraduate student teachers who had been assessed by their tutors as being average or above average ability in secondary school classroom teaching skills. This group was compared to one of a similar size comprising performers, both groups being matched in terms of age, gender, and balance of main study instruments (23 keyboard, 5 strings, 3 woodwind, and one singer). The results very much confirmed the earlier results showing the successful teachers to be extraverted as far as out-goingness (A+) and adventurousness (H+) were concerned. Also in line with the earlier research, they were also more conservative (Q1−) and, in addition, less sensitive (I−), again suggesting that teaching may be an appropriate opening for those less adjusted to life as performers. The teachers' conservatism is an interesting phenomenon, and may relate to an often perceived tendency for music teachers to cling to well-worn methods and approaches that were embedded within their own music education. Although this may be less prevalent than hitherto, with the adoption of the National Curriculum in music, nevertheless, as we shall suggest in a later section of this chapter, it may prevail in other aspects of music teaching.

What emerges from this research is the general notion about the importance of effective methods of selection for training, as well as the critical aspects of the education and training content itself. However, whilst noting this point, the reader might care to refer back to Chapters 8 and 9 in order to speculate as to whether brass players, singers, and possibly pianists might be more temperamentally suited to classroom work than their other colleagues. Of course, it was not too long ago that musicians, purely on the basis of their graduate status in music, were able to take up positions as qualified teachers in schools. This research might account for why some of these people may have experienced considerable difficulties, not only in adjusting to classroom life, but also in meeting the needs and demands of the pupils. We shall be returning to this kind of view later during a discussion of the private studio teacher.

Jungian view of classroom music teachers

The question that arises at this point is whether the Myers–Briggs Type Indicator might reflect the same type of differences between performers and teachers identified with the use of Cattell's inventories. However, as we have observed earlier, the Myers–Briggs dimensions may well possess the capacity to offer a number of additional insights into the discussion. Nevertheless, in line with the Cattellian research, a trend towards extraversion might legitimately be anticipated in the teachers. At the same time, however, their tendencies towards conservatism identified above might be revealed in stronger preferences for the sensing form of perception as well as a thinking type of judgement on the Myers–Briggs. Sensing types tend to restrict their view to the realities of what is immediately experienced, and this type of functioning might reasonably be seen as more conducive to classroom management. The lower sensitivity identified in the student teachers, measured on Cattell's 16PF, might be revealed more in thinking types who are more 'down to earth', practical, and more tough-minded. However, it should be borne in mind that lower sensitivity only emerged in the follow-up research (Kemp 1982c). In line with our earlier conclusions in Chapter 4 about the musician's intuitive perception and its links with pathemia, and also on the basis of the 16PF research with teachers, we might expect the latter to be more distinguishable by their thinking judgement.

Wubbenhorst (1994) undertook a direct comparison of this very kind with postgraduate musicians measured on the Myers–Briggs. In comparing groups of American music educators with performers, the former revealed no heightened extraversion as we might have expected. In fact, a slight reduction occurred, and somehow this may have been due to a particularly extraverted group of performers. Both groups were found to be intuitive, although a small movement towards sensing on the part of the teachers occurred. The slight preference for feeling in Wubbenhorst's performers was not demonstrated by the teachers who emerged equally balanced between feeling and thinking. By far the strongest difference in his groups emerged on the judging–perceiving attitude, the teachers displaying a marked swing towards the judging pole.

The Myers–Briggs results with my (1979) group of 121 student teachers, discussed above in terms of their 16PF profile, are compared again here with the 210 music students specializing in performance. As a direct comparison with Wubbenhorst's results is possible, these are presented together in Table 12.1. Although my groups of teachers and performers both remained introverted, the expected swing in the direction of extraversion did, in fact, occur. As with Wubbenhorst's teachers, my group also displayed a tendency towards sensing, revealing the need for the teacher to be fully aware of the realities of the here and now of classroom work. However, quite contrary to his results and rather unexpectedly, 84 per cent of my student teachers showed a distinct preference for feeling over thinking, whereas in the performers it had been somewhat less at 74 per cent. It should be borne in mind, however, that this group of teachers was *not* the one that had displayed the lower sensitivity on Cattell's 16 PF. As this feature emerged in research that pursued those deemed to be successful teacher practitioners, this tends to suggest that a degree of tough-mindedness might be related to the criteria

Table 12.1 MBTI results for music educators and performers

MBTI dimensions	Music educators (%)		Performers (%)	
	Wubbenhorst (N=56)	Kemp (N=121)	Wubbenhorst (N=56)	Kemp (N=210)
Extraversion	**54**	47	**55**	36
Introversion	46	**53**	45	**64**
Sensing	36	47	34	34
Intuitive	**64**	**53**	**66**	**66**
Thinking	50	16	43	26
Feeling	50	**84**	**57**	**74**
Judging	**70**	**53**	**57**	42
Perceiving	30	47	43	**58**
Thinking–judging	**39**	9	27	14
Thinking–perceiving	11	6	16	11
Feeling–perceiving	20	42	27	**47**
Feeling–judging	30	**43**	**30**	28

used by school practice supervisors in assessing classroom teaching performance. Finally, like Wubbenhorst's teachers, those presented here displayed a tendency towards judgement, although not as strongly as his.

As Table 12.1 reveals, there are certain similarities between Wubbenhorst's performers and the teachers in my study in that both groups were characterized by their tendency towards the feeling-judging temperament. As Myers and McCaulley (1985) suggest, people of this type tend to make plans and decisions on the basis of human factors but their use of intuition tends to be shut off as soon as they have observed enough to come to a decision. They make 'benevolent administrators', 'expressive leaders', and are observant about people and their needs (p. 37). They will expend considerable energy in making people happy and creating interpersonal harmony. On the other hand, Wubbenhorst's educators, being thinking–judging types, are 'logical decision makers'; they are 'tough-minded, executive, analytical, and instrumental leaders' (p. 36). In the classroom these people would tend to make decisions and plans very much on the basis of their ability to think logically and to analyse events. In Myers–Briggs Type Indicator terms we can immediately see a fundamental difference between the temperaments and functioning of Wubbenhorst's performers and teachers. There is a rather more subtle difference between the performers and teachers in my research. Being feeling–perceiving types, the performers would have been what Myers and McCaulley referred to as 'gentle types', concerned with their inner world of subjective values. These individuals are 'adaptable, affiliative harmony seekers who are concerned with the human aspects of problems' (p. 37). Compared with their teaching counterparts, the British performers would have been more introspective and less able to cope in environments that demand a certain degree of resilience and decisiveness. Before moving on we should note that, apart from the differences between American and British music education systems and approaches that may have affected these results, one main difference between the two groups of teachers relates to their levels of experience. As mentioned earlier, those in my research were student teachers whose classroom experience would have been limited to a matter of weeks. On the other hand, those inWubbenhorst's group were older, and their experience probably far more extensive.

Whilst the above research is useful in providing a general description of those musicians who are attracted and drawn to teaching, it can only offer a general context for more detailed analyses that need to focus upon the relationships between personality dimensions and more detailed criteria. For example, research should be able to tell us whether teachers of younger children reveal a kind of temperament different from that of those who teach older students.

One aspect of the research carried out by McCutcheon *et al.* (1991) attempted to do just this, and their results with a group of elementary and secondary student teachers, arising from the use of the Myers–Briggs, are shown in Table 12.2. In terms of our earlier findings presented in Table 12.1, it is interesting to observe that a good proportion of their total group was characterized by feeling–judging, thus confirming my own conclusions.

Table 12.2 MBTI results for student music educators (McCutcheon *et al.* 1991)

MBTI dimensions	Total group (%) (N=79)	Elementary (%) (N=46)	Secondary (%) (N=28)
Extraversion	63	80	39
Introversion	37	20	61
Sensing	62	74	46
Intuitive	38	26	54
Thinking	35	20	57
Feeling	65	80	43
Judging	71	85	46
Perceiving	29	15	54
Thinking–judging	22	15	28.5
Thinking–perceiving	14	4	28.5
Feeling–perceiving	15	10	25
Feeling–judging	49	70	18

More importantly, in terms of our discussions here, is the discovery that this appears to be due to the very high percentage of the elementary teachers being of this type. The results with the secondary student teachers were not so conclusive and, whilst revealing a slight shift in the direction of thinking, were fairly ambivalent on the judging–perceiving dimension. What is also highlighted in these results is a far more conclusive involvement of extraversion than that which emerged in Table 12.1, thus confirming the 16PF research. While a reasonable percentage of the composite group was extraverted, it is clear from the table that this was an effect caused by the elementary teachers' extraversion. On the other hand, the secondary teachers emerged as being somewhat *introverted*. In a similar way, the elementary teachers appeared to discard the musician's intuition, a high percentage adopting the sensing preference, presumably indicating their need to be observant in the classroom environment. On the other hand, the relative retention of intuition in the secondary teachers perhaps demonstrates how their work allows them to operate at more theoretical and abstract levels.

These differences between the teachers of younger and older pupils may well suggest that secondary teachers are more able to retain a temperament that is in line with the pursuit of music, while, at the same time, being required to develop a more tough-minded and logical attitude to their work. This kind of conclusion might well offer an explanation for the inconclusive nature of the results on extraversion presented in Table 12.1 with groups that may well have comprised teachers of both primary and secondary school students.

Teaching style and behaviour

Let us now consider the particular classroom skills that teacher educators and trainers wish to instil in their student teachers. The kind of questions we need to pursue here relate to whether some types of student are more temperamentally suited to the process of developing effective classroom skills than others, and whether some are more receptive to particular forms of help and guidance from their tutors. The research carried out by McCutcheon *et al.* also pursued these questions, seeking to clarify whether supervisors' assessments of students' classroom behaviour were, indeed, related to the Myers–Briggs variables. In terms of the entire group, correlations emerged that suggested that extraversion–introversion and judging–perceiving were linked to particularly beneficial as well as negative features of teaching. For example, extraverts were more likely to take account of the pupils' interests and abilities during their teaching, whereas introverts tended to be overfamiliar with their classes. Another feature of introverts appeared to be their receptiveness to supervisors' criticisms and a willingness to adjust their teaching approaches as a result. Judging types were generally more prepared to provide learners with additional information to aid their enquiry, whereas the perceptives were more likely to modify their teaching according to the interests of the pupils. At the same time, however, the perceptive types' classroom delivery tended to be somewhat more hesitant.

On seeking more detailed information about the classroom behaviour of elementary and secondary student teachers, McCutcheon *et al.* disappointingly found only one single feature that demarcated the former. One well accepted feature of teaching technique with younger children is the teacher's tendency to repeat and reinforce key words and terms with which children are unfamiliar. In the case of these elementary school student teachers, this was found to be linked to their levels of extraversion. In contrast, the secondary school teachers were distinguishable by several features. These particularly related to the thinking types' tendency, not only to commence teaching promptly, but to adopt a style involving considerable amounts of talk, lacking the necessary repetition of key points. On the other hand, feeling types amongst the secondary school teachers tended to be overfamiliar with their students.

In some earlier work, Schmidt (1989a) carried out an interesting investigation with a group of associate instructors employed to supervise the teaching of undergraduate student teachers of orchestral and keyboard instruments, including voice. Each instructor, working with an individual student of average performing ability, was required to rate a recording of the student's teaching on a number of scales. Results showed that, not only did the extraverted instructors use significantly higher levels of approval behaviour and higher reinforcement rates than the introverts, they also taught at a faster pace. Those instructors who were intuitive types were distinguishable by their tendency to provide more approvals, more demonstrations, more reinforcement generally, and also conducted lessons at a faster pace than sensing types. Finally, Schmidt showed that the extraversion and judging dimensions appeared to combine in supporting the use of some of these teaching skills. More particularly, extraverted-judging types also displayed higher degrees of feedback and pace than any of the introverted groups regardless of whether introversion was linked to judging or perceiving.

These results are of considerable interest to us because they highlight a reasonably consistent set of interrelationships between the Myers–Briggs factors and well-defined aspects of teaching behaviours. Whereas other aspects of teaching, such as disapproving feedback, on-task teacher talk, and questioning, did not emerge as being linked to the Myers–Briggs dimensions, those specific aspects of teaching behaviour that might be perceived as being more advantageous for success appeared to be associated with extraverted and judging types.

In a second piece of research, Schmidt (1989b) studied the interrelationships between the Myers–Briggs Type Indicator dimensions of

extraversion–introversion and judgement–perception and the student teachers' perceptions of these different types of teacher-feedback. This research
incorporated a group of undergraduate and graduate student teachers of
singing and instruments, and required them to rate different types of verbal
feedback to a number of short recorded episodes of singing tuition.
Individual members of this group were invited to rate each of these different types of teacher feedback on four seven-point scales indicating whether
they were considered to be good, effective, sincere, or appropriate. The patterns of these responses were then analysed in relation to the Myers–Briggs
dimensions.

The principal outcomes of this research interestingly, and perhaps surprisingly, showed that the introverted students appeared to respond more
favourably to feedback in the classroom than the extraverted. Thus, taken
together, these two pieces of research suggest a complex pattern of behaviours. While extraverts, in their role as teachers, are more disposed to provide their pupils with adequate amounts of feedback, when they find themselves in the position of being learners, they appear not to value it. In a
similar way, the earlier results that found that the extraversion and judging
dimensions in combination were associated with higher amounts of feedback and pace, were also reversed here. In other words, Schmidt found that
the extraverted-judging types were consistently the *poorest* at perceiving the
usefulness of such teacher feedback. In attempting to interpret these patterns
of results in Jungian terms, Schmidt suggests that, in terms of the extraversion–introversion dimension, the difference lies in the extravert directing his
or her energies outwards in an active orientation. Obviously, this is what
teachers, and particularly extraverted teachers, are naturally inclined to do.
Alternatively, the introvert's tendency to direct energy inwards is a natural
process within learning situations where new concepts and skills have to be
accommodated and internally valued. This is entirely compatible with the
phenomenon noted in earlier chapters where students in higher education
have been found to be significantly more introverted than others in the same
age group. Thus we are left with something of a paradox: while extraverts
appear to make effective music teachers, they may not be the most receptive
music learners. Much of the research discussed in this book tends to support
this latter conclusion, and the results here emphasize the need for rigorous
selection of candidates for teacher education and training. Whilst this might
well dwell on aspects of candidates' extraversion, we should not lose sight
of the need to recruit those who have not lost touch with what it is to be a
musician. However, the main point being made here is that, temperamentally, it is by no means the case that high musical achievers necessarily make
the best teachers.

The real dilemma for music teachers, and those who educate them, is
knowing just how much they need to reveal qualities different from those of
the average musician. I am not merely talking about the orientation of their

own personalities, although this will reveal the capacity to adjust to or resist change. Also entangled within teachers' personality make-up will lie their personal rationale about the nature and role of music in ordinary people's lives, its place in the curriculum, and its processes. Within the minds of many music teachers there may be a tug-of-war ensuing. On one side there may exist feelings of loyalty towards their own musicianship which, as we have seen earlier, offers them a real sense of personal identity. Pulling in the opposite direction, there may hover a belief, instilled by their initial courses in teaching, that in order to communicate with 'ordinary' children they need to approach music from a more realistic, day-to-day, and person-orientated stance. This may well involve letting go of some cherished beliefs and deeply seated attitudes.

Let us take a look at the tensions that this might create in the more traditionally trained musician. Firstly, some will see the refocusing of intent away from a narrow set of musical objectives as somehow placing a limit on their own self-concept, believing that their sense of identity emanates from being a 'real' musician. Some of these teachers will deal with this by redirecting much of their energies to extracurricular choirs and orchestras. In this way they manage to retain a sense of their musical persona through the overt direction of concert performances. For others, examination work, and particularly Advanced Level General Certificate of Education teaching, offers the kind of sharing of musical enthusiasms for which many musicians strive. Other, perhaps more flexible types may seek their sense of personal achievement in their classroom teaching activity, obtaining pleasure in experiencing musical development more vicariously through their pupils' personal achievements, albeit sometimes at far more modest levels.

As we have already noted, the work of McCutcheon *et al.* (1991) suggested that, at least in connection with American teachers, the tug-of-war is possibly revealed in the differences between secondary school and primary school teachers. Secondary school teachers seemed to be able to retain elements of their musical introversion and their intuition, but at the same time they revealed a preference for thinking rather than perceiving. On the other hand, the elementary teachers appeared to discard the musicians' introversion and intuition whilst retaining their preference for feeling. What this may well suggest is that teachers of younger pupils need warmth, empathy, and a down-to-earth approach in the classroom. At the same time, however, they will need to generate a climate in which the musicians' sensitivity is not out of place. On the other hand, the secondary teachers' more single-subject-orientated work allows them, within strict limits, to retain certain levels of 'academic' introversion, even to the extent of making greater use of thinking than is usual in musicians. Also, of course, it is possible that primary school classrooms require somewhat higher levels of arousal than required at the secondary level. However, the danger that often occurs is that introverted secondary student teachers do not arouse their classes sufficiently, and boredom can set in particularly for the more extraverted pupils. Singing, of course, can help to raise arousal levels, and it is interesting to consider whether it is the secondary music teacher's introversion that has led to the near disappearance of singing in secondary classrooms. The retention of the musician's intuition may suggest that there is a need for secondary music teachers to be entrepreneurial in developing choirs, bands, and orchestras, and to promote various initiatives such as operas and musicals.

Some of these transformations may be quite difficult for the introverted musician to accomplish. As we have seen, by nature introverts are frequently more interested in their internal lives, their own interests and enthusiasms. Whilst being able to relate to others who are similarly orientated, they will find the emphasis on other people's sometimes very different kinds of needs and responses difficult to handle. This, as I have already suggested, may be particularly challenging for the secondary school teacher who may become anxious over the 'spur of the moment' decisions that have to be made in today's music rooms. Neither should we overlook the sensitivity and feelingfulness of the musician, which may render him or her particularly vulnerable in situations of confrontation with more difficult classes. Any suggestions of vulnerability can be quickly picked up and exploited by pupils and can lead to total downfall. It is not surprising, therefore, that research suggests that in comparison to other musicians music teachers generally appear to demonstrate a significant reduction in sensitivity, and secondary school teachers a greater reliance on thinking as opposed to feeling.

Private teachers

It would be inappropriate to close this chapter without a short discussion about a very different kind of music teacher: the one who tends to work in the privacy of his or her home, frequently teaching on an individual basis. These teachers may be attempting to maintain a modest professional performing life or, alternatively, whilst having ambitions in that direction, may have decided to teach a few pupils to remain financially buoyant in the meantime. Aware that they will never break into the professional circuit for one reason or another, others may decide to put all their energies into making a living by developing a successful private teaching practice.

In the absence of any specific award-bearing training for private teachers until the University of Reading and the Incorporated Society of Musicians recently developed a special post-experience diploma course for them, many of these musicians drifted into teaching without any rigorous preparation for the work. Thus we find a situation in which many thousands of teachers are operating in unregulated and unsupervised circumstances that have no inbuilt process of monitoring or quality control.

Although there is no empirical evidence to support this, we might speculate that the outcome of this situation is likely to be that these teachers will
be distinguishable from school music teachers by their retention of the musician's personality pattern more or less intact. If this is found to be the case,
it would help explain a number of the difficulties that many private teachers
encounter in their work. Let us briefly consider a couple of these. Firstly,
there is the notion of the *private* teacher. Many private teachers are far too
private! Their introversion and their introverted lives may well result in a
serious separation from other similar colleagues with whom they might otherwise have enjoyed the benefits of professional interchange. In spite of the
existence of several professional associations for instrumental and singing
teachers, large numbers remain isolated within the privacy of their own
homes. As a result there is little professionalism amongst many private
teachers; they remain inward-looking, lonely, insecure, and, as a result, little
professional development is possible.

A second aspect of the private teacher that militates against change relates
to what I will refer to as the 'apprentice–master craftsman' model. The lin-
eage of teacher–pupil influence makes fascinating study for the musical his-
torian but, in the absence of substantial professional training and re-
education, the patterns of influence can, theoretically at least, be traceable
back through centuries. In my view, an important part of this dilemma
relates to the musician's high levels of intuition in combination with introversion. Whereas classroom music teachers, particularly at the primary
level, appear to use sensing in their approach to their work, it is likely that
private teachers remain introspective and far more in touch with their
unconscious. This might lead us to contemplate whether the tendency of
these individuals to teach their pupils in the same way as they were taught
themselves is, in fact, due to the strong processes of identification that often
occur between teachers and their pupils. It is a common view amongst
instrumental and singing teachers (perhaps particularly, in terms of the
latter) that the best way to teach is through a process of modelling. This is
probably at its most powerful in pupils' first teachers, but the search for
similar relationships at the conservatoire level may often lead to some students being unsettled and continuously on the lookout for a new teacher.
Students are actively encouraged to identify closely with their teachers, and
to internalize the very essential features of their playing so that these things
may, in due course, become unconscious. What becomes internalized is not
only aspects of physical stance, tonal attributes, and all manner of performance factors, but also teaching style, method, approach, and maybe, repertoire as well.

Thus we may begin to see how, in the absence of any evidence to the contrary, the private teacher's introverted intuition may render him or her as
somehow captured in an inward-looking life in which beliefs and modes of
playing and teaching may remain in a time-warp unless they are challenged

by some form of professional interchange. This whole area is poised for empirical enquiry.

Summary

In examining the personality of music teachers the reader is encouraged to consider the existence of two sets of contrasting job requirements being brought into play. After all, the work and life-style of a practising musician and that of a school teacher may well be very different and involve many conflicting demands. Personality research may well offer some insights into the likely internal conflicts that a musician may suffer when finding him or herself mismatched to the demands of classroom life. Specific questions that arise relate to those qualities considered as inherent in the work of the musician which, nevertheless, may need to be if not eliminated at least reduced, once the musician enters the classroom.

American research tends to suggest that the music teacher needs to be less anxious and imaginative than musicians tend to be, and at the same time to be more conscientious and adventurous. It also indicates that the musician's levels of self-sufficiency do not appear to be debilitating in the music room. In contrast, the British research showed that music teachers need to be more extraverted (more outgoing and group-dependent) and less sensitive than performing musicians in general. Whilst noting that these involve reductions on three musicianship-related traits, we should not be surprised to learn that there is evidence of reduced androgyny as well.

Viewed from the point of view of the Myers–Briggs, differences are apparent between primary and secondary school music teachers. Those teaching younger children appear to be more extraverted, sensing, feeling, and judging, whereas those of older pupils emerge as introverted, intuitive, thinking, and perceptive. These disparities might relate to the need for secondary school teachers to retain more of their musicianly qualities than is necessary for teachers of younger pupils. The Myers–Briggs also seems to be sensitive to certain temperamental differences that relate closely to various classroom techniques. Extraverts appear to be more attentive to pupil needs and give more feedback; judging types are more ready and able to expand on difficult points and to offer additional teaching. On the other hand, there is evidence that introverts and feeling types tend to be overfamiliar with their classes.

Private studio teachers, many of whom do not undergo additional training or processes of selection, may as a result retain many of their musicianly qualities of temperament. The outcome of this may manifest itself, for example, in a very introverted stance towards their work, becoming isolated from the outside world and denying themselves the possibilities of professional contact and interchange. This will militate against professional development taking place, resulting in a perpetuation of approaches and methods adopted by their teachers with whom they may continue to identify particularly closely.

THIRTEEN

Development of musical talent

Introduction

We have now arrived at the final chapter of this book in which I will attempt to draw together some of the threads explored during the course of the earlier chapters, particularly those that relate to issues of bringing up, educating, and training musicians. It is important, however, that we should remain concerned with those issues that relate to personality and motivational aspects of temperament. Clearly, a central theme will revolve round the musician's developing personality and the ways in which this relates to programmes of education and training. The central dilemma for those entrusted with the encouragement and education of a young musician is whether he or she *is* different to most other children. Even in the case where this is very apparent, the question that arises is whether, and in what ways, a special environment should be provided in which the practice of music becomes a principal focus for daily life. The alternative solution is to provide as much good quality music tuition and supporting activities as the child needs whilst retaining as normal a life-style as possible. In this way music continues to feature as a part of a broader, more balanced schedule of everyday activity. This is not merely a dilemma for the parents whose children have been identified as outstandingly gifted who have to decide on school placements, it occurs also for those leaving school and about to embark upon higher education.

Identification of musical talent

Clearly, making a decision of the kind outlined above is dependent in the first place upon the ability of parents and educators to identify those qualities of potential that characterize musical giftedness. I know from my own experience over a number of years of assisting at auditions for new pupils at a specialist music school just how difficult this can be—weighing up the factors of technical proficiency, musical imagination and sensitivity, attitudes, effects of good or bad teaching, age, maturity, and so on. Knowing precisely at what point it is reasonable to operate a dividing line between those that 'have it' and those who do not is one of the central dilemmas, even if we clearly knew what 'it' was. In this we are not helped by the kinds of myths and assumptions concerning the bases of giftedness that are prevalent in musical circles (see Sloboda 1990a).

For the sake of brevity, let us examine two opposing views of the whole problem of identifying the musically gifted. Firstly, the folk-lore attitude has traditionally maintained that prodigies identify themselves in very early childhood; that the very special gifts they inherently possess will, quite naturally and more or less effortlessly, manifest themselves in precocious musical acts. The most celebrated case often cited by those who perpetuate the myth is, of course, Mozart, but others such as Rubinstein, Stravinsky, and Maxwell Davies are often referred to in similar vein (see Shuter-Dyson 1985). But for every one of these there are many, many more internationally recognized performers and composers whose talent did not become apparent until much later in their lives, and after considerable application and hard work.

This rather romantic and misleading notion of the child prodigy has been vigorously challenged by Manturzewska (1990), Sosniak (1990), Sloboda *et al.* (1994), and Howe *et al.* (1995) in an attempt to persuade the profession to place more emphasis on the importance of factors other than those that are often considered to be inborn. These researchers suggest that the development of talent has a much more long-term nature, reflecting considerably more environmental influences than often supposed. Sosniak's (1990) view is that it may well consist of a distinct three-phase process, each with its own distinct set of environmental qualities. As a result of her study of concert pianists she concluded that 'youngsters spent several years acquiring knowledge and developing skills and dispositions . . . before they were "discovered" as the most talented' (p. 153).

This is very much the view shared by Sloboda and Howe (1991) who consider that the identification of musical potential in small children may be a non-starter either for the parent or the educator. All these people can do is to provide an environment that is musically stimulating from infancy onwards, encouraging the child's first responses if and when they occur, and continuing to provide appropriate opportunities and support for the further development of his or her abilities. In fact, Howe *et al.* (1995) suggest that the sole indicator of talent in the young musicians they studied was that they appeared to sing at an earlier age than other children. Other factors such as moving to music, showing a liking for music, musical attentiveness, and requesting musical involvement, surprisingly, were not reported by parents as occurring with any degree of significance in these children in comparison with the less talented.

In the light of these rather unpromising results, some other work by Sloboda (1990b) has a refreshing feel to it. He asked a group of adult musicians to recall early musical events in their lives and the significance that these had for them. What he found was that many musicians reported the kinds of incident that I described near the beginning of Chapter 8 (pp. 140–1), and that Walters and Gardner (1992) refer to as 'crystallizing experiences'. Sloboda *et al.* (1994) describe how a group of musicians recalled these as 'deeply felt and intensely positive early experiences to the "internal" aspect of musical events, which seemed to lift them outside the normal state of awareness' (p. 353). They suggest that this is a form of intrinsic motivation: extrinsic motivation they describe as concerned with achievement, accomplishing goals such as gaining the approval of parents and peers, or perhaps winning competitions. Too early an emphasis on extrinsic motivation, particularly goal-directed activity, he maintains, can inhibit the more intrinsically orientated engagement of 'aesthetic and emotional sensibilities'. Furthermore, Sloboda *et al.* suggest that a musician's capacity to play musically is dependent upon these kinds of internal experiences; those who, whilst being technically competent, tend to play 'unmusically' may be more extrinsically focused.

In this piece of work, and particularly in his statements about 'internal' aspects, Sloboda has perhaps drawn closer to the concerns of this book than at any other time. The reader might wish to take the view, as indeed I have throughout this book, that the kinds of 'internal' experience to which he refers may not only relate to the capacity to play musically but become the essential 'life-force' and value system for the musician. These internal needs are felt so acutely because they connect at the deepest of levels of the psyche, with what and who we are—in other words, our personalities. Sloboda suggests that these experiences tend to occur more when we are allowed to be ourselves, unmanipulated, undisturbed, and free. They occur when a person is fully 'in touch' with him or herself; they

. . . seem to be connected with a relaxed, non-threatening environment where nothing is asked of the child. It seems that such an environment is necessary for music to work its strongest emotional effects on individuals. (Sloboda *et al.* 1994, p. 353)

One cannot help thinking that Sloboda is discussing the perceptual orientation of the introverted, sensitive, and imaginative types I have described throughout the pages of this book. It may not merely be the environment that determines whether a powerful experience occurs; it may involve far more the openness and predisposition of the individual to respond. What may be perceived by others to be a common-place occurrence, becomes for the individual a *peak* experience (see Maslow 1974). Whilst Sloboda and his colleagues may not be able to locate early behavioural factors that indicate musical potential, he himself does not by any means close the door on the notion that personality may have an important contribution to make.

Personality and processes of becoming involved with music

In their attack on the 'folk psychology' that maintains that musicianship is dependent upon innate gifts and talents, Sloboda *et al.* (1994) raised the age-old chestnut—the nature–nurture debate, from which this book has attempted to keep clear. Theoretically speaking, the development of people's personalities appears to be a complex outcome of both genetic and environmental influences and, although Cattell (1973) has moved very close to claiming to have identified different balances of these effects on individual personality traits, genetic determinism is not an issue that we need to get drawn into here. Let it suffice to say that, of the personality factors that we have shown to be connected with musicianship, Cattell maintains that virtually all reveal substantial effects of upbringing and environment (p. 147). In other words, the position frequently implicit in our various discussions has suggested that people are attracted to music by their temperamental predisposition to be so. However, it would be very wrong to suggest that this predilection is predominantly genetically predetermined. Not only will environmental factors and, in particular, styles of upbringing exercise considerable causal effects on the development of this predisposition, the line frequently taken here has also stressed the importance of musical involvement itself contributing to the further development of personality.

Let us take just one example: sensitivity. As we observed back in Chapter 4, sensitivity is a powerful factor in childhood generally. Cattell maintained that it is associated with what might be seen by some observers as overindulgent parenting, as opposed to the kind in which the infant is exposed to a realistically demanding and knock-about childhood. Often from a middle class and fastidiously cultured home, the child is considerably protected and sheltered from trauma and stress, and the child's behaviour will be managed through processes of reasoning rather than punishment. As Chapter 4 showed, sensitivity, the most significant component in pathemia, appears to render the child predisposed towards artistic experience, and music in particular. Because of their inclination to evade the harsh realities of life these children will seek out situations and activities in which their feelings and intuition will find full expression. As Cattell (1973) has pointed out, they will naturally be drawn into occupations that offer the comfort and security of what he calls 'cultural myths' (p. 169). Dews and Williams (1989) appear to support this in maintaining that musicians' sensitivity and motivation often predispose them to entwine their musical experiences with what might be perceived as the cultural myths of religion.

In this way, sensitivity, along with other personality factors such as imagination and introversion, which may also have upbringing antecedents (such as overindulgence, and being an only child), combine to predispose children to respond to aesthetic activity. As we noted in connection with the work of Sloboda *et al.* (1994), these tend to occur when circumstances are appropriate, and when the right opportunities arise. Once attracted to music and drawn into a relationship with it, the young person may move into, and through, Sosniak's (1990) first phase of playful experience; lessons are fun, and teachers are warm and enthusiastic. What is important is that they offer the kind of safe and contained environment, very much valued and sought by the sensitive person. As Sosniak describes, this playful activity pays dividends of considerable consequence.

For relatively little effort, the learner got more than might be expected. The effect of the early years of playful, almost romantic involvement . . . seemed . . . to get the learner involved, captivated, 'hooked'—motivated to pursue the matter further. (p. 155)

Sosniak's second phase is where teaching becomes more focused on a more systematic teaching of skills and knowledge, and during this stage the pupil's attention is directed more towards musical detail. This kind of change is also reported by Manturzewska (1990) who describes it as a distinct move away from playing with music to more active and focused learning of it. Although playfulness is not totally left behind, objectives become far more narrowly defined and there is an expectation that these will be mastered. What I would like to suggest here is that certain aspects of personality become more operative and apparent during this phase through two processes. Firstly, it has been maintained throughout this book that, because these factors are of key importance to musical development in that they *enhance* development, they will become increasingly predominant in musicians' personalities as they proceed through this and further stages. The reader may well ask whether there is evidence for this. A glance at Tables 2.1 (p. 41) and 4.1 (p. 76) will show that each of the main musicianship-related traits (aloofness, A–; sensitivity, I+; imagination, M+; and self-sufficiency, Q2+) bears some relationship to gathering expertise in performance. If more evidence is needed, then Table 11.1 (p. 199) provides it, suggesting also that these factors appear to be related to compositional ability as well. In other words, those of a particular temperamental type, which involves this unique combination of traits, are continuously adjusted and committed to music because of what it offers them in terms of meeting emotional and symbolic needs that are deeply embedded within their personalities. It follows from this view that the more individuals display these traits the more motivated they will be in pursuing activities that they feel satisfy their personal needs.

Those readers who may be uncomfortable with this kind of theory may warm more to the second of the two processes that relates to the opposite causal direction. As children move into Sosniak's second phase, the musical demands become more pronounced, and lessons that started off as pure fun gradually take on a more systematic and precise flavour in which specific skills need to be acquired. The process being suggested here involves the kind of environmental causal effect described earlier: these new musical demands create an environment for the child that impacts upon their personality development. The more the child is drawn into music, the more processes take place in which he or she, probably quite unconsciously, gradually develops the temperament that supports these new levels of involvement. As a result, the young musician may become more introverted, developing a form of introspection that combines with the necessary high levels of imagination and sensitivity.

The time is ripe for further research that might begin to disentangle these two effects. For, if evidence can be produced for the existence of this second process, it would provide music educators with the kind of justification that has always eluded them. Quite apart from any impact upon cognitive development, music, it might be argued, operates as a humanizing influence upon the learner from the point of view of personality development. Certainly, one sometimes hears claims that music learning can enhance pupils' attitudes to other subjects, for example, in the cases of slower learners and the maladjusted. Similarly, this belief appears to underlie some aspects of Hungarian music education.

No claim is being made here that these two processes are alternatives or that they work in opposition to one another: both may well be operative during the complex phenomenon of the education and development of the individual. Both may lead to a dropping out of those who, either because they find that music at the new demanding levels no longer excites them or meets their needs, or, alternatively, they experience increasing discomfort with the demands music tuition makes upon them. The distinction is a subtle one and it would be wrong to equate one with nature, and the other with nurture. As I have argued, both have environmental connotations.

Upbringing of young musicians

The above discussion about the types of upbringing that appear to exercise an impact upon children's personality development brings us to the second-order factor that Cattell actually entitled 'upbringing'. Whilst discussion of this factor has been deliberately left to this point, all its constituent primary factors have already been referred to in connection with one or more other second-order factors. The only exception to this is conscientiousness (G+), which belongs to no other secondary factor although it was briefly discussed in connection with issues relating to independence (see pp. 63–4). Cattell describes the conscientiousness factor as revealing itself in persistence of effort—a 'drive to do one's best'. It is also strongly involved in moral concerns for what is right and wrong, and is often linked with notions about the ego's strength in restraining the id.

Cattell originally gave the second-order factor the psychoanalytically orientated title 'super-ego strength' (see Cattell *et al.* 1970) but later he

FACTOR G

Low score EXPEDIENCY G–	versus	High score CONSCIENTIOUSNESS G+
Disregards rules	vs.	Disciplined
Quitting, fickle	vs.	Persevering, deter- mined
Self-indulgent	vs.	Emotionally disciplined
Slack, indolent	vs.	Consistently ordered
Undependable	vs.	Dominated by sense of duty
Disregards obligations to people	vs.	Concerned about moral standards

Box 13.1

re-named it 'upbringing' (Cattell 1973) maintaining that the factor reflected the 'impress of good upbringing in morals and manners' (p. 187). As Figure 13.1 shows, the four primary traits involved are: the conscientiousness (G+) versus expediency (G–) mentioned above (see also p. 63); high self-sentiment (Q3+) versus low self-sentiment (Q3–) (see pp. 88–9); submissiveness (E–) versus dominance (E+) (see pp. 53–4); and desurgency (F–) versus surgency (F+) (see p. 38). Of these four primaries, conscientiousness and self-sentiment are the two most powerful factors in upbringing. It is not without significance for our full understanding of the impress of upbringing styles on personality that the remaining two are closely related to introversion and dependence.

Cattell shows how each of these factors relates to styles of upbringing, particularly to the methods that parents adopt to control and enforce discipline. Conscientiousness, high self-sentiment, and desurgency are all related to high levels of control by parents. The first two of these are related to a form of upbringing that is based on parental warmth and reasoning, with the result that the child develops a high regard and affection for his or her parents. Family routines are well defined and designed to inculcate strong social values. The conscientiousness and high self-sentiment factors exercise a significant inhibiting effect upon the young child's behaviour patterns, causing levels of restraint and, in turn, lower self-sentiment and reduced dominance. However, research shows that conscientiousness and high self-sentiment are both *negatively* associated with artistic interests in adulthood. At the negative pole, the former is associated with rebellion against imposed values, and the latter, of course, with anxiety. In the case of desurgency,

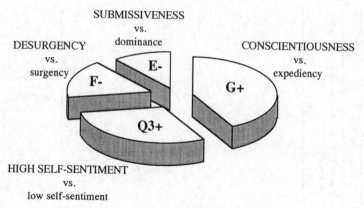

Figure 13.1 Primary factors of 'positive' upbringing in adults.

parental control of the child's behaviour appears to involve the adoption of more severe methods, and its effects appear to relate to aspects of moral inhibition. Finally, submissiveness reflects distinct tendencies towards conforming and conventional behaviour, and children who appear at this end of the factor tend to be obedient, accommodating, and adopt exacting aspirations.

In this way we might wish to speculate whether Cattell's upbringing factor might reveal insights into preferable ways in which young musicians might be nurtured in the home. One of the problems with Cattell's terminology, of course, is that upbringing has to be assigned a positive as well as a negative pole, and this leads him to adopt the rather value-laden 'good' versus 'poor' upbringing labels. Although there may well be readers who wish to argue that the labels might be reversed, particularly in the context of dominance and surgency, we shall side-step a discussion of this. For our purposes, let us agree that upbringing styles can be located somewhere between these two extremes, each with its own pattern of outcomes. Consequently, we shall adopt the less value-laden terms of 'positive' versus 'negative' upbringing, purely on the basis of their statistical polarities.

In line with the kind of theorizing presented in this chapter, I undertook a further analysis of my earlier results (Kemp 1979, 1981a,b). The purpose of this exercise was to develop some additional insights into the developmental patterns occurring from childhood to professional life that might be revealed by the upbringing factor (Kemp 1995). Table 13.1 shows the results of this further study and demonstrates particularly clearly how the main group of young musicians revealed the impact of positive styles of upbringing, in other words, the results of an affectionate, supportive, and structured home nurturing. As the table demonstrates, this was significantly more apparent in those young musicians who were attending junior departments of the conservatoires. This may well be revealing something important, since attendance at these kinds of institution very often involves considerable

Table 13.1 Musicians' results on primary traits associated with upbringing *

	Upbringing †							
	Positive pole				Negative pole			
	Conscientious-ness	High self-sentiment	Submissive-ness	Desurgency	Expediency	Low self-sentiment	Dominance	Surgency
	G+	Q3+	E−	F−	G−	Q3−	E+	F+
Young musicians								
Composite group	G+	Q3+	E−					
At Junior Departments	G+	Q3+						
At special music schools								
Full-time music students								
Composite group	G+			F−				
Performance students					G−		E+	
Composition students					G−	Q3−	E+	
Professional musicians								
Composite group						Q3−‡	E+§	
Composers					G−		E+	

* From Kemp (1995).
† Empty cells indicate non-significant results.
‡ Males only.
§ Females only.

self-sacrifice by parents. As Howe and Sloboda (1991) have suggested, it represents significant levels of investment in their offspring in terms of time, transport, and finance, frequently to the extent of chauffeuring them to the centre of London from the home counties on a regular basis. That the talented youngsters at residential special music schools displayed an absence of these factors tends to suggest that these traits are more linked to parental involvement than levels of musicianship.

The profile of the main group of full-time students reveals a continuation of the same kind of pattern, although with a shift in its detail. These students also show every signs of warm, supportive parenting, together with the only manifestation of desurgency in the table. This suggests the outcome of high levels of parental behavioural control, effecting the establishment of strong work habits and leading to steady achievement. What is of particular interest in Table 13.1 from this point onwards is how all these traits 'go into reverse'. This dramatic about-turn occurring in the full-time students whose levels of performance would have been superior to those of their contemporaries suggests that performance at this level is more associated with negative styles of upbringing. In other words, the profile tends to suggest that these students were from more permissive homes, less controlled by their parents, disobedient, and less responsive to pressure to conform. The pattern is further confirmed by the student composers and, again, in the groups of professional performers and composers.

In what ways might we attempt to interpret these results? Firstly, we might wish to take the view that, in the early stages of their development, young musicians are particularly dependent upon the encouragement and close support that their parents provide in order that the requisite work and practice habits can be developed. The high levels of desurgency in the main group of full-time music students is curious. Most undergraduates are characterized by desurgency as a part of their general introversion: that this trait occurs at significantly higher levels in music students may indicate the continued importance of a learning environment in which work habits and achieving behaviour need to be imposed. These students can be perceived as *dependent* types, still requiring support and encouragement, and they may well look to their conservatoire teachers for the controlling guidance hitherto provided by their parents. One wonders, of course, whether these students will be ultimately successful on completion of their studies, particularly those who wish to enter the world of professional performance. This interpretation is certainly reflected in the profiles of the more talented performers and composers, which tend to suggest that, at a higher level, these individuals are considerably more autonomous types. This seems to be in line with Sosniak's third phase of development in which a sense of personal commitment to the pursuit of excellence is developed, and where the musician becomes a member of a musical community to which there is a shared sense of personal commitment. In line with what we noted in connection with independence (Chapter 3), these musicians take control of their own destiny and are totally self-motivated and self-directed. In common with other artistic types they disregard and reject all pressures to conform to norms that are perceived as peripheral to their own internal values. As Barron (1955) observed, this pattern, which suggests a lack of discipline, is more appropriately interpretable by invoking the notion that creative types adopt their own standards and norms. After all, this is precisely what creative people are required to do—to break away from externally imposed moulds of thinking and behaving and, instead, to conform to sets of personal and internalized rules generated and imposed by themselves.

The important question remains, of course, whether Table 13.1 reveals a population whose personality traits gradually undergo a change or, alternatively, a population that changes through procedures of selection and self-selection, representing a new and more sharply defined membership. Until research is successful in identifying causal direction we are again left to speculate about this and, as above, agree that perhaps the relationship is two-way. Drop-out rates will certainly assist in clarifying the pattern that emerges in the second part of Table 13.1, yet, at the same time, what might be referred to as the 'humanizing' influence of music should not be overlooked. Nevertheless, for the parent and the music educator the question is a real one and not a theoretical construct. To what extent should the young musician be cocooned in an environment in which parents assume the main thrust of responsibility for most aspects of their children's musical development? Might this overlook the importance of Sosniak's first phase of development? Might it place too much stress on Sloboda's notion of external motivation? Is this the best environment for the qualities in the second part of Table 13.1 to be developed?

Perhaps the answer to these questions relates to the idea that parents and educators should provide an encouraging environment in which the deeply internal motivations of the child are respected as being the *central* motivating force. Those parents and teachers who overlook these, or who try to replace these by 'invading' this private space with external pressures and coercion, are inviting rebellion and drop-out at a later stage. The dividing line would appear to be a fine one. As Davidson *et al.* (1996) have shown, those young musicians who appeared to be the most successful possessed parents who became fully involved in their children's lessons and practice routines. What remains unclear is whether their musicians, who were aged between 8 and 18 years, will continue to excel at the higher education level and beyond into the profession. In other words, might their research reveal only the one side of an inverted U relationship between parental support and excellence of the kind suggested by Table 13.1? The thought that this degree of parental support might be intrusive and of relatively short-term benefit is given some credence by Freeman's (1991) work. Whilst supporting the findings of Davidson *et al.* in terms of the links between family support and entry to a specialist music school, in a follow-up study she found that the 'gifts' of these young musicians were not sustainable at an outstanding level, no matter how hard they worked. This view tends to be supported by Butler (1994) who found that a large proportion of drop-outs from a London conservatoire comprised students who had come from special schools.

In respecting the child's individuality by providing a 'facilitating environment' of encouragement, sensitive tuition, space, and freedom, creativity may be allowed to grow. As I have mentioned before, Roe's (1967) claim that too much loving and too little neglect does not produce a creative child appears to be particularly pertinent here. Parents, and particularly the mothers of the gifted need to 'let go', and the biographies of musicians often reveal how traumatic this severance can be. This is especially the case after, what feels like a lifetime of investment of time, energy, and money, the young musician shows signs of taking responsibility for his or her own destiny. A particularly poignant example of this is the case of Joshua Bell, the young American violinist, whose mother assumed so much of the responsibility for his earlier development that considerable difficulty was experienced in the two of them eventually breaking loose.

Special or mainstream schools?

The above discussion raises several issues about the selection of pupils for special music schools as well as their curricula and working environments. Here, also, it is important to keep this focused upon matters which relate to personality. Therefore, perhaps as a starting point, we should take a closer look at some of my own findings (Kemp 1979, 1981a). As mentioned above, in addition to the very telling profile of a group of pupils attending specialist music schools there existed a second subgroup of young musicians attending junior departments of the music conservatoires whilst remaining in mainstream secondary education.

The reader may need reminding about the context of this research. The overall group of secondary school musicians were of fairly modest musical ability (performance criteria being: grade three at 13 years; four at 14, and so on). It will be recalled that, even at this level, these youngsters, were identifiable by their introversion (J+ and Q2+), pathemia (E− and I+), and positive upbringing (E−, G+, and Q3+) (Kemp 1981a). Table 13.2 offers a comparison of this profile with that of the subgroup attending mainstream schools but receiving tuition at the music conservatoires. In comparison with the main group, these young people emerged as less introverted (H+ and J−), of positive upbringing (G+ and Q3+), and significantly more stable. As the table demonstrates, this lack of anxiety, in comparison with that of the main group, emerged on five of the six traits related to stability (C+, H+, O−, Q3+, and Q4−) (Kemp 1979). Whilst it cannot be maintained that these young

Table 13.2 Summary of research with young musicians

Type of group	HSPQ primary factors ¶						
General group *	E−	G+	I+	J+	Q2+	Q3+	
Conservatoire †	C+	G+	H+	J−	O−	Q3+	Q4−
Special school *	A−	D+	H−	J+	O+		

* From Kemp (1981a).
† From Kemp (1979).
¶ A−, aloofness; C+, high ego strength; D+, excitability; E−, submissiveness; G+, conscientiousness; H+, adventurousness; H−, shyness; I+, sensitivity; J+, individualistic; J−, zestful; O+, guilt proneness; O−, self-assurance; Q2+, self-sufficiency; Q3+, high self-sentiment; Q4−, low ergic tension.

musicians were of a comparable performing standard to those attending specialist schools, they would certainly have reflected higher performing standards than those in the composite group. Table 13.2 also shows the results for the pupils at special music schools. These indicate an interesting reversal on two of these traits, although not always involving the same primary factors. In comparison with the overall secondary school group they were significantly more introverted (aloof, A–; timid, H–; and internally restrained, J+) and anxious (excitable, D+; timid, H–; and guilt prone, O+). The contrast between these two profiles is striking, and we can only speculate about their significance, not only in terms of musicianship levels but also in their social and educational circumstances.

Firstly, the relative extraversion of the conservatoire group appeared to occur on traits that are not normally associated with musicianship, and besides, as already mentioned, these young musicians would have been generally *more* talented than the comparison group. We are therefore left to consider explanations that relate to extramusical factors. Their positive upbringing may offer us a clue to an interpretation of the whole profile. As we observed earlier, the positive upbringing reflects a life of utmost stability, parental support and encouragement, a loving yet firm fostering of conscientious and responsible behaviour, leading to the establishment of good working habits. There is just a suggestion here of the 'nurtured by love' concept very much promulgated by Suzuki in his original violin teaching method (see Suzuki 1983). The extraversion may support this notion, reflecting a child who is not left in seclusion to practise for long hours. On the contrary, it may well reveal a situation in which a parent remains present for many of the practice sessions, rendering the routines much more acceptable for an extraverted child to cope with. Incidentally, such an approach might be quite unacceptable to the more introverted types who need, above all, to preserve their periods of seclusion. The group's stability speaks for itself: it reflects an emotional maturity, gregariousness, self-confidence, control of impulse, and relaxed attitude—all qualities of the kind one would expect as a result of a harmonious, caring, and well structured upbringing.

For one reason or another we need to find explanations of a very different kind for the personality characteristics of those receiving their education in special music schools. As the reader will have noted, they did not reveal any substantial departure from the positive upbringing of the main group, although they certainly lack the levels of the conservatoire group. Their aloofness (A–) may well be interpretable in musicianship terms, but less so their timidity (H–) and internal restraint (J+). Cattell *et al.* (1970) suggest that the H– factor is related to a tendency to be embittered, rule-bound, and of restricted interests (pp. 91–2): they interpret the J+ trait as revealing a rigid, guarded uncompromising nature, and mental fastidiousness (pp. 95–6). Associated with this form of introversion are the three factors related to anxiety. Apart from the timidity (H–) already mentioned, in the D+ factor we can locate tendencies for these pupils to be demanding, prone to jealousy, egotistical, and to show many nervous symptoms (pp. 84–5). As we have noted earlier, the guilt proneness (O+) factor describes the depressed, lonely, and moody person, a worrier, with a strong sense of obligation and feelings of inadequacy.

In attempting to account for this kind of profile, one wonders whether separation from their parents and the pressures of a 'hothouse' existence might create some of these phenomena in the young musicians. What this picture describes is an institution of individuals, prone to loneliness and to being overwrought and possibly experiencing difficulties in relating to one another. It appears ironic that, in an institution where pupils, and presumably teachers, will have so much in common from the point of view of interests and temperament, relationship problems seem likely to occur. These children appear to have deep, unarticulated personal needs, and yet, at the same time, emerge as jealous and arrogant. Nigel Kennedy, who attended a specialist music school, describes how at the age of 7 he was required to practise for 4 hours a day on his own, and how lonely and depressed he became, seeking companionship by offering to share his Mars bar with other pupils as a bribe (Lawson 1993).

What is interesting about the description developed above is how so many of these introverted and anxiety related traits reflect aspects of social skills, or a lack of them. In outlining some of the possible dangers of hothousing, Howe (1990b) suggests that one of the negative effects of attempting to accelerate special abilities is that pupils may be deprived of valuable childhood experiences. These, he maintains, are 'related to personality and temperament, and they underlie a person's curiosity, self-motivation, commitment, and self-confidence' (p. 25), and contribute to the overall quality of the child's future life. The picture painted above is a worrying one because it suggests a psychologically unhealthy individualism that may militate against the development of close relationships with other fellow musicians in the special school. But the deprivation may go further than this: a school restricted to striving young musicians precludes the opportunity of relationships with the rich variety of very different types who make up the populations of ordinary schools. In her work with conservatoire students, Butler (1994) claimed that those students who came from specialist music schools tended to have the most reported emotional problems and, as already commented upon, the highest drop-out rate, observing that many of them 'can only identify themselves as a musician, not as a person in their own right, and use their playing as a self-validation' (p. 199).

A key aspect of special music schools, emphasized by the Calouste Gulbenkian Foundation Report (1978) into the training of musicians, was the 'stimulus of competition' within a boarding school environment. One wonders how unhealthy this might be should it get out of hand in a community where, in a sense, all the pupils are in competition with each other, and where, at each level, there are winners and losers, and no escape. The depressive tendencies, timidity, and feelings of inadequacy of these pupils, which are at the same time linked to degrees of jealousy and arrogance, may well ring warning bells for the reader. In the light of the strong interconnection between musicians' levels of self-esteem and personal musical success, one wonders whether such a focused attention on competitive music activity will result in the generation of a particularly debilitating environment. As Howe suggests, most children, however precocious they are, like to have friends of their own age and, what is more, to feel accepted by them. The interpersonal dynamics created by an unduly competitive environment may result in destroying the possibility of pupils developing genuinely close and nurturing relationships. This would particularly appear to be the case in connection with sensitive young people like musicians.

Alongside what may appear to be an unfair criticism of specialist music schools, admittedly as they were some 15 years ago, we should consider the musician's lot in an average mainstream secondary school. Earlier, in Chapter 8, we noted that those children who play gender-mismatched instruments can sometimes be exposed to peer rejection, even to the extent of being bullied (Boulton and O'Neill 1994). Such treatment of, say a boy violinist, is likely to render him isolated, distressed, and deeply psychologically damaged. Of course, this kind of treatment would be likely to occur to a child who was already socially withdrawn and sensitive and, as we noted elsewhere in the same chapter, violinists may well tend to be of this type.

To escape this treatment it would seem obvious and appropriate to transfer the child to a special school if he or she is of a sufficient musical standard. Howe and Sloboda's (1992) research highlights the sense of relief that many of these children feel on being withdrawn from mainstream schools. They offer the case of a male adolescent pianist who explained

... everybody teased me about all the pratty things I used to do. I ... thought, 'Well, I'll be in with people who are similar to myself. They're all musically gifted. People might not treat me the way they used to do at my other primary school. They used to say, 'Look at him over there, brain box', because I played the piano. It wasn't nasty or anything, but it wasn't particularly nice either. (p. 17)

Interestingly, the conservatoire group of pupils did not reveal any temperamental effects of the kind of bullying and ostracism referred to by Boulton and O'Neill, and we are left to consider whether the more resilient pupils are either able to cope with rejection or, alternatively, whether their heightened extraversion and adjustment meant that it did not occur in the first place. What may be revealed here is that those young musicians who are poorly adjusted socially in ordinary schools, perhaps not entirely for musical reasons, are withdrawn in favour of a more sheltered environment.

The notion that the personality problems of the gifted cannot necessarily be directly attributed to the educational context was offered by Jung (1964). It was his view that

. . . great gifts, are the fairest, and often the most dangerous, fruits on the tree of humanity. They hang on the weakest branches, which easily break. In most cases . . . the gift develops in inverse ratio to the maturation of the personality as a whole, and often one has the impression that a creative personality grows at the expense of the human being. (p. 141)

The great problem about educating the gifted, Jung maintained, was making sure that personality develops at the same rate as the particular gift. If not, the gift can prove to be destructive and, he observes, 'there are not a few gifted persons whose usefulness is paralysed, not to say perverted, by their human shortcomings'. What clearly arises from this is the notion that there may well be inherent problems within the condition of giftedness itself. It would therefore appear incumbent upon educational institutions to heed this warning in an attempt to provide programmes of educational activity designed to compensate for any weaknesses in personality development.

It is easy to overstate and polarize these arguments but, nevertheless, the evidence presented here generally supports the above concerns. In making decisions about their children's future, parents need to make sure that undue demands and pressures are not being made upon their children. Placing the mantle of giftedness on a child should not be done lightly; it can be a great burden. As parents we all want to do our best for our children, but when certain methods of developing a special ability appear to preclude growth in other important, yet more general areas, especially emotional and social development, some of these approaches may need challenging. Occasionally, children need protection from exploitation by overambitious parents who appear to manipulate their children for the purpose of satisfying their own egos. The dividing line between active encouragement and what can amount to abuse is a subtle one: perhaps much more subtle than as presented here.

Higher education

This section of the chapter will touch on issues that arise out of the personality research cited in this book. It certainly cannot attempt to pursue some of the fundamental questions about the nature of music undergraduate learning in universities or conservatoires. Nor can it explore in any detail what we *actually* mean by the terms 'education' and 'training' in music. Let it suffice to say that Paynter's (1977) distinction between 'music*al* education' and 'music *in* education' might be helpful to us here. In his discussion of these terms, Plummeridge (1994) points out that, although the former may be seen as essentially training and the latter as education, there is considerable overlap. Whilst agreeing that there will inevitably be elements of each in the other, the distinction may be helpful in terms of teachers' objectives, their teaching styles and approaches, and the developmental outcomes as far as students are concerned.

One of our central concerns here is with the impact that music learning makes on the developing personality, not merely at the higher education level but also in schools. The question that needs raising, particularly in relation to some of the research referred to here, is whether our styles of music teaching adequately consider the development of the whole person. To take an unduly narrow 'training' approach clearly may not give much thought to the impact that music teaching exerts on the rest of the person's emotional development and sense of well being.

In writing about the education of young musicians, Pruett (1990) makes what she considers to be her most important point, that teachers have a responsibility to

. . . encourage the very gifted to avoid the sense of the asymmetric, misshapen, or unfinished life and self . . . The most enduring artistic achievements involve the whole person and his careful understanding and intimate expression of his imagination's light *and* dark components, not just his facile fingerings. (p. 322)

Our discussions in Chapter 5 about self-concept development in musicians tended to show how weak their egos can be, and how that this is linked to low levels of self-esteem particularly in adulthood. Csikszentmihalyi and Getzels (1973) suggested that the low self-esteem (C– and Q3–) of the artist is related more to adverse conditions than to the nature of the task. One is left to consider then whether it is the fact that musicians have been brought up and trained to mobilize so much of their energies and invest an unduly large proportion of themselves in music that results in untold psychological damage. This would be particularly so if the individual's investment of energy does not appear to be offering the kind of return (musical perfection) that was envisaged. The paradox, of course, is that it may well be the person's low self-esteem that attracted them to music in the first place with the study of music seen as an opportunity to unify and make whole a fragmented and vulnerable ego. When this does not occur, the individual's anxiety levels may well rise as a direct result of further disintegration.

And here, of course, the findings of Sloboda *et al.* (1996), which claim that the amount of practice is 'a key variable in the determination of musical expertise', can be grossly misinterpreted. That a person cannot become a musician without engaging in substantial hours of practice appears fairly obvious; the converse may well not be true. The saying, 'practice makes perfect' may, taken in isolation, be misleading and, for some, dubious advice. The other key variables, such as personality and motivation, cannot be overlooked; no amount of practice will result in musical success for those who may lack these other attributes. I believe that Sloboda *et al.*'s question 'how it comes about that high achieving musicians are able to sustain, from the earliest years, levels of formal practice which are greatly in excess of the population norm' is, in part at least, answered in this book. It would perhaps go something like this: for some who are temperamentally suited to long hours in seclusion, practice is not such a hardship; for others it may be at a great cost. The anxiety seen in adult musicians, both students and professionals, of which the low esteem is only a part, may be interpreted as revealing, amongst all the other explanations we have considered, a maladjustment and discomfort with 'what life offers'. In the light of this low self-esteem, one worrying aspect is the musician's tendency to project a 'grandiosity and omnipotence' which, as we noted on page 100, Pruett (1991) has remarked upon. It is particularly worrying that, because of their high rates of investment of themselves in music, musicians feel the need to mask their lack of self-worth in this way.

At this point we return to the earlier question. To what extent is a higher education in music an educative process? If the musician's well-being is to be considered, the demands of a higher education must be seen to be educative. That what is learned deeply impacts upon individuals and extends their understanding of themselves in relation to the world as it exists around them would appear to be a fundamental characteristic. Although it sounds like a truism: education makes for a better person—more aware, more human, more able to relate to the society in which he or she lives. We are forced to ask ourselves therefore whether music teaching always reflects these kinds of aims, or whether somewhere along the line the needs of the person may somehow be lost sight of.

It certainly goes beyond the scope of this book to suggest ways in which higher education in music gives full consideration to educative processes. What can be said here is that the warning signs inherent in the musician's personality structure might begin to offer insights. One issue relates to the degree of specialism required of the professional performer, which, in itself, demands training with clear, relevant, and specific objectives. But what percentage of music students actually take up a performing career? Has the remainder undergone the same forms of training to no avail when a broader education would have been more beneficial? This question appears to be particularly pertinent if, as one suspects, large numbers of these students emerge at the conclusion of their courses with feelings of failure at not 'making the grade'.

It may often be the case that it is during higher education that problems of maladjustment can arise for music students, particularly in respect of the role that their parents had occupied in the build-up to their arrival in higher education. As we observed in our discussions about upbringing, a change of pattern, which appears to be associated with musical success, certainly occurs during studentship. It appears that those who continue into the profession reveal something of a different form of upbringing to others who do not. In this respect, Butler's (1994) work may offer some particular insights. In her research with conservatoire students, which was, in part, psychodynamically orientated, she observed that, in those students who had enjoyed a good relationship with their fathers, this appeared to be associated with higher levels of musical achievement and self-esteem. In her discussion of this, Butler suggests that music students are driven by two forms of superego: one focused upon the mother, the parental conscience, and the other on the father, the artistic superego. These two, she maintains, need to be kept in balance, and those who were too dominated by their mothers to the exclusion of their fathers would be likely to experience problems. In both cases these are highly internalized 'drivers' and may well affect a student's relationship with his or her teachers. It appears so very often the case that it is the mother who not only takes on the upbringing role generally, but who also becomes the driving force, taking on the supporting, encouraging, and controlling aspects of the young musician's development. Those students who are too dominated by their mothers in this way may find it increasingly difficult to relate to their teachers in a mature and satisfactory manner, continuing to seek out childlike nurture and containment.

Finally, in closing this chapter, perhaps it might be worth returning to Pruett's (1990) view about the need for parents and teachers to provide musical students with opportunities to have 'diverse experiences that permit them to reflect upon their whole life, such as the other arts and humanities outside music, i.e., a fundamental, abiding reverence for one's entire imagination' (p. 322). Dews and Williams (1989) took the view that young musicians who had taken part in informal music-making prior to receiving more formal tuition appeared to reveal a looser, yet not disadvantageous, connection between their musical capabilities and their self-esteem. This may relate to Sosniak's first 'playful' stage, but the message appears clear. Too early systematic music tuition can narrow down a child's focus prematurely to the detriment of engaging in wider, more socially rich activities that help to develop a more gregarious and adjusted person. Perhaps there is an argument here for a wider curriculum in the education of the musician, and, certainly, many higher education institutions now offer a broader range of contextual studies with this in mind. From my own work with postgraduate music students I have witnessed the beneficial impact that first-hand experience in another expressive art, particularly dance or drama, can exercise on a student's musical imagination. The rationale for this may well relate to offering students an opportunity to engage in a shared aesthetic activity, encouraging openness, receptivity, and different forms of aesthetic sensitivity that all their preconceptions and narrower training may prevent from occurring in their own art. In this way musical processes can frequently become more deeply personal and significant.

Summary

The notion of the child prodigy is dismissed by research as a myth. Studies show that most young performers, far from inheriting a 'gift', need to work hard at developing their abilities over a long period of hard work and appli-cation. In many cases the emergence of talent appears to be due to parental support and encouragement, but this alone may not be sufficient. Evidence suggests that such external factors may need augmenting by the individual receiving some form of 'crystallizing experience'. During such events a young person may become powerfully aware of a deep need to engage in a particular mode of expression, and this thereafter becomes an internal and motivating life force.

Personality research certainly supports both belief in environmental effects on motivation and the internal drive theory. Alongside genetic influ-ences, styles of upbringing exert a major impact upon the child's personali-ty development including those non-cognitive qualities that are conducive to musical involvement. These may become entwined with, and indistin-guishable from, the more overt parental practices used to encourage and support musical interests. Clearly, teachers engage in this process as well, ensuring that tuition passes through an initial fun phase that gradually gives way to more explicit demands as the learner begins to show the necessary signs of personal commitment.

Currently, research appears to be poised at a point at which it may, per-haps wrongly, conclude that parental and teacher influence is the strongest factor in ensuring that pupils engage in extensive hours of practice, and thereby develop the desired levels of talent. This may need to be challenged by other research that suggests that, although parental and teacher influence may allow a pupil to achieve certain degrees of success, it may not ensure success at the highest levels. The essential difference might lie in the degree to which parental and teacher support ceases to be facilitative and becomes unduly manipulative.

Apart from the difficulties of distinguishing giftedness, several issues arise concerning the provision of special schooling for the musically talent-ed. For example, research identifies particularly high levels of anxiety in pupils at special schools and, for the moment, its causes remain largely obscure. We are left to speculate whether separation from parents may be an issue, or if the 'hothouse' environment with its pressures and interpersonal competitive elements may manifest itself in these negative effects.

Finally, research highlights some of the implications for higher education in music. One issue relates to the ways in which music students may be in danger of investing too much of themselves in their quest for musical per-fection. For many it can become an 'all or nothing' issue and, as a result, they become narrowly fixated on their identities purely as musicians, and with all the attendant anxiety about failure. This manifests itself in their search for adulation through music, whilst developing feelings of omnipotence within the narrow confines of their musical existence. There is evidence here to suggest that, if a higher education in music is to be truly educational, it may need to taker a broader view of the way in which music relates to other areas of human experience.

References

Ables, H. F. and Porter, S. Y. (1978). The sex-stereotyping of musical instruments. *Journal of Research in Music Education*, **26**, 65–75.

Adcock, N. V., Adcock, C. J., and Walkley, F. H. (1974). Basic dimensions of personality. *International Review of Applied Psychology*, **23**, 131–6.

Allport, G. W. (ed.)(1960). *Personality and social encounter*. Boston: Beacon Press.

Allport, G. W. and Odbert, H. S. (1936). Trait-names a psycho-lexical study. *Psychological Monographs*, 47, Whole no. 211.

Babikian, H. M. (1985). The psychoanalytic treatment of the performing artist: superego aspects. *Journal of the American Academy of Psychoanalysis*, **13**, 139–48.

Bachmann, M-L. (1991). *Dalcroze today: an education through and into music* (trans. D. Parlett). Oxford: Clarendon.

Bandura, A. (1977). Self-efficacy: towards a unifying theory of behavior therapy. *Psychological Review*, **84**, 191–215.

Barron, F. (1955). The disposition towards originality. *Journal of Abnormal and Social Psychology*, **51**, 478–85.

Barron, F. (1957). Originality in relation to personality and intellect. *Journal of Personality*, **25**, 730–42.

Barron, F. (1963). *Creativity and psychological health: origins of personal vitality and creative freedom*. Princeton, New Jersey: Van Nostrand.

Bayne, R. (1994). The 'big five' versus the Myers–Briggs. *The Psychologist*, **7**, 14–16.

Bell, C. R. and Cresswell, A. (1984). Personality differences among musical instrumentalists. *Psychology of Music*, **12**, 83–93.

Bem, S. L. (1974). The measurement of psychological androgyny. *Journal of Consulting and Clinical Psychology*, **42**, 155–62.

Bem, S. L. (1975). Sex-role adaptability: one consequence of psychological androgyny. *Journal of Personality and Social Psychology*, **31**, 634–43.

Bem, S. L. (1981). Gender schema theory: a cognitive account of sex typing. *Psychological Review*, **88**, 354–64.

Bentley, A. (1966a). *Musical ability in children and its measurement*. London: Harrap.

Bentley, A. (1966b). *Bentley measures of musical abilities*. London: Harrap.

Ben-Tovim, A. and Boyd, D. (1990). *The right instrument for your child: a practical guide for parents and teachers*. London: Gollancz.

Bernreuter, R. G. (1933). The theory and construction of the personality inventory. *Journal of Social Psychology*, **4**, 402–3.

Boult, A. C. (1963). *Thoughts on conducting*. London: Phoenix.

Boulton, M. J. and O'Neill S. (1994). Children's perceptions of the social consequences of playing most and least favoured musical instruments: being liked, bullied and ignored by one's peers. Unpublished research paper, University of Keele.

Bowen, M. (1981). *Michael Tippett*. London: Robson.

Brebner, J. and Flavell, R. (1978). The effect of catch-trials on speed and accuracy among introverts and extraverts in a simple RT task. *British Journal of Psychology*, **69**, 9–15.

Broadhurst, P. L. (1959). The interaction of task difficulty and motivation: The Yerkes–Dodson Law revived. *Acta Psychologica*, **16**, 321–38.

Brodsky, W., Sloboda, J. A., and Waterman, M. G. (1994). An exploratory investigation into auditory style as a correlate and predictor of musical performance anxiety. *Medical Problems of Performing Artists*, **9**, 101–12.

Bruce, R. and Kemp, A. E. (1993). Sex-stereotyping in children's preferences for musical instruments. *British Journal of Music Education*, **10**, 213–18.

Builione, R. S. and Lipton, J. P. (1983). Stereotypes and personality of classical musicians. *Psychomusicology*, **3**, 36–43.

Burns, D. (1980). *Feeling good: the new mood therapy*. New York: New American Library.

Burns, R. B. (1979). *The self concept: theory, measurement, development and behaviour*. London: Longman.

Burt, C. (1939). The factorial analysis of emotional traits. *Character and Personality*, **7**, 238–54; 285–99.

Butler, C. (1994). The effects of psychological stress on the success and failure of music conservatoire students. Unpublished MPhil dissertation, Keele University.

Caldwell, A. E. (1972). La malinconia: final movement of Beethoven's quartet op. 18, no. 6: a musical account of manic depressive states. *Journal of the American Medical Women's Association*, **27**, 241–8.

Calouste Gulbenkian Foundation (1978). *Training musicians: a report to the Calouste Gulbenkian Foundation on the training of professional musicians*. London: Calouste Gulbenkian Foundation.

Cattell, R. B. (1945). The principal trait clusters for describing personality. *Psychological Bulletin*, **42**, 129–61.

Cattell, R. B. (1947). Confirmation and clarification of primary personality traits. *Psychometrica*, **12**, 187–220.

Cattell, R. B. (1956). Validation and intensification of the sixteen personality factor questionnaire. *Journal of Clinical Psychology*, **12**, 205–14.

Cattell, R. B. (1957). *Personality and motivation structure and measurement*. New York: World Book Co.

Cattell, R. B. (1971). *Abilities: their structure, growth, and action*. Boston: Houghton Mifflin.

Cattell, R. B. (1972a). The 16PF and basic personality structure: a reply to Eysenck. *Journal of Behavioural Science*, **1**, 169–87.

Cattell, R. B. (1972b). The nature and genesis of mood states; a theoretical model with experimental measurements concerning anxiety, depression, arousal, and other mood states. In *Anxiety: current trends in theory and research*, Vol. 1 (ed. C. D. Spielberger), pp. 115–83. New York: Academic.

Cattell, R. B. (1973). *Personality and mood by questionnaire: a handbook of interpretive theory, psychometrics, and practical procedures*. San Francisco: Jossey-Bass.

Cattell, R. B. (1981). *Personality and learning theory*. New York: Springer.

Cattell, R. B. (1995). The fallacy of the five factors in the personality sphere. *The Psychologist*, **8**, 207–8.

Cattell, R. B. and Anderson, D. R. (1953a). *The IPAT Music Preference Test of Personality*. Champaigne, Illinois: Institute for Personality and Ability Testing.

Cattell, R. B. and Anderson, D. R. (1953b). The measurement of personality and behavior disorders by the IPAT Music Preference Test. *Journal of Applied Psychology*, **37**, 446–54.

Cattell, R. B. and Butcher, H. J. (1968). *The prediction of achievement and creativity*. Indianapolis: Bobbs-Merrill.

Cattell, R. B. and Cattell, M. D. (1969). *The High School Personality Questionnaire*. Champaign, Illinois: Institute for Personality and Ability Testing.

Cattell, R. B. and Child, D. (1975). *Motivation and dynamic structure*. London: Holt, Rinehart and Winston.

Cattell, R. B. and Dreger, R. N. (ed.) (1975). *Handbook of modern personality theory*. New York: Appleton-Century-Crofts.

Cattell, R. B. and Kline, P. (1977). *The scientific analysis of personality and motivation*. New York: Academic.

Cattell, R. B. and Saunders, D. R. (1954). Musical preferences and personality diagnosis: a factorization of one hundred and twenty themes. *Journal of Social Psychology*, **39**, 3–24.

Cattell, R. B., Sealey, A. P., and Sweney, A. B. (1966). What can personality and motivation source trait measurement add to the prediction of school achievement? *British Journal of Educational Psychology*, **36**, 280–95.

Cattell, R. B., Eber, H. W., and Tatsuoka, M. M. (1970). *Handbook for the sixteen personality factor questionnaire (16 PF)*. Campaign, Illinois: Institute for Personality and Ability Testing.

Chambers, J. A. (1969). Beginning a multidimensional theory of creativity. *Psychological Reports*, **25**, 779–99.

Cooke, D. (1959). *The language of music*. London: Oxford University Press.

Cooley, J. C. (1961). A study of the relation between certain mental and personality traits and ratings of musical abilities. *Journal of Research in Music Education*, **9**, 108–17.

Cooper, C. L. and Wills, G. I. D. (1989). Popular musicians under pressure. *Psychology of Music*, **17**, 22–36.

Copland, A. (1952). *Music and imagination*. London: London University Press.

Costa, P. T. Jr. and McCrae, R. R. (1985). *The NEO personality inventory manual*. Odessa, Florida: Psychological Assessment Resources.

Costa, P. T., Jr and McCrae, R. R. (1992a). *Revised NEO Personality Inventory (NEO-PI-R) and NEO Five-Factor Inventory (NEO-FFI) professional manual*. Odessa, Florida: Psychological Assessment Resources.

Costa, P. T., Jr and McCrae, R. R. (1992b). Four ways five factors are basic. *Personality and Individual Differences*, **13**, 653–65.

Craske, M. G. and Craig, K. D. (1984). Musical performance anxiety: the three-systems model and self-efficacy theory. *Behaviour Research and Therapy*, **22**, 267–80.

Csikszentmihalyi, M. and Getzels, J. W. (1973). The personality of young artists: an empirical and theoretical exploration. *British Journal of Psychology*, **64**, 91–104.

Csikszentmihalyi, M. and Robinson, R. (1986). Culture, time, and the development of talent. In *Conceptions of giftedness*, (ed. R. J. Sternberg and J. Davidson), pp. 264–84. Cambridge University Press.

Daoussis, L. and McKelvie, S. J. (1986). Musical preferences and effects of music on a reading comprehension test for extraverts and introverts. *Perceptual and Motor Skills*, **62**, 283–9.

Davidson, J. W., Howe, M. J. A., Moore, D. G., and Sloboda, J. A. (1996). The role of parental influences in the development of musical performance. *British Journal of Developmental Psychology*, (In press).

Davies, J. B. (1976). Orchestral discord. *New Society*, **35**, 46–7.

Davies, J. B. (1978). *The psychology of music*. London: Hutchinson.

Deary, I. J. and Matthews, G. (1993). Personality traits are alive and well. *The Psychologist*, **6**, 299–311.

Delzell, J. K. and Leppla, D. A. (1992). Gender association of musical instruments and preferences of fourth-grade students for selected instruments. *Journal of Research in Music Education*, **40**, 93–103.

Dews, C. L. B. and Williams, M. S. (1989). Student musicians' personality styles, stresses, and coping patterns. *Psychology of Music*, **17**, 37–47.

Dickson, J. H. (1992). The training of conductors through the methodology of kinaesthetics. *Journal of the American Choral Directors Association*, **XXXII** (8), 15–19.

Dollinger, S. J. (1993). Research note: personality and music preference: extraversion and excitement seeking or openness to experience? *Psychology of Music*, **21**, 73–7.

Drevdahl, J. E. (1956). Factors of importance for creativity. *Journal of Clinical Psychology*, **12**, 21–6.

Drevdahl, J. E. and Cattell, R. B. (1958). Personality and creativity in artists and writers. *Journal of Clinical Psychology*, **12**, 21–6.

Dunbar-Wells, R. (1995). The use of metaphor in voice teaching: a comparative study of sinus tone production and vocal cord theories. *Australian Voice*, **1**, 55–64.

Durrant, C. (1994). Towards a model of effective communication: a case for structured teaching of conducting. *British Journal of Music Education*, **11**, 57–76.

Dyce, J. A. and O'Connor, B. P. (1994). The personalities of popular musicians. *Psychology of Music*, **22**, 168–73.

Easton, C. (1989). *Jacqueline du Pré: a biography*. London: Hodder & Stroughton.

Ekman, K. (1946). *Jean Sibelius: his life and personality* (trans. E. Birse). New York: Tudor.

Elkind, D. (1981). *The hurried child: growing up too fast too soon*. Reading, Massachusetts: Addison Wesley.

Ellis, M. C. (1995). Research note: Field dependence–independence and texture discrimination in college non-music majors. *Psychology of Music*, **23**, 184–9.

Ellis, M. C. and McCoy, C. W. (1990). Field dependence/independence in noncollege music majors and their ability to discern form in music. *Journal of Research in Music Education*, **38**, 302–10.

Entwistle, N. J. (1972). Personality and academic attainment. *British Journal of Educational Psychology*, **42**, 137–51.

Ericsson, K. A., Tesch-Römer, C., and Krampe, R. T. (1990). The role of practice and motivation in the acquisition of expert-level performance in real life: an empirical evaluation of a theoretical framework. In *Encouraging the development of exceptional skills and talents* (ed. M. J. A. Howe), pp. 109–30. London: British Psychological Society.

Eysenck, H. J. (1959). *Maudsley Personality Inventory*. London: University of London Press.

Eysenck, H. J. (1965). *Fact and fiction in psychology*. Harmondsworth: Penguin.

Eysenck, H. J. (1967). *The biological basis of personality*. Springfield, Illinois: Thomas.

Eysenck, H. J. (1970). *The structure of human personality* (3rd edn). London: Methuen.

Eysenck, H. J. (1976). *The measurement of personality*. Lancaster: MTP.

Eysenck, H. J. (1992a). Four ways five factors are *not* basic. *Personality and Individual Differences*, **13**, 667–73.

Eysenck, H. J. (1992b). The definition and measurement of psychoticism. *Personality and Individual Differences*, **13**, 757–85.

Eysenck, H. J. and Eysenck, S. P. G. (1964). *Manual of the Eysenck Personality Inventory*. San Diego: Educational and Industrial Testing Service.

Eysenck, H. J. and Eysenck, S. B. G. (1969). *Personality structure and measurement*. London: Routledge & Kegan Paul.

Eysenck, H. J. and Eysenck, S. B. G. (1976). *Psychoticism as a personality dimension*. London: Hodder & Stroughton

Eysenck, H. J. and Wilson, G. D. (1991). *The Eysenck Personality Profiler*. London: Corporate Assessment.

Eysenck, H. J., Nias, D. K. B., and Cox, D. N. (1982). Sports and personality. *Advances in Behavior Research and Therapy*, **4**, 1–56.

Eysenck, S. P. G. and Eysenck, H. J. (1969). Scores on three personality variables as a function of age, sex and social class. *British Journal of Social and Clinical Psychology*, **8**, 69–76.

Festinger, L. (1957). *A theory of cognitive dissonance*. Evanston, Illinois: Row Peterson.

Fogel, D. O. (1982). Towards effective treatment for music performance anxiety. *Psychotherapy: Theory, Research and Practice*, **19**, 368–75.

Fortney, P. J., Boyle, J. D., and DeGarbo, N. J. (1993). A study of middle school band students instrumental choices. *Journal of Research in Music Education*, **41**, 28–39.

Freeman, J. (1979). *Gifted children: their identification and development in a social context*. Lancaster: MTP.

Freeman, J. (1991). *Gifted children growing up*. London: Cassell.

Freud, S. (1905). *Three essays on the theory of sexuality*, standard edition, Vol. 7. London: Hogarth.

Freud, S. (1925). *An autobiographical study*, standard edition, Vol. XX (trans. J. Strachey). London: Hogarth.

Freud, S. (1949). *An outline of psychoanalysis*. New York: Norton.

Freud, S. (1964). *New introductory lectures on psychoanalysis*, standard edition, Vol. XXII (trans. J. Strachey). London: Hogarth.

Friedman, M. and Rosenman, R. H. (1974). *Type A behaviour and your heart*. London: Wildwood House.

Frith, C. D. (1971). Strategies in rotary pursuit tracking. *British Journal of Psychology*, **62**, 187–97.

Gale, A. (1987). Arousal, control, energetics, and values: an attempt at review and appraisal. In *Personality dimensions and arousal* (ed. J. Strelau and H. J. Eysenck), pp. 287–316. New York: Plenum.

Gall, H. (ed.) (1978). *The musician's world: letters of the great composers*. Thames and Hudson.

Galton, F. (1884). Measurement of character. *Fortnightly Review*, **42**, 181.

Garder, C. E. (1955). Characteristics of outstanding high school musicians. *Journal of Research in Music Education*, **3**, 11–20.

Gardner, H. (1983). *Frames of mind: the theory of multiple intelligences*. New York: Basic Books.

Gaudrey, E. and Spielberger, C. D. (1971). *Anxiety and educational achievement*. Sydney: Wiley.

Gibbons, C. F. (1990). The personality of the performing musician as measured by the Myers–Briggs Type Indicator and the reported presence of musical performance anxiety. Unpublished doctoral dissertation, University of Arkansas.

Gold, B. D. (1987). Self-image of punk rock and nonpunk rock juvenile delinquents. *Adolescence*, **22**, 535–44.

Goldsmith, M. and Wharton, M. (1993). *Knowing me—Knowing you*. London: SPCK.

Gordon, E. E. (1991). A study of the characteristics of the instrument timbre preference tests. *Council for Research in Music Education Bulletin*, **110**, 33–51.

Gordon, E. E. (1993). *Learning sequences in music: skill, content, and patterns* (2nd edn). Chicago, Illinois: G. I. A.

Gray, J. A. (1982). *The neuropsychology of anxiety*. New York: Oxford University Press.

Griswold, P. A. and Chroback, D. A. (1981). Sex-role associations of music instruments and occupations by gender and major. *Journal of Research in Music Education*, **29**, 57–62.

Groves, C. (1960). The conductor. In *A career in music* (revised edn) (ed. R. Elkin), pp. 114–33. London: Novello.

Guilford, J. P. (1959). *Personality*. New York: McGraw Hill.

Hall, W. B. and MacKinnon, D. W. (1969). Personality inventory correlates of creativity among architects. *Journal of Applied Psychology*, **53**, 322–6.

Hamann, D. L. (1982). An assessment of anxiety in instrumental and vocal performances. *Journal of Research in Music Education*, **30**, 77–90.

Hamann, D. L. (1985). The other side of stage fright. *Music Educators Journal*, **71** (8), 26–7.

Hamann, D. L. and Sobaje, M. (1983). Anxiety and the college musician: a study of performance conditions and subject variables. *Psychology of Music*, **11**, 37–50.

Hansen, C. H. and Hansen, R. D. (1991). Constructing personality and social reality through music: individual differences among fans of punk and heavy metal music. *Journal of Broadcasting and Electronic Media*, **35**, 335–50.

Hargreaves, D. J. (1986). *The developmental psychology of music*. Cambridge: Cambridge University Press.

Hargreaves, D. J. and Coleman, A. M. (1981). The dimensions of aesthetic reactions to music. *Psychology of Music*, **9** (1), 15–19.

Hedden, S. K. (1973). Listeners' responses to music in relation to autochthonous and experiential factors. *Journal of Research in Music Education*, **21**, 225–38.

Henderson, B. B. N. (1984). Music major matriculants in North Carolina colleges and universities: Their personality types as measured by the Myers–Briggs Type Indicator. Unpublished doctoral dissertation, University of North Carolina, Greensboro.

Henson, R. A. (1977). The language of music. In *Music and the brain: studies in the neurology of music* (ed. M. Critchley and R. A. Henson), pp. 233–54. London: Heinemann.

Hindemith, P. (1952). *A composer's world: horizons and limitations*. Cambridge, Massachusetts: Harvard University Press.

Hines, J. (1994). *Great singers on great singing* (7th edn). New York: Limelight.

Hoffnung, G. (1954). *The Hoffnung symphony orchestra*. London: Dobson.

Howard, V. A. (1982). Artistry: the work of artists. Indianapolis: Hackett.

Howarth, E. (1976). Were Cattell's 'personality sphere' factors correctly identified in the first instance? *British Journal of Psychology*, **67**, 213–30.

Howarth, E. and Brown, J. A. (1971). An item factor-analysis of the 16PF. *Personality*, **2**, 117–39.

Howe, M. J. A. (1989). Child development: the hot house effect. *Child Education*, **66** (3), 20–21.

Howe, M. J. A. (1990a). *The origins of exceptional abilities*. Oxford: Blackwell.

Howe, M. J. A. (1990b). *Sense and nonsense about hothouse children: a practical guide for parents and teachers*. Leicester: British Psychological Society.

Howe, M. J. A. and Sloboda, J. A. (1991). Young musicians' accounts of significant influences in their early lives. 1. The family and their musical background. British *Journal of Music Education*, **8**, 39–52.

Howe, M. J. A. and Sloboda, J. A. (1992). Problems experienced by young talented musicians as a result of the failure of other children to value musical accomplishments. *Gifted Education International*, **8**, 16–18.

Howe, M. J. A., Davidson, J. W., Moore, D. G., and Sloboda, J. A. (1995). Are there early signs of musical ability? *Psychology of Music*, **23**, 162–76.

Howells, K. (1986). Sex roles and sexual behaviour. In *The psychology of sex roles* (ed D. J. Hargreaves and A. M. Colley), pp. 268–86. Cambridge: Harper and Row.

Hull, C. L. (1943). *Principles of behaviour*. New Haven, Connecticut: Yale University Press.

Jamison, R. (1993). *Touched with fire: manic-depressive illness and the artistic temperament*. New York: Free Press.

Judd, T. (1988). The varieties of musical talent. In *The exceptional brain* (ed. L. K. Obler and D. Fein), New York: Guilford.

Jung, C. G. (1923). *Psychological types* (trans. H. G. Baynes). London: Routledge and Kegan Paul.

Jung, C. G. (1928). *Contributions to analytical psychology*. New York: Harcourt, Brace & World.

Jung, C. G. (1964). *The development of personality*, collected works, Vol. 17 (trans. R. F. C. Hull) (Original edition 1954). London: Routledge & Kegan Paul.

Kaplan, L. (1961). The relationship between certain personality characteristics and achievement in instrumental music. Unpublished doctoral thesis, New York University.

Karp, S. (1977). Psychological differentiation. In *Personality variables in social behavior* (ed. T. Blass), pp. 135–78. Hillsdale, New Jersey: Erlbaum.

Keister, M. E. and McLaughlin, R. J. (1972). Vigilance performance related to extraversion–introversion and caffeine. *Journal of Experimental Research in Personality*, **6**, 5–11.

Kemp, A. E. (1971). A pilot study of the personality pattern of creative music students. Unpublished MA dissertation, University of Sussex.

Kemp, A. E. (1979). The personality structure of composers and performing musicians. Unpublished D. Phil thesis, University of Sussex.

Kemp, A. E. (1981a). The personality structure of the musician. I. Identifying a profile of traits for the performer. *Psychology of Music*, **9** (1), 3–14.

Kemp, A. E. (1981b). The personality structure of the musician. II. Identifying a profile of traits for the composer. *Psychology of Music*, **9** (2), 69–75.

Kemp, A. E. (1981c). Personality differences between the players of string, woodwind, brass and keyboard instruments, and singers. *Council for Research in Music Education Bulletin*, **66–67**, 33–8.

Kemp, A. E. (1982a). The personality structure of the musician. III. The significance of sex differences. *Psychology of Music*, **10** (1), 48–58.

Kemp, A. E. (1982b).The personality structure of the musician. IV. Incorporating group profiles into a comprehensive model *Psychology of Music*, **10** (2), 3–6.

Kemp, A. E. (1982c). Personality traits of successful music teachers. *Psychology of Music* (Special Issue) Proceedings of the Ninth International Seminar on Research in Music Education, 72–5.

Kemp, A. E. (1983). *Considering the mind's ear*. Romford: Curwen Institute.

Kemp, A. E. (1985). Psychological androgyny in musicians. *Council for Research in Music Education Bulletin*, **85**, 102–8.

Kemp, A. E. (1990). Kinaesthesia in music and its implications for developments in microtechnology. *British Journal of Music Education*, **7**, 223–9.

Kemp, A. E. (1992). Music education and psychodynamic theory: The manifestation of separation and loss in music. In *Music education: sharing musics of the world* (ed. H. Lees), pp. 119–26. Proceedings of the 20th world conference of the International Society for Music Education held in Seoul, Korea. Christchurch, New Zealand: University of Canterbury.

Kemp, A. E. (1995). Aspects of upbringing as revealed in the personalities of musicians, *Quarterly Journal of Music Teaching and Learning*, **5** (4), 34–41.

Keniston, K. (1968). *Young radicals*. New York: Harcourt Brace & Jovanovich.

Kenrick, D. T. and Funder, D. C. (1988). Profiting from controversy: lessons from the person–situation debate. *American Psychologist*, **43**, 23–34.

Keston, M. J. and Pinto, I. M. (1955). Possible factors influencing musical preference. *Journal of Genetic Psychology*, **86**, 101–13.

King, D. (1983). Field dependence/field independence and achievement in music reading. *Dissertation Abstracts International*, **43**, 2534A.

Kline, P. (1972). *Fact and fantasy in Freudian theory*. London: Methuen.

Kline, P. (1973). The IPAT preference test of personality in Great Britain: a study of validity. *British Journal of Projective Psychology*, **18**, 27–9.

Kline, P. (1993). Comments on 'Personality traits are alive and well.' *The Psychologist*, **6**, 304.

Kline, P. and Storey, R. (1977). A factor analytic study of the oral character. British *Journal of Social and Clinical Psychology*, **16**, 317–28.

Kline, P. and Storey, R. (1980). The etiology of the oral character. *Journal of Genetic Psychology*, **136**, 85–94.

Krueger, R. J. (1974). An investigation of personality and music teaching success. Unpublished Ed.D thesis, University of Illinois.

Krug, S. E., Scheier, I. H., and Cattell, R. B. (1976). *Handbook for the IPAT anxiety scale*. Champaign, Illinois: Institute for Personality and Ability Testing.

Kuhn, T. S. (1963). The essential tension: tradition and innovation in scientific research. In *Scientific creativity: its recognition and development*, (ed. C. W. Taylor and F. Barron), pp. 341–54. New York: Wiley.

Langer, S. K. (1953). *Feeling and form: a theory of art*. New York: Scribner.

Lanning, A. M. (1990). Personality characteristics of music majors in selected Oklahoma universities: An investigation of relationships as measured by the Myers–Briggs Type Indicator. Unpublished doctoral dissertation, University of Oklahoma, Norman, Oklahoma.

Lawson, M. (1993). The importance of being Nigel. *BBC Music Magazine*, **1** (9), 17–20.

Lehrer, P. M. (1987). A review of the approaches to the management of tension and stage fright in musical performance. *Journal of Research in Music Education*, **35**, 143–52.

Lester, D. A. (1974). *A physiological basis for personality traits*. Springfield, Illinois: Thomas.

Lewis and Schmidt (1991). Listeners' response to music as a function of personality type. *Journal of Research in Music Education*, **39**, 311–21.

Lipton, J. P. (1987). Stereotypes concerning musicians within symphony orchestras. *Journal of Psychology*, **121**, 85–93.

Litle, P. and Zuckerman, M. (1986). Sensation seeking and music preferences. *Personality and Individual Differences*, **7**, 575–7.

Loo, R. (1976). Field dependence and the Eysenck personality inventory. *Perceptual and Motor Skills*, **43**, 614.

McAllister, D. E. and McAllister, W. R. (1967). Incubation of fear: an examination of the concept. *Journal of Experimental Research in Personality*, **2**, 180–90.

McClelland, D. C. (1961). *The achieving society*. Princeton, New Jersey: Van Nostrand.

McCrae, R. R. and Costa, P. T., Jr (1985). Openness to experience. In *Perspectives in personality*, Vol. 1 (ed. R. Hogan and W. H. Jones), pp. 145–72. Greenwich, Connecticut: JAI.

McCrae, R. R. and Costa, P. T., Jr (1989a). Reinterpreting the Myers–Briggs Type Indicator from the perspective of the five factor model of personality. *Journal of Personality*, **57**, 17–40.

McCrae, R. R. and Costa, P. T., Jr (1989b). More reasons to adopt the five factor model. *American Psychologist*, **44**, 451–2.

McCutcheon, J. W., Schmidt, C. P., and Bolden, S. H. (1991). Relationships among selected variables, academic achievement and student teaching behavior. *Journal of Research and Development in Education*, **24**, 38–44.

McDougall, W. (1932). *Energies of men*. London: Methuen.

MacKinnon, D. W. (1962). The nature and nurture of creative talent. *American Psychologist*, **17**, 484–95.

Manturzewska, M. (1990). A biographical study of the life-span development of professional musicians. *Psychology of Music*, **18**, 112–39.

Marchant-Haycox, S. E. and Wilson, G. D. (1992). Personality and stress in performing artists. *Personality and Individual Differences*, **13**, 1061–8.

Martin, P. J. (1976). Appreciation of music in relation to personality factors. Unpublished PhD thesis, University of Glasgow.

Maslow, A. (1974). What is a Taoistic teacher? In *Facts and feelings in the classroom* (ed. L. J. Bubin), pp. 147–70. London: Ward Lock.

Maslow, A. H. (1987). *Motivation and personality* (3rd edn). New York: Harper and Row.

Matson, D. L. (1978). Field dependence–independence in children and their response to musical tasks embodying Piaget's principle of conservation. *Dissertation Abstracts International*, **39** 4798A.

Michael, W. B., Barth, G., and Kaiser, H. F. (1961). Dimensions of temperament in three groups of music teachers. *Psychological Reports*, **9**, 701–4.

Mischel, W. (1968). *Personality and assessment*. New York: Wiley.

Mischel, W. (1973). Towards a cognitive social learning reconceptualization of personality. *Psychological Review*, **80**, 252–83.

Myers, I. B. (1993). *Gifts differing: understanding personality type* (original edition 1980). Palo Alto, California: Consulting Psychologists Press.

Myers, I. B. and McCaulley, M. H. (1985). *Manual: a guide to the development and use of the Myers–Briggs Type indicator* (2nd edn). Palo Alto, California: Consulting Psychologists Press.

Nagel, J. J., Himley, D. P., and Papsdorf, J. D. (1989). Cognitive-behavioural treatment of musical performance anxiety. *Psychology of Music*, **17**, 12–21.

Nass, M. L. (1971). Some considerations of a psychoanalytic interpretation of music. *Psychoanalytic Quarterly*, **40**, 303–16.

Nass, M. L. (1975). On hearing and inspiration in the composition of music. *Psychoanalytic Quarterly*, **44**, 431–47.

Noller, P., Law, H., and Comrey, A. L. (1987). Cattell, Comrey, and Eysenck personality factors compared: more evidence for the five robust factors? *Journal of Personality and Social Psychology*, **53**, 775–82.

Norman, W. T. (1963). Toward an adequate taxonomy of personality attributes: replicated factor structure in peer nomination personality ratings. *Journal of Abnormal and Social Psychology*, **66**, 574–83.

O'Neill, S. and Boulton, M. J. (1996). Boys' and girls' preferences for musical instruments: a function of gender? *Psychology of Music*, **24**. (In press).

Payne, E. (1967). Musical taste and personality. *British Journal of Psychology*, **58**, 133–8.

Payne, E. (1980). Towards an understanding of musical appreciation. *Psychology of Music*, **8** (2), 31–41.

Paynter, J. (1977). The role of creativity in the school music curriculum. In *Music education review: a handbook for music teachers*, Vol. 1 (ed. M. Burnett), pp. 3–26. London: Chappell.

Piers, P. (1978). A voice is a person. BBC Radio 4 Programme (first broadcast on 4 October 1978).

Piperek, M. (1981). *Stress and music: medical, psychological, sociological, and legal strain factors in a symphony orchestra musician's profession*. Vienna: Braumüller.

Plummeridge, C. (1994). *Education and training: criteria and processes*. Reading: International Centre for Research in Music Education.

Pollack, B. (1991). The effective conductor: a matter of communication and personality. In *Psychology and performing arts*, (ed. G. D. Wilson), pp. 155–62. Amsterdam: Swets and Zeitlinger.

Porter, R. B. and Cattell, R. B. (1959). *The children's personality questionnaire (CPQ)*. Champaign, Illinois: Institute for Personality and Ability Testing.

Post, F. (1994). Creativity and psychopathology: a study of 291 world-famous men. *British Journal of Psychiatry*, **165**, 22–34.

Powell, T. J. and Enright, S. J. (1990). Anxiety and stress management. London: Routledge.

Pruett, K. D. (1990). Coping with life on a pedestal. In *Music and child development* (ed. F. R. Wilson and F. L. Roehmann), pp. 309–22. St. Louis, Missouri: MMB Music.

Pruett, K. D. (1991). Psychological aspects of the development of exceptional young performers and prodigies. In *Textbook of performing arts medicine* (ed. R. T. Sataloff, A. Brandfonbrenner, and R. Lederman), pp. 337–49. New York: Raven.

Quenk, N. L. (1993). *Beside ourselves: our hidden personality in everyday life*. Palo Alto, California: Consulting Psychologists Press.

Rawlings, D., Hodge, M., Sherr, D., and Dempsey, A. (1995). Toughmindedness and preference for musical excerpts, categories and triads. *Psychology of Music*, **23**, 63–80.

Raychaudhuri, M. (1966). *Studies in artistic creativity: personality structure of the musician*. Calcutta: Express.

Reber, A. S. (1985). *The Penguin dictionary of psychology*. London: Penguin.

Renzulli, J. S. (1986). The three-ring conception of giftedness: a developmental model for creative productivity. In *Conceptions of giftedness*, (ed. R. J. Sternberg and J. Davidson), pp. 53–92. Cambridge University Press.

Robertson, P. (1993). The great divide. *BBC Music Magazine*, **1** (9), 23–6.

Roe, A. (1961).The psychology of the scientist. *Science*, **134**, 454–9.

Roe, A. (1967). Parent-child relations and creativity. Paper prepared for conference on child-rearing practices for developing creativity. Macalester College, MN, November 2–4.

Ruch, L. O. (1984). Dimensionality of the Bem sex role inventory: a multidimensional analysis. *Sex Roles*, **10**, 99–117.

Sample, D. and Hotchkiss, S. M. (1971). An investigation of relationships between personality characteristics and success in instrumental study. *Journal of Research in Music Education*, **19**, 307–13.

Saville, P. (1972). *The British standardisation of the 16PF: supplement of norms*. Windsor: National Foundation for Educational Research.

Saville, P. and Blinkhorn, S. (1976). *Undergraduate personality by factored scales: a large scale study on Cattell's 16PF and the Eysenck Personality Inventory*. Windsor: National Foundation for Educational Research.

Saville, P. and Finlayson, L. (1973). *British supplement to the high school personality questionnaire (Form A) Anglicised 1968/69 edition*. Windsor: National Foundation for Educational Research.

Scheier, M. F., Carver, C. S., and Matthews, K. A. (1983). Attentional factors in the perception of bodily states. In *Social psychophysiology: a sourcebook* (ed. J. T. Cacioppo and R. E. Petty), pp. 510–42. New York: Guilford.

Schleuter, S. L. (1972). An investigation of the inter-relation of personality traits, musical aptitude, and musical achievement. *Studies in the Psychology of Music*, No. 8. Iowa City, Iowa: University of Iowa Press.

Schmidt, C. P. (1984). The relationships among aspects of cognitive style and language-bound-optional perception to musicians' performance in selected aural discrimination tasks. *Journal of Research in Music Education*, **32**, 159–68.

Schmidt, C. P. (1985). Cognitive styles and musical behavior. Unpublished paper presented at the Southeastern Music Education Symposium, Athens, Georgia, April 1985.

Schmidt, C. P. (1989a). Applied music teaching behavior as a function of selected personality variables. *Journal of Research in Music Education*, **37**, 258–71.

Schmidt, C. P. (1989b). Individual differences in perception of applied music teaching feedback. *Psychology of Music*, **17**, 110–22.

Schmidt, C. P. and Lewis, B. A. (1987). Field-dependence/independence, movement-based instruction and fourth graders' achievement in selected musical tasks. *Psychology of Music*, **15**, 117–27.

Schmidt, C. P. and Sinor, J. (1986). An investigation of the relationships among music audiation, musical creativity, and cognitive style. *Journal of Research in Music Education*, **34**, 160–72.

Schultz, C. and Lang, G. (1963). The reliability of music preferences under varying mood conditions. *Journal of Clinical Psychology*, **19**, 506.

Seashore, C. E. (1936). The psychology of music V: measurement of musical talent: the Eastern experiment. *Music Educators Journal*, **23** (3), 24–25.

Seashore, C. E. (1967). *The psychology of music* (Original edition 1938). New York: Dover.

Seashore, C. E., Lewis, D., and Saetveit, J. (1939). *Seashore measures of musical talents*. New York: Psychological Corporation.

Shatin, L., Kotter, W., and Longmore, G. (1968). Personality traits of music therapists. *Psychological Reports*, **23**, 573–4.

Shaw, G. (undated). *A book of hidden tunes*. London: Thomas Nelson.

Shaw, G. B. (1962). *G.B.S. on music*. Harmondsworth: Penguin.

Shuter, R. (1974). The relationship between musical abilities and personality characteristics in young children. Unpublished paper delivered at the Fourth International Seminar on Research in Music Education.

Shuter-Dyson, R. (1985). Musical giftedness. In *The psychology of gifted children* (ed. J. Freeman), pp. 159–83. Chichester: Wiley.

Shuter-Dyson, R. and Gabriel, C. (1981). *The psychology of musical ability* (2nd edn). London: Methuen.

Simon, R. S. (1979). Jungian types and creativity of professional fine artists. Unpublished doctoral dissertation, United States International University.

Sloboda, J. A. (1985). *The musical mind: the cognitive psychology of music*. Oxford: Oxford University Press.

Sloboda, J. A. (1990a). Musical excellence—how does it develop? In *Encouraging the development of exceptional skills and talents* (ed. M. J. A. Howe), pp. 165–78. Leicester: British Psychological Society.

Sloboda, J. A. (1990b). Music as a language. In *Music and child development* (ed. F. R. Wilson and F. L. Roehmann), pp. 28–43. St. Louis, Missouri: MMB Music.

Sloboda, J. A. (1991). Musical structure and emotional response: Some empirical findings. *Psychology of Music*, **19**, 110–20.

Sloboda, J. A. and Howe, M. J. A. (1991). Biographical precursors of musical excellence: an interview study. *Psychology of Music*, **19**, 3–21.

Sloboda, J. A., Davidson, J. W., and Howe, M. J. A. (1994). Is everyone musical? *The Psychologist*, **7**, 349–54.

Sloboda, J. A., Davidson, J. W., Howe, M. J. A., and Moore, D. G. (1996). The role of practice in the development of performing musicians. *British Journal of Psychology*, (In press).

Smith, J. D. (1987). Conflicting aesthetic ideals in a musical culture. *Music Perception*, **4**, 373–92.

Sosniak, L. A. (1990). The tortoise, the hare, and the development of talent. In *Encouraging the development of exceptional skills and talents* (ed. M. J. A. Howe), pp. 149–64. Leicester: British Psychological Society.

Spence, J. T. and Helmreich, R. (1978). *Masculinity and femininity: their psychological dimensions, correlates, and antecedents*. Austin: University of Texas.

Spielberger, C. D. (1966). Theory and research on anxiety. In *Anxiety and behavior* (ed. C. D. Spielberger), pp. 3–22, New York: Academic.

Spielberger, C. D., Gorsuch, R. L., and Lushene, R. E. (1970). *Manual for the state-trait anxiety inventory*. Palo Alto, California: Consulting Psychologist Press.

Spielberger, C. D., Barker, L., Russell, S., Silva de Crane, R., Westberry, L., Knight, J., and Marks, E. (1979). Preliminary manual for the state-trait personality inventory. Unpublished manuscript, University of South Florida.

Stelmack, R. M. (1990). Biological bases of extraversion: psychophysical evidence. *Journal of Personality*, **58**, 293–311.

Stelmack, R. M. and Campbell, K. B. (1974). Extraversion and auditory sensitivity to high and low frequency. *Perceptual and Motor Skills*, **38**, 875–9.

Steptoe, A. (1989). Stress, coping and stage fright in professional musicians. *Psychology of Music*, **17**, 3–11.

Steptoe, A. and Fidler, H. (1987). Stage fright in orchestral musicians: a study of cognitive and behavioural strategies in performance anxiety. *British Journal of Psychology*, **78**, 241–9.

Sternberg, C. (1955). Personality trait patterns of college students majoring in different fields. *Psychological Monographs*, **69**, No. 18 (Whole No. 403).

Storms, M. D. (1980). Theories of sexual orientation. *Journal of Personality and Social Psychology*, **38**, 783–92.

Storr, A. (1963). *The integrity of the personality*. Harmondsworth: Penguin.

Storr, A. (1976). *The dynamics of creation*. Harmondsworth: Penguin.

Storr, A. (1988). *The school of genius*. London: Deutsch.

Storr, A. (1989). *Solitude*. London: Fontana.

Storr, A. (1992). *Music and the mind*. London: Harper Collins.

Stricker, L. J. and Ross, J. (1964). An assessment of some structural properties of the Jungian personality typology. *Journal of Abnormal and Social Psychology*, **68**, 62–71.

Suzuki, S. (1983). *Nurtured by love: the classic approach to talent education* (2nd edn) (trans. W. Suzuki). Smithtown, New York: Exposition Press.

Thayer, R. W. (1972). The inter-relation of personality traits, musical achievement and different measures of musical aptitude. *Studies in the Psychology of Music*, No. 8. Iowa City, Iowa: University of Iowa Press.

Thorndike, R. L. and Hagen, E. (1955). *Measurement and evaluation in psychology and education*. New York: Wiley.

Tobacyk, J. J. and Downs, A. (1986). Personal construct threat and irrational beliefs as cognitive predictors of increases in musical performance anxiety. *Journal of Personality and Social Psychology*, **51**, 779–82.

Tripp, C. A. (1975). *Homosexual matrix*. New York: McGraw Hill.

Tucker, A. B. (1982). Jungian psychological traits and personal perceived values associated with university band affiliation. Unpublished doctoral dissertation, Texas Tech University, Lubbock, Texas.

Van Wyk, P. H. and Geist, C. S. (1984). Psychosocial development of heterosexual, bisexual and homosexual behavior. *Archives of Sexual Behavior*, **9**, 199–203.

Vernon, P. E. (1953). *Personality tests and assessments*. London: Methuen.

Vernon, P. E. (ed.) (1970). *Creativity: selected readings*. Harmondsworth: Penguin.

Walters, J. and Gardner, H. (1992). The crystallizing experience: discovering an intellectual gift. In *Genius and eminence* (2nd edn) (ed. R. S. Albert), pp. 135–55. Oxford: Pergamon.

Watson, P. and Valentine, E. (1987). The practice of complimentary medicine and anxiety levels in a population of musicians. *Journal of the International Society for the Study of Tension in Performance*, **4**, 25–30.

Weaver, J. B. III (1991). Exploring the links between personality and media preferences. *Personality and Individual Differences*, **12**, 1293–9.

Weisen, A. (1965). Differential reinforcing effects of onset and offset of stimulation on the operant behavior of normals, neurotics, and psychopaths. Unpublished doctoral dissertation, University of Florida.

Wheeler, B. L. (1985). Relationship of personal characteristics to mood and enjoyment after hearing live and recorded music and to musical taste. *Psychology of Music*, **13**, 81–92.

Wills, G. and Cooper, C. L. (1988). *Pressure sensitive: popular musicians under stress*. London: Sage.

Wilson, G. D. (1977). Introversion/extraversion. In *Personality variables in social behavior* (ed. T. Blass), pp. 179–218. Hillsdale, New Jersey: Lawrence Erlbaum.

Wilson, G. D. (1984). The personality of opera singers. *Personality and Individual Differences*, **5**, 195–201.

Wing, H. D. (1968). Tests of musical ability and appreciation (2nd edn). *British Journal of Psychology*, Monograph Supplement no. 27.

Winnicott, D. W. (1965). *The maturational process and the facilitating environment: studies in the theory of emotional development.* London: Hogarth.

Witkin, H. A. (1965). Psychological differentiation. *Journal of Abnormal Psychology*, **70**, 317–36.

Witkin, H. A., Oltman, P. K., Raskin, E., and Karp, S. A. (1971). *A manual for the embedded figures tests.* Palo Alto, California: Consulting Psychologists Press.

Witkin, H. A., Lewis, H. B., Hertzman, M., Machover, K., Meissner, P. B., and Wapner, S. (1975). *Personality through perception.* Westport, Connecticut: Greenwood.

Witkin, H. A., Moore, C. A., Goodenough, D. R., and Cox, P. W. (1977). Field-dependent and field-independent cognitive styles and their educational implications. *Journal of Educational Research*, **47**, 1–64.

Wubbenhorst, T, (1994). Personality characteristics of music educators and performers. *Psychology of Music*, **22**, 63–74.

Zalanowski, A. (1986). The effects of listening instructions and cognitive style on music appreciation. *Journal of Research in Music Education*, **34**, 43–53.

Author index

Subject index